PERGAMON INTERNATIONAL
of Science, Technology, Engineering and

The 1000-volume original paperback library ir
industrial training and the enjoyment of leisure
Publisher: Robert Maxwell, M.C.

Food Science
SECOND EDITION

BEDALE AGRICULTURAL CENTRE
Benkhill Drive, Bedale, N. Yorks. DL8 2EA

THE PERGAMON TEXTBOOK
INSPECTION COPY SERVICE

An inspection copy of any book published in the Pergamon International Library will gladly be sent to academic staff without obligation for their consideration for course adoption or recommendation. Copies may be retained for a period of 60 days from receipt and returned if not suitable. When a particular title is adopted or recommended for adoption for class use and the recommendation results in a sale of 12 or more copies, the inspection copy may be retained with our compliments. The Publishers will be pleased to receive suggestions for revised editions and new titles to be published in this important International Library.

Some other titles of interest:—

BROWN	By Bread Alone
DUCKWORTH	Fruit and Vegetables
EARLE	Unit Operations in Food Processing
GAMAN & SHERRINGTON	The Science of Food An Introduction to Food Science, Nutrition & Microbiology
HICKLING	The Farming of Fish
KENT	Technology of Cereals 2nd Edition
LAMB & HARDEN	The Meaning of Human Nutrition
LAWRIE	Meat Science 2nd Edition
RHODES & FLETCHER	Principles of Industrial Microbiology
YEATES et al	Animal Science: Reproduction, Climate, Meat, Wool

Food Science
SECOND EDITION

GORDON G. BIRCH, BSc, PhD, FRIC, MRSH
MICHAEL SPENCER, BSc, DCC, FIFST, FRIC
National College of Food Technology, University of Reading

ALLAN G. CAMERON, BSc, FIFST
College of Food and Domestic Arts, Birmingham

PERGAMON PRESS
OXFORD · NEW YORK
TORONTO · SYDNEY · PARIS · FRANKFURT

U.K.	Pergamon Press Ltd., Headington Hill Hall, Oxford OX3 0BW, England
U.S.A.	Pergamon Press Inc., Maxwell House, Fairview Park, Elmsford, New York 10523, U.S.A.
CANADA	Pergamon of Canada Ltd., 75 The East Mall, Toronto, Ontario, Canada
AUSTRALIA	Pergamon Press (Aust.) Pty. Ltd., 19a Boundary Street, Rushcutters Bay, N.S.W. 2011, Australia
FRANCE	Pergamon Press SARL, 24 rue des Ecoles, 75240 Paris, Cedex 05, France
WEST GERMANY	Pergamon Press GmbH, 6242 Kronberg-Taunus, Pferdstrasse 1, Frankfurt-am-Main, West Germany

Copyright © 1977 G. G. Birch, A. G. Cameron, M. Spencer

All Rights Reserved. No part of this publication may be reproduced, stored in a retrieval system or transmitted in any form or by any means: electronic, electrostatic, magnetic tape, mechanical, photocopying, recording or otherwise, without permission in writing from the publishers

First Edition 1972
Reprinted 1973
Second Edition 1977

Library of Congress Cataloging in Publication Data

Birch, Gordon Gerard.
Food Science.

(Pergamon international library)
Includes bibliographies and index.
1. Food. I. Spencer, Michael, joint author.
II. Cameron, Allan Gillies, joint author. III. Title.
TX354.B57 1977   641.3   76-46261
ISBN 0-08-021347-2 (Hardcover)
ISBN 0-08-021346-4 (Flexicover)

Printed in Great Britain by Biddles Ltd., Guildford, Surrey

Contents

	Preface to Second Edition	vii
1.	Introduction	1
2.	Components of Food and Drink	5
3.	Why do we need Food?	27
4.	From Farm to Table	52
5.	Drink	74
6.	Food Poisoning and the Preservation of Food	87
7.	Changes in Food during Storage and Preparation	106
8.	Flavour, Colour and Texture	131
9.	Eating Chemicals	151
10.	Fads, Fallacies and the Future	166
	Appendix	182
	Index	183

Preface to Second Edition

"TELL me what you eat, and I will tell you who you are." We may not agree with this provocative remark attributed to Brillat Savarin, but it serves to remind us that our bodies are built up from the food we eat. We cannot escape from the fundamental importance of food in our lives and though a few people may claim that they "live to eat", everyone must acknowledge that they must "eat to live". Indeed the importance of food in our lives is emphasized by the knowledge that on average we consume 30 tons of food during our lifetime at a total cost of about £10,000. It is evident—even on narrow financial grounds—that it is to our advantage to know something about a subject which is so fundamental to our existence.

In this book we attempt to give a simple but up-to-date account of the science of food. We have tried to write a book that will be both intelligible, and of interest, to the layman. We also hope it may stimulate interest among students in schools and colleges—including arts students who wish to explore a "liberal" science that is intimately connected with everyday life, and science students who wish to understand how the basic sciences they have studied at school are used and dovetailed together in exploring the realms of food science.

After a brief *hors-d'oeuvre* to whet the appetite in Chapter 1, the main course follows in the succeeding two chapters. These discuss the nature of food and what happens to it in the body after it has been eaten. If these topics prove indigestible at a first reading, their study may be deferred until later when the reader will have been mellowed by the account of liquid refreshment given in Chapter 5. We believe that readers will want to know about the food they store, cook and eat in their homes and these topics are considered in Chapters 6 and 7 following an account of the stages by which food progresses from farm to table given in Chapter 4. To be attractive food must be of good flavour, colour and texture; moreover, nowadays almost every meal that we eat contains "additives" —a subject of intense public concern at the present time. These important topics are considered in Chapters 8 and 9. Finally, in Chapter 10, when the appetite has been satisfied and the coffee is served we should be in a suitably relaxed and expansive mood to consider our (often strange) attitudes to the food we eat: we may even feel sufficiently fortified to contemplate the greatest problem facing us today—namely, that of how to provide enough food to satisfy a growing and hungry world.

This new edition incorporates several new references and updated developments.

The authors would like to express their thanks to Mrs. Nancy Goodwin for her help in the typing of the manuscript, and in the compilation of the index to this edition.

CHAPTER 1

Introduction

THIS is not a history book! The story of food through the ages is too huge and unwieldy a subject to be included in an introductory book. What is more, a modern reader is more interested in the hows and whys of food as it is today than in what it was like yesterday or in the remoter past.

Why do we want to read about food? Is it not enough that we eat it? Does it matter that we know what it is? All of these questions belong more properly to the unenlightened pool of social wisdom which existed in the nineteenth century or at latest early twentieth century. Unfortunately, however, they or others like them, are all too prevalent today. Take, for example, a recent survey by nutritionists of "the man in the street" and his responses, such as:

"I don't go looking for the vitamins. But I know what's good for me—butter, liver, eggs and cheese."
or "How did I learn what's best? Call me a big'ead, but I remember what me Mum done and I goes on from there."
or "They were healthier *and* worked harder in the old days. *And* had plenty of stodge."
or "You see all these vitamins in babies' foods and you think it must be good. You don't know what it is of course."

These quotations indicate a complete lack of applied thought and also a disinclination to think on the part of the respondent about the value of what he eats. They also suggest that the man in the street bases his eating habits almost entirely on emotionalism.

Vitamins appear to be the class of nutrients which have the greatest impact on the public via mass-media advertisement. This does not necessarily mean, however, that the impact is a truthful one. Many people assiduously read their corn flakes packet every morning at breakfast where they see such names as thiamine and riboflavine, but really they have no idea at all what thiamine or riboflavine are. More overtly informative advertisements are often misleadingly descriptive. For example, "Thiamine is the happiness vitamin, and is needed to keep your cat happy". We hope that when the reader has completed this book he will be better able to see through the fallacies of advertisements such as this. For while it is true that a cat deprived entirely of thiamine would certainly not be happy it is at the same time completely misleading to describe it as "the happiness vitamin".

People are more willing to air their ill-considered opinions about food than about any other subject under the sun, and resulting from this is a series of inaccurate rumours which have a curious habit of persisting for many years. For example, agene was once used to bleach flour and was subsequently discontinued because it was shown to be toxic to dogs. Even today, however, many people believe that white bread could make their pets hysterical, although this is quite untrue.

Recently in Britain and the United States, among other countries, the artificial sweetening agents, cyclamates, have been banned. The person who questions the need to read and find out about his food, however, may not know why. Nor would he have known a year beforehand that there was any possibility of their being banned. In this respect he is therefore at a disadvantage compared to readers of serious books on food science, such as this one. We may, of course, know the more sensible questioner who comes with a newly discovered pearl of wisdom: "God gave us our sense of taste and smell long before we knew all this science and technology, as a safeguard to enable us to reject what was bad and offensive. Therefore what we like must be what is best for us." This clever questioner has presumably never heard of the metallic sweetening agents which were discovered and used in the Middle Ages. Sugar of lead and beryl, for example, had the most delicious flavour and rapidly caused fatal results. Furthermore, a host of other food components, both natural and synthetic, have, after a period of use, been completely banned from foods because of their toxic properties, and these substances have no flavour whatsoever. On the less dramatic plane of nutrition, however, the flavour of food is quite likely to be unrelated to its nutritional value, especially nowadays with so many artificial flavours and flavour enhancers on the market.

There are many known international differences in foods. Is there, therefore, any point in reading a book like this when foods in Britain, for example, are so different from those in the East? Oriental readers please do not despair. Although most of the examples we give relate to European type foods, this book approaches the whole subject from fundamental principles which, if properly understood, are applicable to all foods. Basic similarities and differences between foods eaten in different countries may become clearer on reading, and the nature and significance of what we eat will thus become appreciated.

Perhaps it is true that there are as many basic dietary variations nationally as internationally. Thus it has been said that more puddings and starchy foods are consumed in the north of England, and more salads and light foods in the south. Yorkshiremen eat ten times as much fish and chips as Scotsmen. Welshmen eat four times as much cheese as Londoners. The Scots eat much more beef and less pork than Londoners. Haggis is peculiar to Scotland, while larva bread (made from seaweed) is probably unheard of except in Wales, where it is treated as a delicacy equivalent to caviare! Perhaps in any one nation the diet depends more on social class than on locality. Certainly it is easy to recognize differences in character between food at one end of the scale, e.g. fish and chips or baked beans on toast, and the sophisticated food at the other—e.g. *pâté de foie gras*, real turtle soup, or truffles (a black subterranean fungus) which is known as the food of kings. All of these foods, however, can be split up into the same basic components (which are dealt with in the next chapter) and differences between them exist only in species, shape and flavour, and not in real nutritional effect.

Nowadays most of our food (canned or otherwise) is treated in some way or other to improve its texture, colour, or appearance. There is no possibility of avoiding this, and hence it is in the interest of readers to understand the principles of the treatment of food. An additive may not in fact change the food but may either enhance or depress a flavour already present. This is where the realms of food and drugs begin to overlap. An interesting example of this, which has been known in Africa for many years, but which has only of recent times been known to food scientists, is the Miracle Fruit. The berries when kept in the mouth cause all sour food which is eaten to taste sweet. Furthermore, the effect lasts for 2 hours after the berries are removed from the mouth, indicating that some sort of drug action is involved. It could be that this type of effect is a signal for the future in food technology and as recently as 1969 at a symposium organized by the British Food Manufacturers Industrial Research Association it was given as the opinion of several authoritative speakers that the next decade in flavour research would move toward modification of the individual rather than modification of the food.

Our world goal must be enough safe, nutritious, pleasing and top quality food for all, and the consequent banishment of starvation. Looking back over the past few years we have already done something toward this by a huge increase in food manufacture, and more fundamentally by the setting up of food science and technology courses at universities and colleges throughout the world. The latter is basically much more productive than simply increasing our output of food in tonnage per year, because the ideas which these graduates from universities and colleges will spread across the world will be the seeds of a stable and far-reaching improvement in quality and quantity of food production. Looking forward we now have within our grasp a chance to help all mankind.

CHAPTER 2

Components of Food and Drink

WHEN people use the word "Food" they can, as with so many other words in the English language, mean all sorts of different things. The primitive tribesman uses his word "food" for a few familiar substances such as flesh, fruit or roots, which satisfy his pangs of hunger when he eats them. The concept of food in an advanced society, however, is highly sophisticated and, moreover, varies from individual to individual. We can perhaps divide the meaning of the word "food" under two headings—"gastronomic food" and "scientific food". Gastronomists are interested in fulfilling their sense of appetite by eating extremely attractive meals, garnished exotically, flavoured exquisitely and embellished by the consumption of fine old wines. So long as they achieve at least normal satisfaction of their hunger and meet normal nutritional requirements in the consumption of their food, all that they are interested in is the appearance, smell, flavour and general "beauty" of what they eat. This gastronomical conception of food is, of course, perfectly legitimate, and provides one of the joys of life to many people including the authors of this book. However, it must be made clear at this point that scientifically such concepts are practically irrelevant.

Scientifically, "food" is defined as that which is necessary for the health, growth and normal functions of living organisms, and whether we talk about the food of simple unicellular organisms such as bacteria, or the food of plants or the food of mammals such as man, we mean a collection of substances which are necessary to keep them alive and functioning in their normal healthy way.

"What are foods made of?" is the sort of intelligent question we would nowadays expect from anyone who really wants to know exactly what he eats or is liable to eat. He will not be satisfied by the type of answer which he can get from a recipe in a cookery book, however, and he would more likely be interested in what sorts of atoms and molecules were present in food, how they might change and what harm or good they might do him. This chapter and the next will attempt to satisfy the curiosity of a modern informed questioner on these points.

Basically, we now know that food is in reality a mixture of chemicals and the reader should appreciate this fundamental point before proceeding further. When we say that food is a mixture of chemicals we mean that we could separate any food of our choosing into different parts which are chemically identifiable—i.e. we could recognize the chemical class to which each of the separated parts belonged, and could thus predict how these parts of the food would behave on cooking or, after eating, how they would behave in the body. Each class of chemical substance in food has a chemical name and these are—carbohydrates, fats, proteins or amino acids, vitamins, minerals, and water. Together they constitute more than 99.9% of all foods and therefore any other traces of material present are probably additives or adulterants. The chemical reality of food components can be illustrated by the fact that if we were to take any one of the above substances out of food (e.g. glucose, a carbohydrate, out of grapes) and place it in a bottle, a chemist would be able to synthesize the same substance entirely from laboratory reagents and place it in a similar bottle so that the two bottles of chemical (i.e. glucose) could not be distinguished by any means whatever.

Apart from the minerals and water which are present in foods, the remaining chemical matter is said to be "organic". This does not simply mean that the matter has been obtained from once living organisms, which is obvious, but that the chemical compounds involved all contain *carbon* atoms which are chemically joined to other atoms, mostly hydrogen, oxygen and nitrogen or sometimes phosphorus. It is the way in which these atoms are joined together which decides to which class of chemical each part of our food belongs, and although most foods contain mixtures of all the chemical classes mentioned in the last paragraph some foods consist mostly of one class of chemical. An example of the latter type is honey, which consists mostly of carbohydrate (mixtures of sugar) and a small proportion of water. Table 2.1 gives the approximate percentage of some classes of food chemical in selected foods. The reader must realize, however, that these are only approximate, as considerable variation is possible between different samples of the same food.

The "inorganic" part of our food consists largely of the minerals which we require in our diet to keep us healthy, and even though the

COMPONENTS OF FOOD AND DRINK

TABLE 2.1. AMOUNTS OF MAJOR FOOD CHEMICALS IN SOME SELECTED FOODS

Food	Amounts of food chemical (g/100 g of food)				
	Water	Carbohydrate	Fat	Protein	Ash
Milk	88	4·7	3·6	3·3	0·1
Cheddar cheese	37	0	34·5	24·9	1·0
Egg	74	0·9	11·5	12·5	0·1
Sirloin beef	59	0	23·0	16·0	1·0
Herring (Jan.–Aug.)	66	0	15·0	16·0	1·5
White bread	37	51·4	1·2	8·5	1·0
Apples	85·8	12·2	0	0·3	0·1
Cabbage	92	5·0	0	1·5	0·1
Jam	30	69	0	0·6	0·2
Chocolate (plain)	0	52·5	35·2	5·6	0·8

mineral part of our food is very small compared with the remainder, it is just as important dietetically. The column headed "Ash" in Table 2.1 gives an indication of the mineral content which is present in those foods listed. The word *ash* means the inorganic part of any food which remains after we burn all the organic part away, and consists largely of salts of the various metals which are present in food. The vitamins consist of such different sizes and shapes of molecules that we cannot really say much about them in this chapter, except to mention the ways in which we might lose them when food is cooked. As far as water and the "organic" part of our food is concerned, however, we can discuss the molecules of all the main chemical classes. Understanding the nature of these molecules will help us to discover why food changes when we cook it, and what happens to it after it is eaten when it undergoes further chemical changes within the body.

Water

Water is one of the most important chemicals in foods and drinks, being present in all drinks and most foods. Even those foods which contain virtually no water have usually been cooked or grown by a method in which water must have played a part. Nearly all chemical changes that take place in nature need water to make them work, both in the animal and vegetable kingdoms.

Most people nowadays know that the chemical formula for water is H_2O, and in fact the two hydrogen atoms are each attached to the oxygen atom as shown in Fig. 2.1. The dotted line in Fig. 2.1 shows that if water molecules are close enough together they are joined by a weak bond which has the characteristic of being largely electrostatic in nature. This type of bond is called a hydrogen bond, and since each water molecule in any mass of water may form this type of bond with its nearest neighbours, and two hydrogen bonds can hold every oxygen atom with its neighbours, the result is one great network of bonds in which all the water molecules are held together as a "giant molecule". The ordinary chemical bond (solid lines in Fig. 2.1) is several times stronger than the hydrogen bond

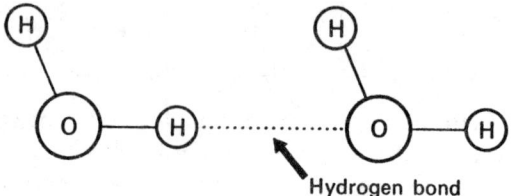

FIG. 2.1. Two water (H_2O) molecules weakly held together by a hydrogen bond.

and differs from the hydrogen bond in that it involves sharing of electrons between oxygen and hydrogen atoms. The difference in strength between the two types of bond which we find in water can be illustrated by the fact that we would need temperatures of hundreds of degrees centigrade higher than the boiling point of water to break the molecule down chemically (i.e. change it into another substance), whereas the process of heating water alone "loosens" and breaks the hydrogen bonds so that at its boiling point they all break down as the liquid changes to steam. Thus at the boiling point of water the "giant molecule" effect of hydrogen bonding collapses altogether and the individual water molecules fly off as vapour (steam).

Hydrogen bonds also form between other molecules and other types of molecule found in food. We know that the water which is present in some foods (e.g. flour) is held by hydrogen bonds in this way because it is extremely difficult to remove it; in other words we are not able to dry flour completely because of the hydrogen bonds between the protein and water molecules which it contains.

Water is necessary for all chemical reactions which take place in living organisms, but because of this too much water in foods can be a danger as far as bacteria and other micro-organisms are concerned. Moist foods are good media for spoilage bacteria and it is the aim of modern food technology to keep the water content of many foods as low as possible to increase their shelf life. This process is taken to its ultimate conclusion in modern techniques of dehydration which enable foods to be stored, free of water, for extremely long periods after which they can be reconstituted by the addition of water before eating. Some foods and all drinks, however, need a certain minimum water content to be recognizable as normal constituents of our diet. Jam, for example, contains a considerable amount of water, and to preserve foods of this type from bacterial growth we simply make the jam with plenty of sugar in it (about 70%). This preserves the jam from the action of micro-organisms such as bacteria, yeasts and moulds in spite of the high water content.

Carbohydrate

Carbohydrate is the name given to a class of chemicals occurring in foods which contain atoms of carbon, hydrogen and oxygen in their molecules. The hydrogen and oxygen atoms are always present in the same proportion (i.e. 2H : O) as they are found in water, and they are attached to carbon atoms; hence the name carbohydrate. There are a number of different carbohydrates in food but broadly speaking they can be classed under two headings—sugars and polysaccharides. Sugars usually consist of small sweet-tasting molecules; but these molecules may be joined into long chains in which case they no longer taste sweet. If this happens we can get carbohydrate molecules which consist of chains of sugar units joined together, of many different lengths. If only between two and nine sugar units are joined together to form a chain in this way we call the resulting carbohydrate an *oligosaccharide*, but if ten or more sugars join together in this way the resulting carbohydrate is called a *polysaccharide*. Figure 2.2 shows how oligosaccharides and polysaccharides may be formed by the joining together of *two* different types of sugar unit *(monosaccharide)*. However, chains like these may form from only *one* type of sugar unit, or as many as *four* different types of sugar may be present in one polysaccharide molecule.

The carbohydrate of some foods (e.g. jam or honey) consists almost

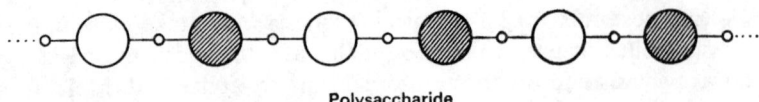

Polysaccharide

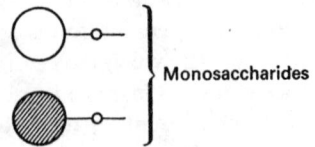

Monosaccharides

Fig. 2.2. Part of a polysaccharide molecule made up from two different monosaccharide molecules.

entirely of simple sugars. In other foods (e.g. flour) it consists of the polysaccharide (starch) while there are certain types of confectionery and other manufactured foods which contain both sugars and polysaccharides (e.g. cakes).

The three most common sugars found in foods are called *sucrose* (common sugar, cane sugar, or beet sugar), glucose (grape sugar) and fructose (fruit sugar). Others, such as lactose (milk sugar) and maltose (malt sugar), occur in smaller quantities in foods and, moreover, do not taste as sweet. The various types of brown sugar available today are *all* sucrose of different degrees of purity and in general the darker the sugar the more impure it is. During the last century people paid much higher prices for refined white sugars than for the more impure brown varieties. Nowadays, ironically, the respective prices are reversed, although normal white granulated sugar, being at least 99·9% pure sucrose, is chemically one of the purest foods on the market. All the other sugars which are now available on the retail market consist of sucrose with the addition of permitted colouring agents. Icing sugar is simply powdered sucrose to which an anticaking agent (starch or an inert inorganic material) has been added.

Sucrose molecules are formed when glucose molecules join up with fructose molecules. In other words, each sucrose molecule consists of one glucose molecule joined to one fructose molecule. Since each sucrose molecule is made up of *two* sugar units (monosaccharides) we refer to it as a *disaccharide*. Maltose is also a disaccharide but is made up of two glucose molecules only.

COMPONENTS OF FOOD AND DRINK   11

Fructose molecules can join together in long chains to form a polysaccharide called inulin, which is present in chicory. Glucose molecules can join together to form the very important polysaccharide called starch, and another polysaccharide which is formed entirely out of glucose units is cellulose, a tough fibrous substance present in wood, vegetables and cocoa shell and nothing at all like starch in the way it behaves either chemically or in the human stomach. Why is it then, that two polysaccharides, both of which contain only glucose molecules joined together in a chain, can in fact appear to be so different? It is the way in which the glucose molecules are joined together which decides the particular characteristics of the polysaccharide. Also, the glucose molecules in starch probably join together to form spiral chains whereas in cellulose they

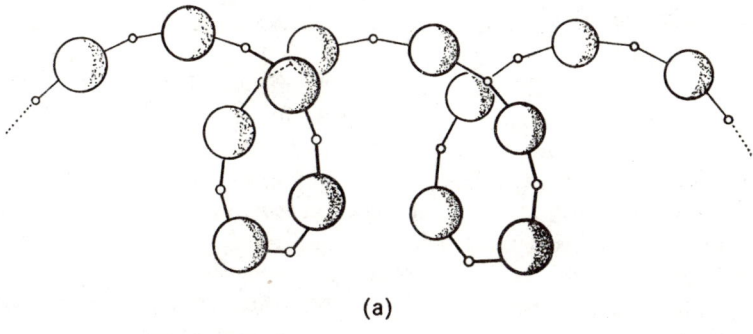

(a)

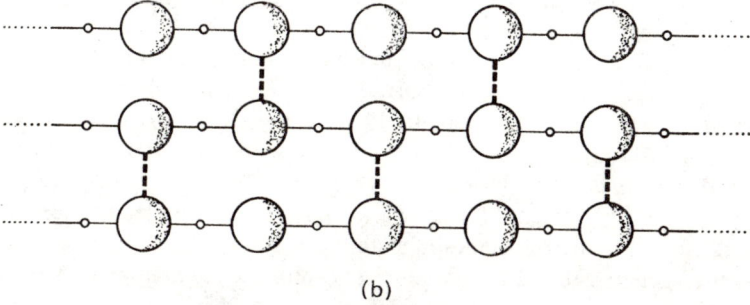

(b)

FIG. 2.3. Part of (a) starch molecule showing spiral structure and (b) cellulose molecule showing stiff chains held together by hydrogen bonds (thick dotted lines).

form stiff, extended, parallel chains held together, side by side by means of hydrogen bonds, as shown in Fig. 2.3 a and b.

Since polysaccharides are formed by joining sugars together the reverse process should also be possible, and sugars can be broken down either on a small scale in the laboratory or on a large scale industrially by a process of *hydrolysis* which will be explained later. For example, when corn starch is heated with an acid it is converted into a sweet sticky mixture of sugars called "glucose syrup". This substance is now widely used in food manufacture having useful nutritional and medical properties. Commercial methods for turning starch into sweet sugars in this way were first devised by countries such as Germany, undergoing naval blockades in times of war and therefore unable to import sugar.

During cooking, starch molecules can become *gelatinized* and this is very useful in giving "body" and thickness to desserts such as blancmanges. What happens to starch molecules when they are cooked at ordinary temperature is that the chains of glucose units are forced out of their tight-packed spiral arrangements and are thus able to mix intimately with water molecules. An ordered arrangement of starch and water molecules gives a characteristic smooth jelly-like substance in which the water molecules present are hydrogen bonded to the starch molecules. This arrangement is necessary in any blancmange if it is to have the correct "mouth feel".

Cellulose, which forms most of the tough fibrous part of wood, can also be changed into glucose by heating it with a dilute acid. This can be useful commercially and industrial processes therefore exist, particularly in Russia, for example, for converting wood into glucose—i.e. grape sugar!

When polysaccharides are converted into sugars by heating them with acids, each link in the polysaccharide chain is chemically broken by a water molecule which then joins itself on to the sugar unit which is next to the link. Because water molecules are necessary for the process it is referred to as *hydrolysis*. However, molecules other than polysaccharides may also undergo hydrolysis because proteins and fat molecules can also be attacked by water molecules in a similar way as will be described later in this chapter. Table 2.2 lists some carbohydrates, examples of foods in which they occur, and their importance (other than dietary).

Pectin is a complex polysaccharide which occurs in fruits. Although its structure is quite well understood it is beyond the scope of this book

TABLE 2.2. FOOD CARBOHYDRATES AND THEIR IMPORTANCE

Carbohydrate	Food in which it occurs	Importance
Glucose	Jams, honey, grapes	Sweetness*
Fructose	Jams, honey, many fruits	Sweetness and prevents crystallization*
Sucrose	Jams, honey, condensed sweetened milk	Sweetness*
Lactose	Milk, condensed sweetened milk	Sweetness, texture
Maltose	Malt, "glucose syrup"	Sweetness, fermentation
Starch	Flour, puddings, blancmanges	Thickness, body, filling
Cellulose	Vegetables and fibrous foods	Mostly waste
Inulin	Chicory	Caramelizes on heating
Pectin	Fruits	Jam and jelly formation
Edible gums	Various plants	Thickening and emulsifying
Caramel	Strongly heated carbohydrate foods	Colouring and flavouring

to discuss it in detail. The molecules have a certain degree of acid character, however, and understanding this helps food technologists to make foods such as jams and jellies of desired consistency. The pectin contents of some fruits are much higher than others—apples, for example, being a good source of the polysaccharide.

When pectin is boiled with sugar and acid in the correct proportion it forms a jelly of the desired consistency for use in jams and marmalades, and the same principle operates here as for starch gelling in puddings. In other words an ordered arrangement of pectin and water molecules is formed and held together largely by a network of hydrogen bonds. Other polysaccharides of importance in foods are the edible gums which are far too complex to discuss in this book. They contain about four different types of rare sugar unit linked together as long chains, which are also attached to one another to form complex, branched, tree-like structures. These edible gums are only used in small amounts (about 1%) in foods and have useful thickening and *emulsifying* properties. Emulsification is a process by which two immiscible liquids in a food are brought together as a smooth product, e.g. vinegar and oil are emulsified in the preparation of salad cream.

Sugars and polysaccharides all have similar *Calorific Values* or heating effects on the body but apart from this effect, which will be dealt with in the next chapter, they tend to confer different properties on foods. Thus polysaccharides cause gelling, thickening, bodying, filling and emulsification effects in foods, whereas sugars are used mainly for sweetening. This brings us to the natural questions "What is sweetness, why do sugars taste sweet, and why do some sugars taste sweeter than others?"

Now although sweetness could be said to be a matter of taste it is in fact basically a chemical phenomenon and sweetness depends on the chemical nature of each sugar molecule. The molecule of glucose, for example, contains six carbon atoms, six oxygen atoms, and twelve hydrogen atoms which can protrude into surrounding space in all manner of different ways, according to what shape the molecule adopts. It is the shape of each sugar molecule which therefore determines whether it will *fit* into the molecules of the taste-bud proteins (as a hand fits into a glove). No sugar molecule can taste sweet unless it fits into taste-bud proteins on the tongue in this way, and in order to produce the sensation of sweetness they must be held at the taste bud for a short time by a weak bond. These bonds are most probably hydrogen bonds and because sugars vary in their molecular structure they also vary in their ability to fit closely into the molecules of the taste buds. Hence their sweetness varies.

All carbohydrates, whether they be sugars or polysaccharides, turn into caramel when heated strongly. Most people nowadays know that caramel is a brown substance which smells and tastes sweet and is used in the flavouring and colouring of foods. In fact it is a substance which chemists do not yet understand. It is probably a mixture of many chemicals containing big and small molecules. Obviously sugar molecules will change very markedly under strong heat or roasting conditions but other less obvious changes in food carbohydrates can take place under milder cooking conditions. Industrial processes in which carbohydrates are heated to temperatures rather less than roasting, but still very high, often convert them into *rare food sugars*—a subject of much current research. Rare food sugars have molecules which the body is not used to dealing with. The body may not be able to digest them either in the stomach or the intestines and they therefore sometimes produce cramping pains, flatulence and diarrhoea. Not all rare sugars do this, however, and these unpleasant symptoms are therefore not often encountered.

Fats

All fats are substances which consist of glycerol (i.e. glycerine, the same substance of which throat pastilles are made) *chemically combined* with an acid. This means that each molecule of a fat consists of a molecule of glycerol attached by a chemical bond to one, two or three molecules of an acid as shown in Fig. 2.4 and that it cannot be detached unless we treat it with another chemical which will react with it. A fat molecule which is formed chemically in this way no longer has the acid character of the acid molecules which are used to make it, nor does it possess the characteristics of the glycerol molecule. In fact its properties (i.e. the way in which it will react with other substances) are similar only to other fats. Fats are therefore a separate class of chemical substance from either glycerol or acids. Oils belong to the same class as fats and there is really no scientific difference between oils and fats, but it is usual to mean liquids when we speak of oils and solids when we speak of fats. However, we could heat a solid fat until it melted but would not necessarily refer to the

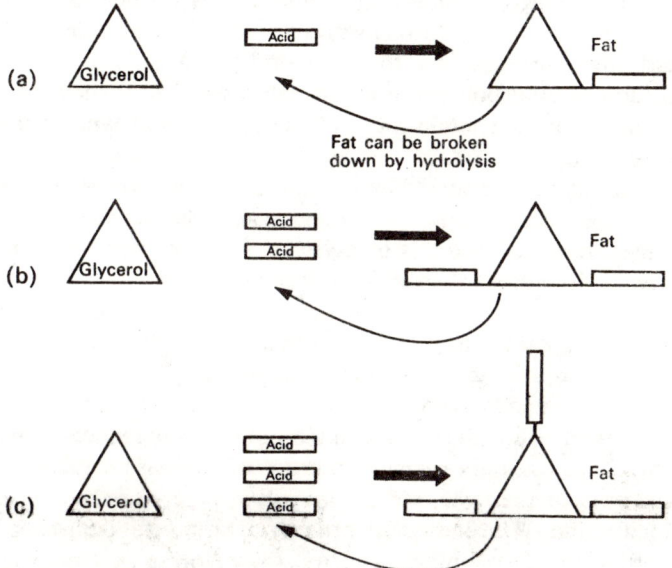

Fig. 2.4. Formation of different types of fat molecule by reaction of glycerol with (a) one, (b) two, and (c) three acid molecules.

liquid we would obtain this way as an oil. Conversely olive oil, for example, often solidifies when cooled, but we still refer to it as olive oil. When this latter process occurs the fat is said to crystallize and the way in which the cooling or freezing is carried out will govern the form which the fat crystals will adopt, and hence the consistency of the solid. Fat crystallization is important in many foods, and in chocolate-making, for example, unless the chocolate sets to the correct consistency it will not have the "snap" which appeals to the consumer.

In Fig. 2.4 the acid molecules are represented as long rods because they are in reality made up of chains of carbon atoms joined together by chemical bonds to give a long molecule. All the carbon atoms are also chemically combined with hydrogen atoms and sporadically along the chain of carbon atoms there are sometimes pairs of adjacent carbon atoms held together extra firmly by a second chemical bond. These points along the chain where an extra bond exists between two carbon atoms are called *double bonds* and any fat which contains double bonds is called an *unsaturated* fat. The word "unsaturated" here refers to the fact that carbon atoms held together by means of double bonds do not have as many hydrogen atoms attached to them as other carbon atoms and are therefore said to be unsaturated with respect to hydrogen. Fats which do not contain any double bonds are called saturated fats. Vegetable fats in general are likely to contain more of the unsaturated type of molecule than animal fats.

In Fig. 2.4 the lower curved arrow shows that the process whereby fat molecules are formed from glycerol and acid molecules may be reversed by chemical means. Since this involves a water molecule attacking a fat molecule the process is called *hydrolysis* and it results in breakdown of the fat molecule to smaller molecules just as the hydrolysis of polysaccharides results in the breakdown of these molecules into smaller one (sugars). Fat molecules breaking down to acids in this way result in a condition referred to as rancidity in which the acid produces an unpleasant sour taste. However, although spoilage of a fat in this way renders it unattractive to the consumer, only a small proportion of the fat is likely to be broken down in spite of the taste, and the fat will not therefore have lost much nutritional value. The industrial process of frying food in deep fat in large kettles gradually causes rancidity to develop in this way. This will cause changes in the nutritional quality of the food because the rancid fat will destroy vitamins in the food and will be much more effective in doing this than the fresh oil or fat would be. In the industry it is common practice to change the fat in these frying kettles after 15 to 20 days, and this point is worth noting by housewives who carry out the practice of keeping a chip pan full of fat in the cupboard and then using it time after time. Furthermore, quantities of fat should always be stored away from odoriferous materials because the molecules of such substances (e.g. paraffin) have a great tendency (being themselves chemically related to oils) to dissolve in fats or oils. Chip pans or butter dishes can therefore easily become very smelly.

A different type of rancidity which can occur in foods is *oxidative rancidity*. In this type of rancidity the double bonds of unsaturated fats are selectively attacked by oxygen in the air. When unsaturated fats or oils are exposed to the atmosphere the double bonds in the fat or oil molecule are chemically changed by the oxygen (oxidized) after which the molecule breaks down further and tastes rancid.

All fats have a characteristically greasy texture, and unlike sugars which dissolve freely in water, they are completely immiscible with water. For this reason the fatty parts of food can generally be considered as separate from the other parts. Even well-mixed foods such as meat pastes actually consist of separate pieces of fat and water-soluble components, so small that great magnification would be necessary to distinguish them visually. The fatty parts of foods also show different chemical behaviour from other parts. Fats can often stand higher temperatures then other food components and are therefore useful for frying and roasting purposes when they can cause the desired amount of browning or crisping to occur in the product. On the other hand, once the fat has been heated above a certain critical temperature (the flash point) it will burn very fiercely and it is therefore a potentially dangerous cooking hazard as every housewife knows. In some foodstuffs, such as butter and margarine, the fat is very evenly dispersed or emulsified with the water which is present, so that the product appears to be smooth and uniform in texture. This process of forming a uniform dispersion of two immiscible liquids may be assisted by additives called emulsifying agents and will be dealt with in a later chapter.

Flavouring oils. As well as the major fatty foods like butter, cheese and cream in which a high fat content (18–80%) is desirable, there are a number of foods containing extremely small amounts of an oil (less than 1%) in which the oil content is nevertheless highly important, chiefly for odour and flavour reasons. These oils are often synthetic chemicals added specifically as flavouring agents and an example is the oil *amyl acetate* which has a very strong odour and flavour of pears and is therefore used in boiled sweet manufacture. There are a number of naturally occurring substances which are oily in nature and which are responsible for the natural odour of many fruits and vegetables. These substances form the characteristic odour or essence of the fruit or vegetable concerned and are therefore referred to as essential oils or volatile oils. It should be pointed out, however, that these substances are in reality mixtures of chemicals, many of which are *not* formed from glycerol and acids and which do not therefore justify inclusion in the fat group of chemicals.

Amino Acids and Proteins

The molecules of the amino acids all have nitrogen atoms attached to hydrogen atoms in their make up. There are always two hydrogen atoms attached to one nitrogen atom and this particular grouping (NH_2) is called the *amino* group. Thus amino acid molecules consist of carbon atoms to which are attached amino groups and groups of other atoms which have an acid character. In a sense the words "amino acid" are not a good way to describe these molecules because most amino acids are not actually acids at all, being in fact neutral in character. This is because the amino groups have an alkaline character and this therefore *neutralizes* the acid group in each molecule. However, amino acid molecules may contain more than one amino group or more than one acid group. If there are more acid groups than amino groups in each molecule the amino acid is in fact a true acid, but if there are more amino groups than acid groups in the molecule the amino acid is alkaline. All three types—acid, neutral and alkaline—of amino acid are known and altogether there are about twenty different types of amino acid which are of importance in food.

When amino acids join together into long chains the resulting molecules are called polypeptides, and this can occur with either one, two, three, or *any number* of different amino acids linking up. Figure 2.5a and b shows the sort of polypeptide molecule we would obtain if three different amino acid molecules (represented as squares) are joined together repetitively into a chain. Figure 2.5c shows the result of coiling the polypeptide

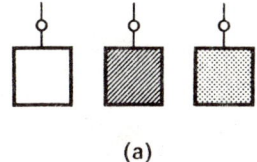

(a)

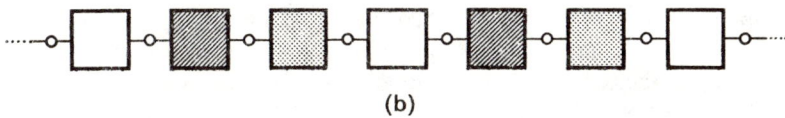

(b)

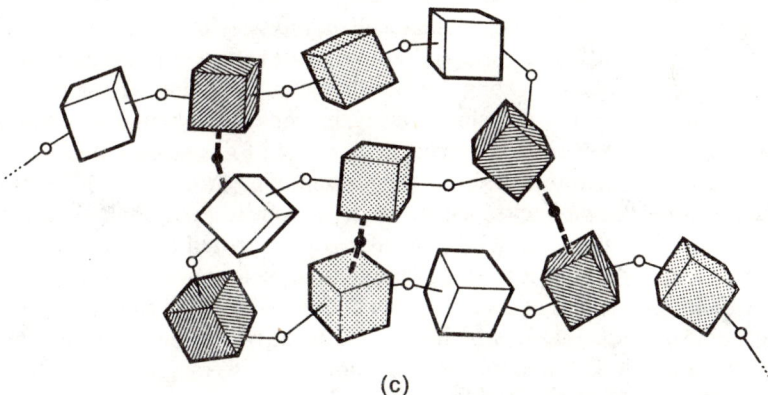

(c)

FIG. 2.5. (a) Amino acid molecules, (b) part of a polypeptide molecule and (c) part of a protein molecule showing the three-dimensional coiling of the polypeptide molecule.

chain into a particular shape in three dimensions. The molecule which we now have in Fig. 2.5c is called a protein and it is an essential dietary constituent of food (see next chapter).

Just as we can convert polysaccharides into sugars (i.e. break up the chain) by heating them with acids, so we can split up polypeptides or proteins into amino acids in the same way. This process is called *hydrolysis* being similar to the breakdown of fats or carbohydrates according to the same basic principle. In other words water molecules attack each link along the polypeptide or protein chain. Hydrolysis of proteins is carried out commercially, chiefly to produce meat flavouring materials.

Proteins are the most complex of the main food chemicals in our diet because not only do they contain many different types of amino acid in their make up, but the special three-dimensional structure which they adopt by coiling (Fig. 2.5c) will determine what sort of physical properties the protein will have. Thus the toughness, rubberiness, elasticity and solubility of the protein foods we eat all depend on the molecular structure of the protein molecules.

The type of bond which holds the polypeptide chain in a particular *coiled* three-dimensional structure as shown in Fig. 2.5c is called a *bridge* and may be a chemical bond or hydrogen bond. The bridges are often broken quite easily by either chemical or physical methods, e.g. acids, heat, cold, or even mechanical agitation may be sufficient to destroy them. This in turn may cause a considerable change in the characteristic properties (or nature) of the protein because the molecules, being deprived of bridges, begin to uncoil. The process is referred to as *denaturation* of the protein, and an example of this is the protein of egg-white, which changes from a slimy transparency to a firm, white, opaque solid on cooking. Freezing may also damage protein molecules so that frozen and subsequently thawed meat often tastes more "stringy" than fresh. Mechanical agitation may denature protein in a similar way and an example of this is provided by cheese manufacture in which the curd from which the cheese is made needs to be skilfully manipulated. Bad handling will result in denaturation of the curd protein and produce a rubbery, unattractive cheese.

The more we learn about the molecular structure of proteins the more thoroughly we come to understand the ways in which changes will be expected to occur in our food. However, the structure of proteins is so immensely complex that very few of them are as yet fully understood. The sequence of amino acids in the molecule of the hormone insulin (a substance secreted from the pancreas into our blood-streams to control the level of blood glucose) was the first to be elucidated, and since then a number of enzymes and other molecules of biological interest have been worked out. However, a vast amount of research taking several years is necessary to work out the structure of one protein molecule, and a lot more is needed to help food scientists on this subject. A knowledge of the structure of muscle protein, for example, would be of immense value if completely understood. Many people are not fully aware of the chemical changes in fresh meat protein which must occur after slaughter of an animal in order for our meat dishes to be fully acceptable. First of all, a polysaccharide substance called glycogen, which is present in muscle tissue, gradually breaks down to another chemical called lactic acid (the same acid that is present in sour milk and cheese incidentally) which is very important as it has both a preservative action and a tenderizing action in the meat. Only after the lactic acid has had enough time to change the three-dimensional character of the protein molecules (the hanging time) will the meat be tender enough to cook in the home. If an animal becomes excited and over-exercised before slaughter the glycogen in its muscles will be depleted and there will not be enough available to change into lactic acid. Hence the tenderizing action in the muscle will not take place. This is the reason why animals should be fully rested and quiet before slaughter.

Enzymes

Enzymes are protein molecules which are able to cause particular chemical reactions to take place and which are manufactured by living organisms for this purpose. They are *catalysts* which means that they are able to cause chemical reactions to take place without being used up themselves. Only very small amounts of each enzyme are necessary to catalyse chemical reactions in living cells and every single chemical reaction in a living cell is controlled by an enzyme. Some enzymes can cause sugars to turn into fats and others cause changes to take place in fats, proteins, etc. Living organisms in fact contain many different sorts of enzymes each causing particular chemical reactions to take place in one direction or another, manufacturing and breaking down chemicals according to their own needs.

This is a fascinating picture of biological control and provokes the immediate question: "How do enzymes work in this amazing way?" Perhaps the best way to answer this is to consider the analogy of an escalator which is travelling upwards and onto which we step. Obviously this escalator will carry a lot more people up, and a lot more quickly than if it were standing still. As we step off the top of the escalator more of it becomes available at the bottom for other people to step onto, and so it goes on without the escalator being changed in the process. The escalator is thus like the enzyme and the people like the molecules being continuously changed from one state to another. There is one other point about the escalator: it is a surface. It is only the surface of the escalator which is being used by the people. In the same way it is the surface of the enzyme molecule which is being used by the molecules which are undergoing change. Thus if we take the case of the enzyme *sucrase*, which hydrolyses the disaccharide sucrose (this is the way enzymes are usually named, by putting the suffix *-ase* onto the stem of the name of the molecule being changed), sucrose and water molecules must first of all fit into particular places on the surface of the enzyme. Having "fitted in" to the surface

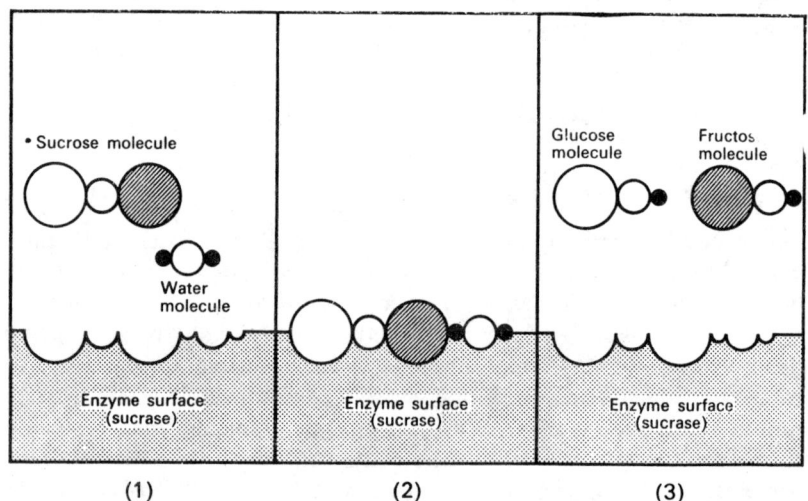

FIG. 2.6. Lock and key diagram showing how an enzyme catalyses sucrose hydrolysis. (1) Before reaction, (2) reaction taking place at the enzyme surface and (3) after reaction, showing the molecules of glucose and fructose formed.

this way they then interact to form a molecule of glucose and a molecule of fructose which are then released from the surface of the enzyme thus making room for more molecules of sucrose and water. This is shown in Fig. 2.6.

The way the molecules of sucrose and water fit into the surface of the enzyme may be likened to the analogy of a lock and key, the sucrose and water being the key and the enzyme surface being the lock. Enzyme surfaces will only fit the particular molecules taking part in the reaction which they are catalysing and generally no "foreign" molecules are able to fit into the enzyme surface at all. This means that enzymes are *specific* for the particular reactions that they catalyse or, referring to our analogy, the enzyme surface provides a burglar-proof lock.

In the context of food there are two very important functions of enzymes. Firstly the digestion of food in the stomach or intestine is carried out by mixtures of enzymes and other substances (see next chapter), and secondly the early stages of many food-manufacturing processes require the action of enzymes. The fermentation of tea and the malting of barley are examples of this. In the latter process an enzyme called diastase breaks down the barley starch to the sugar maltose, which is then fermented by an enzyme system in yeast. Sometimes it is possible to extract an enzyme preparation from an organism, purify it, and then use it for particular food-manufacturing purposes. For example, the enzyme sucrase (also known as invertase) which breaks down cane sugar or beet sugar (sucrose) to glucose and fructose is often used in confectionery to assist the manufacture of fondants or cream centres for chocolates.

Enzymes will only continue to work so long as their particular three dimensional molecular character is maintained. Thus heat, acids, alkalis or other chemicals might cause uncoiling of the polypeptide chain and hence denaturation of the enzyme protein, which would not then function in its particular way. This can be useful, however, as there are many enzymes which cause undesirable changes in foods making them unsightly and unnutritious, and these can be destroyed by heating the food in boiling water and steam for a few minutes. This process, which is called "blanching", removes the offending enzyme without cooking the food and is carried out during the industrial canning of vegetables. In particular it destroys enzymes which cause "browning" reactions to occur in the food and others which cause destruction of vitamins A and C.

Vitamins

Vitamins are essential constituents of the diet but they are required in amounts so small that they probably function as catalysts in a similar way to enzymes. The observations which first led up to our present understanding of vitamins occurred during the eighteenth century when it was noticed that British sailors on long voyages who had no access to fresh fruit often suffered from the disease called scurvy. To overcome this, near the beginning of the nineteenth century it was made compulsory for British sailors to drink lime juice and hence they became known as "limeys" by sailors of other nations. Since then we have discovered that the active principle in lime juice or any fresh fruit which prevents scurvy is vitamin C and because of its anti-scurvy or antiscorbutic effect it has become known chemically as *ascorbic acid*.

Although the word vitamin conjures up mysterious or even magical meaning for some people, all vitamins are in fact ordinary chemicals nearly all of which can be synthetically prepared by chemists entirely out of laboratory reagents. Vitamin A, for example, is a yellow solid which will dissolve in organic solvents such as chloroform while vitamin C is a white crystalline powder with a sharp taste. The molecular structure of all the vitamins is thoroughly understood.

The most important vitamins in food science and technology are vitamins A, B, C, D and E, and with the exception of vitamin C (ascorbic acid) the others are actually families of chemicals, one member of each being much more biologically active than the others. Vitamin B differs from the others in that it is actually a complex of many vitamins each having different functions.

Vitamins B and C differ from vitamins A, D and E in that the first two are water soluble and the others are oil soluble. Each vitamin has a unique physiological role in human metabolism which will be dealt with in the next chapter, but on the basis of their chemical properties alone we are able to predict how the vitamin content of foods will depend on the type of the food or its method of preparation.

Well-informed housewives know that heating of foods causes losses in their vitamin content but unfortunately as a result a popular misconception has grown up about the value of cooking food. Some people believe that raw foods are always better for us than cooked. This is not true. The sensible cooking of foods not only improves their taste, odour, tenderness and digestibility, but also need not entail great losses of vitamins.

The most sensitive of all the vitamins to cooking temperatures is vitamin C and the next most sensitive after this one is thiamine. The oil-soluble vitamins tend to be a good deal more stable than the others, but high cooking temperatures such as occur in frying or roasting will cause all of them to be partly destroyed. Vitamin C is particularly easily destroyed by atmospheric oxygen, especially in the presence of sunlight. Warm foods should not be allowed to stand in the open in metal containers for long periods before eating because the metal in the container may catalyse the breakdown of vitamin C in this way.

Other methods of preparing foods such as cutting, freezing and thawing, or dehydrating also contribute to loss of the vitamins. Freezing itself, however, does not destroy vitamins and is in fact the best way of preserving the vitamin content of food.

Minerals and Trace Elements

Minerals and trace elements constitute the *inorganic* matter of our food. In other words, these substances are not chemically combined with carbon. In fact, they are all present mostly in the form of simple salts and we can obtain them from foods most easily by burning off all the organic matter. The ash which remains is the inorganic part of the food.

All of the mineral and trace elements which are of any importance in foods are listed in Table 2.3 under three different physiological headings.

It must be pointed out here that certain of the elements in column 1 of Table 2.3 are toxic in anything but very small amounts, examples of these being selenium and fluorine. Even the toxic elements in column 3 (e.g. arsenic) are often present in our bodies in trace quantities, but we do not yet know whether these tiny amounts are actually needed by the body for some purpose. Most of the metals in column 1 of Table 2.3 are needed to help enzymes function in the body. Cobalt is actually part of the molecule of vitamin B_{12}, which is also called cobalamin, the anti-pernicious anaemia vitamin.

No quantities are given for any of the trace elements in Table 2.3 because these are so small that they are hardly worth recording at this point. Some idea of the weight of each present, however, may be grasped by knowing that meat, for example, contains about 100,000 times as much protein as copper and at least 10 million times as much protein as arsenic.

TABLE 2.3. CLASSIFICATION OF IMPORTANT MINERAL SUBSTANCES IN HUMAN FOOD

The essential nutritive elements	The non-essential, non-nutritive, non-toxic elements	The non-nutritive, toxic elements
Hydrogen Oxygen Nitrogen Sulphur Phosphorus Fluorine Chlorine Iodine Sodium Potassium Calcium Magnesium Iron Zinc Manganese Copper Cobalt Molybdenum Selenium	Aluminium Boron Chromium Nickel Tin	Arsenic Antimony Cadmium Lead Mercury

Suggestions for Further Reading

ALTSCHUL, A. M. *Proteins: their Chemistry and Politics*, Chapman & Hall, 1965.
BENDER, A. E. *Dictionary of Nutrition and Food Technology*, Butterworths, 4th ed., 1975.
BENDER, A. E. *Dietetic Foods*, L. Hill, 1967.
BENDER, A. E. *Nutrition and Dietetic Foods*, 2nd ed., L. Hill, 1973.
FISHER, P. and BENDER, A. E. *The Value of Food*, Oxford University Press, 2nd ed., 1975.
FOX, B. A. and CAMERON, A. G. *Food Science—a Chemical Approach*, Hodder and Stoughton, 3rd edn., 1976.
MARKS, J. *A Guide to the Vitamins—their role in health and disease*, Medical and Technical Publishing Co., 1975.
MARKS, J. *The Vitamins in Health and Disease*, Churchill, 1968.
MCCANCE, R. A. and WIDDOWSON, E. M. *The Composition of Foods*, Medical Research Council, H.M.S.O., 1960.
TAYLOR, R. J. *Carbohydrates*, Unilever Booklet, 1975. A well presented fairly advanced chemical review of the structure of carbohydrates.
TAYLOR, R. J. *The Chemistry of Glycerides*, Unilever Educational Booklet, 2nd edn., 1968. A clear, simple and well-illustrated account.
TAYLOR, R. J. *The Chemistry of Proteins*, Unilever Educational Booklet, 2nd edn., 1969. A very clear and concise introduction to a complex subject.

CHAPTER 3

Why Do We Need Food?

Now that the reader has some idea of the types of chemical of which ordinary foods consist, it is of interest to consider why these particular chemicals are able to nourish the body or, in other words, to provide it with its essential nutrients. What do these chemicals actually do to enable the body to fulfil its normal functions? How do these substances actually change chemically within the body?

The food we eat always contains some indigestible material which will not be absorbed by the body and will therefore be unable to nourish it in any way. This indigestible part of our diet is eventually eliminated from the body although it serves a purpose in that it provides roughage and stimulates intestinal movement. The body actually selects the nutrients in our diet by means of a pipeline called the *alimentary canal*, shown diagrammatically in Fig. 3.1, which passes from the mouth to the anus. The part of this pipe connecting the mouth to the stomach is called the oesophagus and after leaving the stomach it becomes highly convoluted and is called the small intestine. The small intestine runs into the large intestine which consists of the caecum and then the colon, which passes to the rectum and the anus.

It is essential to get this picture clear before we proceed to examine the fate of food within the body because digestion takes place at various places along the alimentary canal and, in this way, the body selects particular classes of chemical from the food we have eaten and absorbs them, through the wall of the pipe into the bloodstream. The nutrients released into the blood in this way pass to different parts of the body where they may be changed chemically to enable the body to carry out its normal functions.

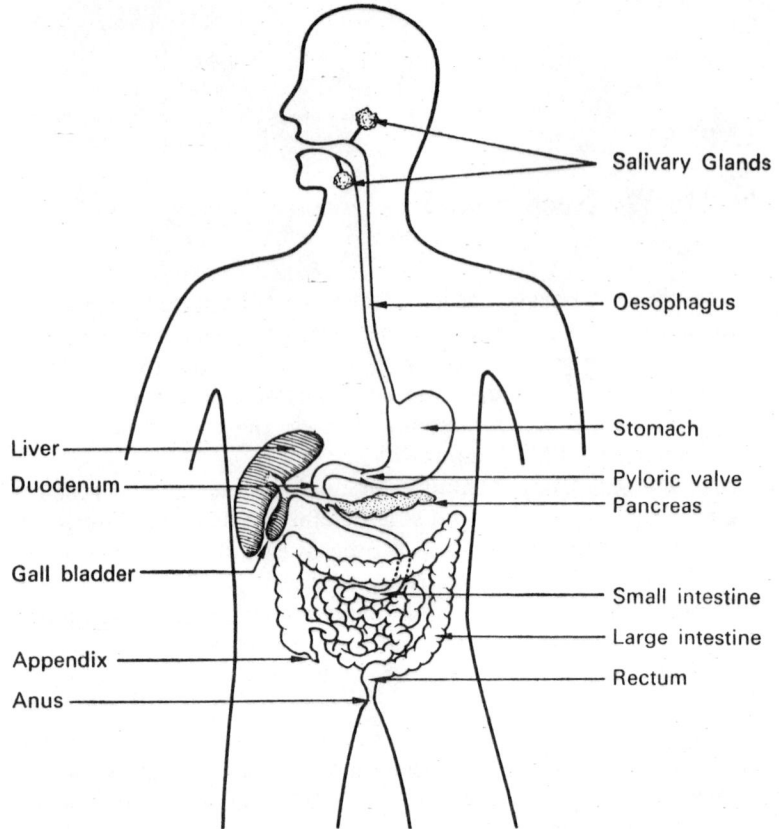

Fig. 3.1. The alimentary system.

Functions of Food

The chief effects of the major food chemicals within our bodies are production of energy (including heat), the supply of "building bricks" for the building and repair of body tissues, and the formation of substances which control and regulate bodily processes. Since each food chemical can cause some or all of these effects to take place, we need to control our diet to achieve a balance of all the effects, to enable our bodies to function healthily. Let us therefore consider each of these effects in turn.

The first function of food within the body is to produce energy, in two main forms, i.e. mechanical energy and heat energy. The products of digestion of food, having passed into the bloodstream, are oxidized by oxygen (taken into the lungs from the atmosphere) to produce all the mechanical energy which we require for movement, muscular contraction, or any other bodily function, whether voluntary or involuntary. In fact the body consists of a vast number of chemical substances undergoing change, each change also being a chemical reaction which requires energy to take place, and every change that takes place is controlled by enzymes which are continually breaking down chemicals into simpler substances and building up other complex substances out of simpler ones, the whole process being regulated with fantastic precision. The body could thus be likened to a vastly complicated engine, producing energy for a variety of purposes and growing and repairing itself in the process. Like all engines however, it is not perfectly efficient, and not all the energy required for a particular purpose is therefore produced by a particular reaction. In other words, in all engines some energy is always lost as heat, and our bodies similarly lose a certain amount of heat each day. The heat which is produced this way as the end product of all the chemical reactions which go on in the body also serves, however, to maintain the temperature of the body at 98·6°F, which is the temperature necessary for most of the enzymic reactions in the body to take place. The heating effect which food provides for us is essential for the normal healthy functioning of our bodies, for unless the temperature of the body is kept at a constant level (98·6°F) most of the chemical reactions and enzymic changes within the body cannot take place. The three main classes of chemical in our food—carbohydrate, fat and protein—each contribute heat to our bodies and the amount of heat provided by each of them is measured in units called calories.

There has been much confusion in food books written in the past about the word *calories*. One gramme of any carbohydrate, for example, can supply us with about 4000 of these heat units called calories, so to save time writing "4000 calories" authors have written 4 kilocalories (the prefix kilo meaning thousand). This was further shortened to 4 kcals and then to 4 Calories (or 4 Cals), the capital C indicating that Calories are 1000 times bigger than calories. Since then many other authors of food subjects have forgotten to use the capital C and much confusion has resulted. We have therefore used the term *Calories* meaning *kilocalories*, in this book, and we refer to the *Calorific Value* of food meaning its energy value in thousands of calories.

Food chemicals differ in their *Calorific Values* and the number of Calories which we would obtain from eating a meal weighing 100 grammes would be given by the formula:

Calories/100 g = 4 × no. of grammes protein + 4 × no. of grammes carbohydrate + 9 × no. of grammes fat.

It can be seen from this formula that fat is much more effective in producing energy than either carbohydrate or protein. A new development has been the use of the joule as a unit of nutritional energy. 1 kilocalorie (Cal.) equals 4,200 joules or 4·2 kilojoules (kJ) See Appendix, page 181.

An important function of the components of our diet is to form a reserve of energy. Our bodies need a store of energy which may be readily drawn on for the purpose immediately required—e.g. heat production or muscle contraction. In other words we need a store of energy to enable us to endure harsh conditions or sustain physical effort without the *immediate need of further food intake*. The energy reserve depots of the body may be likened to chemical warehouses in which a great store of energy-containing molecules are located, and from which fresh supplies of energy may quickly be obtained. The energy reserve depot consists of two main types of body chemical. The first of these is polysaccharide in type and is called *glycogen*. The main store of glycogen in the body is the liver, but muscles also contain small amounts (see p. 21). Glycogen being a carbohydrate rather like starch in its molecular structure, provides a compact store of readily available glucose for the body. Thus, whenever energy is required *without food intake*, enzymes in the liver or muscles release glucose from glycogen into the bloodstream, and the glucose is carried in the blood to whatever part of the body requires energy. Glucose parts with its energy by the action of further enzymes which convert it into other substances like lactic acid. The second type of energy reserve depot within the body is the fat depot (adipose tissue for example) and when excess fat (or carbohydrate) is eaten, fat will be deposited in these depots. The process of storing energy in this way is a normal, healthy function of the body. However, an excessive food intake will cause too much fat to be deposited in this way and thus lead to the "disease" of *obesity*. If food intake is restricted the body will release fat from these depots, changing it by means of enzymes into energy required for its normal internal func-

WHY DO WE NEED FOOD? 31

tioning and external bodily exercise. This is the reason why diet control and physical exercise are the best ways of reducing overweight.

The third function of our diet is to provide "building bricks" for the body to synthesize the chemicals required for its own particular needs. Most of the chemicals which the body needs to synthesize are proteins; for instance, new blood has to be made continuously and the cells forming the lining of the stomach have to be replaced every day. Obviously if the body needs to make new proteins all the time for its own use it can best do this by means of protein in the diet, and as the basic units of the protein chain are amino acid molecules (p. 18) it is actually the amino acid constituents of the proteins which are the true "building bricks" for the body. Before using these building units the body must obtain them from the protein in the diet by breaking down the proteins or digesting them, and this process of digestion of protein takes place in the stomach and small intestine. In the stomach and small intestine, enzymes called *pepsin* and *trypsin* hydrolyse the protein chains converting them to amino acids. Now as proteins differ in the types of amino acid which they contain, obviously not all of the amino acid produced in this way from the proteins in the diet will be required by the body to make into its own proteins. All the amino acids are absorbed through the wall of the small intestine but those not required by the body are disposed of by special sets of enzymes which change them chemically before excretion in the urine. Those amino acids which are required by the body but which cannot be synthesized by the body are called the *essential amino acids*. These amino acids along with all others that are required for the nitrogen pool are absorbed into the bloodstream through the intestinal wall and are then carried to different parts of the body where they are built up into the proteins which the body requires.

TABLE 3.1. HIGH AND LOW PROTEIN FOODS

High protein foods	Low protein foods
Egg	Cabbage
Meat	Carrot
Fish	Apple
Cheese	Orange
	Jam
	Honey

Some foods are deficient in some of the essential amino acids. Wheat flour, for example, is very deficient in lysine. If our diet does not contain enough of certain essential amino acids it is said to be of poor biological value and we may then have to eat more in order to take in the required amount of these essential amino acids. Table 3.1 lists some typical foods of high and low protein value.

Whether we eat enough or not, everything we do eat starts to undergo various changes as soon as we start eating it. The changes which occur in the digestive system, bloodstream and beyond eventually result in turning the food into constituents of our own bodies. As de la Mare has observed in a pithy little verse:

> It's a very odd thing—
> As odd as can be—
> That whatever Miss T. eats
> Turns into Miss T.

Our bodies are therefore in a constant state of chemical reaction with food passing down the alimentary canal and chemical substances in this food being selectively absorbed through the walls of the canal at various places along its length. Perhaps the best way of illustrating this dynamic state of the human digestive system is to follow the passage of a standard three-course meal through the alimentary system and note the various biological effects.

The Digestion of a Standard Three-course Meal

Let us consider the changes which take place among the major types of food chemical where a meal of clear soup, followed by roast beef, roast potatoes, Yorkshire pudding and cabbage, and followed by steamed jam roll and custard is eaten. In considering the digestion of this meal we must learn to recognize in which parts of the meal the major chemical substances—i.e. carbohydrates, fats and proteins—are most likely to be found.

In the first place the clear soup is probably a very dilute solution of meat extract in hot water. There may well be food additives also present in the soup, but these will be present in extremely small quantities so that we may consider the soup as containing practically nothing else than meat extract and water. Furthermore, there will be very little of the meat extract in the water and the soup consists, therefore, mostly (over 90%) of water.

The meat extract is nearly all protein so that the soup is really a very small amount of protein in a lot of water. After passing down through the mouth and then the gullet into the stomach which always contains some hydrochloric acid, the soup stimulates the secretion of digestive juices such as pepsin in the stomach. Pepsin is an enzyme which immediately begins the task of hydrolysing the protein of the meat extract in the soup to amino acids of which the protein chain is composed. Probably far too much pepsin will be secreted for this purpose as there is only a little protein in the stomach after drinking the soup, but the excess pepsin secreted is probably very useful because it prepares the stomach for the mass of protein which will follow after ingestion of the main course. As the digestion of the protein begins under the influence of the pepsin the watery digest is expelled from the stomach into the small intestine where it is made alkaline by the secretion of bile salts from the gall bladder and liver. Trypsin, another enzyme, is then secreted and this, together with erepsin from the intestine, completes the job of hydrolysing the already partially digested protein into amino acids, which can then be absorbed through the wall of the intestine into the bloodstream. Water from the soup also passes through the wall of the intestine into the bloodstream where it is needed to keep the concentration of food substances in the blood at the right level. Any excess water in the blood is passed, along with other unwanted substances, from the bloodstream into the kidneys and then to the bladder from where it is eventually excreted as urine.

The main course of the meal is more complicated. It contains all the three major classes of food chemicals—proteins, carbohydrates and fats—which will be absorbed by the body as nutrients. The insoluble (indigestible) carbohydrate cellulose is present in the cabbage. The main classes of food chemical present in our standard three-course meal are listed in Table 3.2.

Each mouthful of food which we take is first chewed or masticated in the mouth and this process releases the first digestive enzyme into the food. The enzyme is present in saliva and is called amylase. This enzyme only acts on the starch which is present in the mouthful of food, i.e. the roast potato and the Yorkshire pudding. However, it does not have very long to act as after only a very few seconds the mouthful of food is swallowed and thus drops into the stomach. In the stomach the hydrochloric acid prevents the amylase from acting so that it is only after the food enters the small intestine that hydrolysis of starch takes place to any extent under

TABLE 3.2. MAIN CLASSES OF FOOD CHEMICAL IN A STANDARD THREE-COURSE MEAL

First course	Second course	Third course
Water (Soup)	Water (cabbage, potato, meat, gravy)	Water (custard, jam roll)
Protein (Soup)	Protein (meat, gravy, Yorkshire pudding)	Protein (not much, jam roll)
	Carbohydrate (potato, Yorkshire pudding)	Carbohydrate (custard, jam roll)
	Fat (meat, Yorkshire pudding)	Fat (jam roll)

the influence of the amylases secreted from the pancreas. Other enzymes are present in the small intestine which convert maltose into glucose and sucrose into glucose and fructose. This means that nearly all of the carbohydrate which is present in the food, whether it is present originally as starch as we are now considering, or sugar (and there will, of course, be a small amount of sugar present perhaps in the Yorkshire pudding), it will nearly all be finally absorbed through the wall of the intestine into the bloodstream as glucose and/or fructose. There will not be much sucrose in the Yorkshire pudding and roast potato which we are now considering and hence there will be very little fructose appearing in the bloodstream. However, what there is will be rapidly transported to the liver where it will be converted into glucose. Apart from the starch the other major food chemical present in the main course is the protein which we obtain in each mouthful of meat. This is broken up into small pieces during mastication in the mouth and then swallowed down the gullet to the stomach where the pepsin begins the process of hydrolysing the protein into amino acids as already explained for the soup course. From the stomach, the partially hydrolysed protein is passed to the small intestine where it becomes alkaline and trypsin and other enzymes complete the hydrolysis of proteins to amino acids as for the soup. The amino acids formed now pass through the walls of the intestine into the bloodstream where they are transported to those parts of the body which need "building bricks" for making new cells. For example, some will be taken by the blood to the bone marrow where they will be used for the formation of fresh blood cells, others will be taken to the liver to help form new liver cells. In the case of young humans in particular the amino acids in the bloodstream will be dispersed all over the body to help it form all the new tissues required for general growth. The digestion of the meat this way provides the main amino acid intake of the entire meal which we are now considering.

The gravy in the main course is probably identical with the soup of the previous course, so that all that was said about the digestion of the soup also applies to the gravy except that the gravy may contain some starch. Sometimes housewives make gravy by mixing flour with the fatty juice which is obtained during the roasting of meat. Gravy is therefore obviously a dilute solution of meat extract and possibly starch in water, and the digestive fats of the meat extract (protein) and starch have now been dealth with. Apart from the minerals and vitamins which are trace nutrients in the cabbage the major chemical constituents of this vegetable are the insoluble polysaccharide cellulose and water. Since we obtain plenty of water in our diet and since the cellulose of the cabbage is indigestible, it is clear that the major part of cabbage is not very significant nutritionally. However, the extreme importance of the tiny amounts of vitamins and minerals which are present in the vegetable make it a valuable part of the meal. We will discuss the nutritional importance of the vitamins and minerals at a later stage of this chapter, but at this stage we need only know that the insoluble (indigestible) cellulose in the cabbage simply passes right through the small intestine to the large intestine, whence it is eventually expelled as faeces.

The only other major class of food chemical in the main course of our meal is fat. This is present in the beef and roast potatoes, especially on the outside of the latter and is also present in the Yorkshire pudding as this was probably made from a batter of flour, eggs and fat. As with the starch, very little of the fat is broken down in the stomach, but after passage of the food into the small intestine enzymes from the pancreas called lipases break down the fats into fatty acids and glycerol. These chemicals then pass through the wall of the intestine when they recombine as fats in the blood and may be transported to the fat depots of the body.

We can now imagine the situation in which the soup and main course have been eaten, have undergone some digestion in the stomach, and are being expelled in short bursts as a slurry into the small intestine. While this is going on and long before the stomach is anywhere near empty we will have begun our third course—jam roll and custard. This pudding contains all the major classes of food chemical—i.e. carbohydrate, fat and protein, but there is less protein and it is less important nutritionally than that in the roast beef. Nevertheless, all the three major classes of food chemical from the pudding will be digested in the stomach and small intestine by the same enzymes which were used for the digestion of the main course of the meal and in the same way. One big difference between this course and the main course, however, is that a considerable part of the carbohydrate which is present (mostly in the jam, but some in the custard) is the sugar sucrose, and some of the sucrose is already hydrolysed in the jam to glucose and fructose. Sucrose differs from the polysaccharide starch in undergoing some hydrolysis to glucose and fructose in the stomach. However, it eventually arrives in the bloodstream as glucose and fructose. A very high proportion (over 70% of the solid matter) in the jam roll consists of carbohydrate, which will be broken down to glucose (from starch) or glucose and fructose (from sucrose) in this way. Likewise, a very high proportion of the solid matter in the custard will consist of the carbohydrate starch and the rest of the custard is mostly water. All that we have already said about the digestion of carbohydrate, fat and protein will also therefore apply to this third course of our meal. Considerable mixing of the second and third courses of our meal will occur in the stomach and this provides a gentle churning effect on the components of these two courses and what remains of the first course. There will be two most immediate noticeable effects of eating this three-course meal. The first is the feeling of satiety which results from having a full stomach and the second is an effect of digestion of the carbohydrate, which occurs more quickly than that of the fat or protein, and results in a rise in blood glucose level. This immediately provides energy which is rapidly transported in the blood to all parts of the body and provides a sense of well being.

The feeling of satiety will slowly diminish with time as the contents of the stomach are gradually expelled into the small intestine, and the time taken for this to occur will be probably not more than 6 hours, while for some individuals the stomach will be emptied of food within 4 hours or considerably less. Six or 7 hours after eating our meal the digested food mass will have reached the large intestine and the small intestine will probably have emptied it all into the large intestine after about 9 hours. Food chemicals and/or water will be absorbed through the walls of the intestine at various points throughout the length of travel through the intestine. What remains (largely insoluble) after passage through the rectum is expelled as faeces.

Now that we have followed the digestion and absorption of the major food chemicals in our standard meal we will pass on to the examinaton of our nutritional requirements in food and will refer to our standard meal to illustrate these requirements.

Our Nutritional Needs

Water. Water is important in our diet as it is the medium in which all our bodily chemical reactions take place. Our bodies consist of more than 50% water and indeed without water these reactions would not be able to work in the smooth interrelated way in which they do. Furthermore, water prevents our bodies changing temperature too rapidly—everyone knows how long it takes for water to heat up or cool down—and in this way it prevents sudden damage to our tissues. Water functions as a transport system, i.e. transports nutrients in the bloodstream and enables unwanted materials to be eliminated. In addition to the water which we take in while drinking, water is all the time being formed by the chemical reactions which are going on in our bodies. We are continuously losing water from our bodies by perspiration, breathing (the air we exhale contains water vapour) and urine, and we therefore need to replace this by including drink in our diet. A man leading a sedentary life in a temperate climate will lose about $2\frac{1}{2}$ litres of water a day from his body. One and a half litres of this will be as urine and the remainder by perspiration and breathing. If violent exercise is undertaken loss from the last two causes may reach several litres a day. Water is replaced in our bodies as we react to the stimulus of thirst which causes us to drink enough to satisfy our need. The reader is referred to Chapter 5 for an account of this subject. We also, of course, obtain water from soups in meals such as we have considered, and even in part from solid food.

Carbohydrate, Fat and Protein

For reasons already stated the body needs to obtain energy from the food chemicals which we consume and also needs to synthesize new cells for itself with chemicals from the same source. The Calories and mechanical energy which we need may be supplied by either the carbohydrate, fat or protein which we eat but whereas the protein (Table 3.1, p. 31) and fat (essential fatty acids, i.e. linoleic acid and linolenic acid) are needed for purposes other than energy production (or energy storage) the carbohydrate is not. It is true that we need a very small amount of carbohydrate in our diet to prevent a disease called ketosis occurring but this is such a small amount that we could not normally avoid obtaining it in what we eat. Therefore, scientifically speaking there is no need for us to bother about including carbohydrate in our diet. Gastronomically speaking, on the other hand, we would certainly not tolerate many of our traditional confections, ices and desserts if they were not sweet enough; nor would we be attracted by many traditional baked goods if they were not of a pleasant golden brown colour. Both of these effects of taste and appearance are produced by carbohydrates.

Sweetness is a property of those carbohydrates which have small molecules, i.e. sugars, and no other major food chemical can produce anything like the same degree of sweetness as the sugars. To produce sweetness in foods which do not contain sugars we have to use artificial sweetening agents such as saccharin or the cyclamates, about which there has been so much controversy in the national press during the last few years. The brown colour on the crusts of our baked goods is produced by the chemical reaction of sugars with amino acids in the dough during the baking process. Therefore it can be seen that unless we pay attention to technological effects like browning or organoleptic effects like sweetness in the preparation of our food there could easily be a great upset in the normal pattern of our dietary intake because we do not eat much of a food we dislike. This in turn might cause an incorrect balance of the nutrients in our diet and in particular Calorie and protein intake might be upset.

First of all we need a certain minimum number of Calories in our food in order to maintain the body at its normal temperature of 98·6°F for healthy functioning. This minimum number of Calories is equal to the heat output from the body when the subject or patient is resting completely on a bed (not necessarily asleep) without exerting any physical effort. It is heat which results from the normal functioning of the body (i.e. breathing, heart-beating, etc.) under completely restful conditions. Of course, chemical reactions are taking place in the body between products which have come from digestion of previous meals and every one of the normal functions of the body which take place under restful conditions is in fact a complex of chemical reactions. These chemical reactions, which are usually measured in terms of heat output over 24 hours, are referred to as the *basal metabolism* of the body. The amount of energy required for basal metabolism varies according to age, sex and size of individuals, but for adults it lies between 1400 and 1800 Calories in 24 hours. In our daily lives most of us exert some degree of physical effort (even if this is only to walk to our car and get in) and we therefore need quite a lot more than 1800 Calories. In fact probably most people in the United Kingdom, for example, consume between 2500 Calories and 5000 Calories in every 24-hour cycle. In tropical countries such as Africa, heat losses from the body are correspondingly less than in Britain and less Calories are required in the diet for this reason. However, the Calorie intake depends very much on the degree of exertion so that a coal-miner for example will need almost twice as many Calories as a clerk every day of his working life. While most people in the United Kingdom and the United States eat rather too much every day and obesity in some degree is a frequent problem, people in some developing countries obtain insufficient Calories from their diet. This means that they are short of energy and so they become apathetic and their general productivity of food or other essentials in life goes down. These unfortunate people are therefore caught in a vicious circle. Reports coming out of China 15 years ago, for example, showed that the average Calorie intake per adult was about 1800 per day. This means that at that time a considerable number of people in China were existing near starvation level.

Although we do not need to include carbohydrate in our diet except for the small amount needed to avoid ketosis we would in fact have to be very careful of our dietary balance if we decided to omit carbohydrate from our meals. For example, although we could get enough Calories from the protein and fat which we consume we would have to make sure that there was a lot of fat in our food because the consumption of too much protein rapidly gives a feeling of satiety and if we were to judge our intake requirements on the basis of appetite in this case we might easily consume too few Calories. In fact for most people in the United Kingdom carbohydrates supply 50–60% of the Calorie intake and the most important sources of these in our diets are starch and sucrose in baked goods, puddings and jams. In the standard meal which we have already considered the most important suppliers of Calories are the starch in the roast potatoes, Yorkshire pudding, jam roll and custard, and the sucrose in the jam roll and custard, but we must not forget that some of the Calories will be supplied by the protein of the beef and also the fat, which although present as a small part by weight of the whole meal, nevertheless supplies a considerable number of Calories. Certainly there is no need to bother about insufficient Calorie intake in a well-balanced meal such as we have been considering. In fact the only danger is that we might eat too much and thus gain too many. In the poor and developing countries a nutritionally well-balanced meal like this is often a rarity especially during periods of famine. Carbohydrate, being one of the cheapest food constituents, then often constitutes an unbalanced and very high proportion of the diet (up to 70%). It is usually recommended on medical grounds that carbohydrate should not constitute more than 66% of the diet.

Fat is important in our diet, not only because it is a rich source of energy, but because it contains fat-soluble vitamins necessary for the normal chemical reactions of the body. It is also important for technological and gastronomical reasons. For example, the characteristic crispness of the roast potato and the texture of the jam roll in our standard meal would not be possible if we did not include fat in the recipe for the pudding or in the pan in which we roasted the potatoes. However, provided that the supply of fat-soluble vitamins and essential fatty acids (linoleic and linolenic) is adequate it is otherwise not essential to include fat in the diet.

In the United Kingdom the fat intake is about 150 g per head per day and constitutes about 35% of the total Calories. The diets of tropical countries are much lower in fat while in the cold countries they are much higher. An Eskimo, for example, can eat 300 g of fat a day whereas this amount could not be tolerated by an average European. Although it is difficult to be absolutely certain of intake requirements for humans it can be said that when the dietary intake is less than 3000 Calories per day fat should account for at least 25% of the total Calories. If the intake is greater than 3000 Calories per day the fat should account for at least 30% of the total Calories. Once again in the standard meal which we have described an adequate fat content is assured.

Although it is not essential to have much fat or much carbohydrate in the diet providing we have enough Calories, the requirement for adequate protein in the diet is essential. Protein is the one class of major food chemical for which we have a minimum daily requirement. Now we know that proteins consist of chains of amino acids linked together and that during digestion the chain is broken down or hydrolysed by digestive enzymes into amino acids. All the protein must be broken down this way before it can be used by the body. In other words we must make sure that the protein which we consume in our meals contains all the essential amino acids in large enough quantities and, furthermore, they must all be present simultaneously in one meal because we are not able to store amino acids in our bodies in the same way that we can store fat. The amount of essential amino acids in the proteins which we eat is therefore a measure of the quality of the protein and we refer to this as the *biological value* of the protein. It is important to pay attention to the biological value of the protein in our meals because proteins vary enormously this way and in general plant proteins are inferior to animal proteins in this respect. Usually, however, plant proteins are deficient in only one or two essential amino acids. For example, wheat is deficient in lysine and maize is deficient in lysine and tryptophan; but other plant proteins may be deficient in different amino acids so that it is possible to obtain enough essential amino acids from a diet made up entirely of mixtures of vegetable proteins providing we pay sufficient attention to the selection of suitable foods. In general animal proteins contain all the essential amino acids, the egg being an excellent example of an animal protein of high biological value. Moreover, animal proteins contain these essential amino acids in about the right proportion for man's needs. The one notable exception among the animal proteins is gelatin which is of poor biological value, being deficient in tryptophan and tyrosine. It should be noted, however, that gelatin contains all the other essential amino acids and if it could be compounded with a vegetable protein such as wheat (which is not deficient in tyrosine or tryptophan) into an attractive "food of the future" it could provide a meal of good biological value. Despite these possibilities animal proteins are thought to be digested and absorbed more easily than plant proteins and it is therefore recommended that at least 50% and preferably 60% of the protein in a mixed diet should be of animal origin.

Let us now reflect for a moment on the importance of protein (really essential amino acids) in our diet. We now know that proteins of high biological value provide not only the "building bricks" (i.e. essential amino acids) that the body needs to make new cells but are also capable of providing Calories to the same extent as carbohydrate for the body. Whereas it is not absolutely essential to have either much carbohydrate or much fat in our diet it *is* absolutely essential to have a considerable amount of protein, otherwise we would be liable to suffer from the protein deficiency disease (kwashiorkor) which will be discussed later.

What would happen, therefore, if we lived on a diet composed almost entirely of protein? The answer to this question is that it would probably not matter so long as the meals which we ate were of sufficiently high biological value and so long as we ate enough to meet all energy requirements. If sufficient carbohydrate and fat are included in the diet to meet energy requirements this avoids the necessity of our bodies having to use amino acids for this purpose instead of as "building bricks". Carbohydrate and fat are therefore said to exert a *protein sparing* action, and the smallest amount of protein which we need when energy requirements are completely met by fat and carbohydrate is the minimum but not necessarily the optimum protein intake for our diet.

How much protein do we actually eat each day? This varies according to the part of the world in which we live, but in the United Kingdom people usually take between 10 and 12% of their total Calorie intake as protein, of which about 60% is animal protein. In cold parts of the world it may be a lot higher than this. Eskimoes, for example, may take up to 40% of their total Calories as protein, while it has already been mentioned that in many famine areas of tropical countries diets contain only small amounts of low value vegetable protein. The chief factor limiting protein intake is price, because high-value protein is relatively expensive. In the United Kingdom the cheapest sources of high quality, or animal, protein are milk, cheese and herring. Official recommendations of daily protein intake for adults suggest an intake of about 1 g per kg of body weight. This means that a "reference man" weighing 70 kg would have 70 g of protein a day while a "reference woman" weighing 60 kg would have 60 g per day. However, during pregnancy women probably need more than men to allow for the growth of the foetus. Children need much more protein per unit of body weight, in fact, 3–4 per kg. This means that a child of 10–12 years requires as much protein as a man, and older children even more. There is some dispute about the official recommendation of protein intake for people engaged in very hard physical work. The Dept. of Health and Social Security in the United Kingdom recommends that there should be no increase in protein intake for hard physical work. In the case of pregnant women, nursing women, infants, children and adolescents the protein intake should be 14% of the total Calorie intake: for others only 10%.

There is no need for us to worry about protein contained in a standard meal of roast beef and Yorkshire pudding such as we have been considering. The beef is, of course, the most important source of protein in this meal. Nevertheless, it is worth noting that the biological value of beef protein is only about three-quarters of that of egg albumen protein, the latter being another constituent of our standard meal as it was used in the batter from which the Yorkshire pudding was made.

Vitamins

The vitamins were discovered near the beginning of this century by a scientist called Funk who referred to them as *vitamines* (meaning vital amines, or amines essential to life). Funk thought that all the vitamins belonged to the class of chemicals called amines, but we now know this to be incorrect as only certain members of the B complex fit this definition. Funk, of course, was only able to find the facts about vitamins in the same way that any scientist would go about a chemical problem of this type. He had to spend years of constant effort until he was able to extract the biologically potent trace substances from food and then feed the small quantities of products which he obtained, in controlled studies, to rats. The skill and personal expertise of these early scientists must have been considerable and modern food technologists who are engaged in the manufacture, improvement and fortification of foods are indebted to them:

> How grateful we are to Doctor Funk,
> Who by science, skill and knack,
> Extracted the vitamins out of foods
> So we have to put them back.

Vitamins A, B, C, D and E are the most important vitamins for us to consider in the diet because they are the best understood in terms of food distribution. With the exception of vitamin C all of these are actually families of chemicals and one member of each family is often more biologically active than the others. As pointed out in Chapter 2 some vitamins are water soluble and some are oil soluble. They are therefore found in either the aqueous or fatty parts of food respectively. Even so the amounts of the vitamins which are necessary for normal functioning of the body and prevention of deficiency diseases are so small that it is inconvenient for us to talk about them even in terms of grammes, because if we did the quantities involved would be a few thousandths of a gramme or so. In dealing with vitamins we therefore often use quantities called International Units (I.U.s), and the size of an international unit varies from vitamin to vitamin. One international unit of vitamin A, for instance, is only one-third of one-millionth of a gramme.

Vitamin A is called the anti-xerophthalmia vitamin, which means that it prevents a disease called xerophthalmia which results in the hardening of the cornea of the eye. For reasons related to this it is able to prevent deterioration of our eyesight under conditions of poor lighting, e.g. at night. As mentioned in Chapter 2, we obtain vitamin A from two major sources in our diet. First of all the vitamin itself is present in fatty parts of animals, particularly fish oils, and secondly many vegetable foods, while not containing the vitamin itself, contain chemicals called *carotenes*, which are converted into vitamin A in the body. Carotene is not as biologically potent as vitamin A itself but if we eat enough carrots and green vegetables it contributes a very high proportion of our daily vitamin A requirements. It should be noted here that simply to ensure an adequate intake of vitamin A in our diet may not be enough to meet actual needs because vitamin A, although present in many foods, varies enormously in its *availability* to the body. In cod or halibut liver oil, for example, it is well absorbed by the body, but if we are consuming liquid paraffin or similar mineral oils for medical or other reasons this could seriously affect the availability of the vitamin A contained in our food. The recommended daily allowance for vitamin A for an adult is 2500 I.U.s with an increase to 4000 I.U.s for women during pregnancy and lactation. Unless foods make a claim on their label about their vitamin A content they are not normally fortified with vitamin A in the United Kingdom. An example of this is margarine, which has to contain between 760 and 940 I.U.s per ounce by law.

Vitamin B is a complex of vitamins which we normally obtain mostly from vegetable sources and which are necessary to prevent a variety of physiological disorders. Vitamin B_1 or thiamine, for example, is necessary to prevent the disease of beriberi which is a disorder of the nerves and muscles. This disease has been observed and well documented particularly among Asian people who consume too much polished rice in their diets —i.e. rice from which the bran and cortical parts, and hence most of the thiamine content, have been removed. Baby foods and breakfast cereals are frequently fortified with thiamine in the United Kingdom but the only food which has to be fortified by law in the United Kingdom is flour, which must contain at least 0·24 mg thiamine per 100 g of flour. The recommended daily intake of thiamine is about 1 mg.

Other members of the B complex of vitamins for which allowances have been calculated are riboflavine and nicotinic acid. For the former we need a daily intake of 1·5–1·8 mg (higher during pregnancy) to prevent disorders of the skin and eyes, while for the latter we need 15–18 mg per day to avoid the disease of pellagra. The great stability of nicotinic acid compared with all the other vitamins is worthy of note at this point. We expect very little loss of this vitamin to occur during the cooking of food—for example in our standard three-course meal—whereas both thiamine and riboflavine might, and probably would suffer extreme loss during the roasting process. Riboflavine and nicotinic acid are also used to fortify foods in the United Kingdom, but only nicotinic acid is required by law for fortification, and this again only in the case of flour. Flour has to contain at least 1·6 mg nicotinic acid per 100 g. The intake requirement of nicotinic acid is complicated by the fact that the amino acid tryptophan is chemically related to nicotinic acid and possesses about one-sixteenth of its biological effectiveness. Quite a lot of the nicotinic acid effect which we require in our diet is therefore supplied by this amino acid rather than by nicotinic acid itself.

Pyridoxine and the other members of the vitamin B complex are less well understood in terms of human intake requirements, although physiological disorders attributable to lack of them in the diet are well documented. A few years ago, for example, a number of American schoolchildren were afflicted with violent seizures all at about the same time. The disorder was traced to a common supply of milk which they had all been drinking. The milk had been pasteurized by a technique which had resulted in the destruction of its pyridoxine content. Administration of the vitamin to the children overcame the symptoms.

There is one other very probable source of the B vitamins for humans which we have not yet mentioned, and this is the human intestine itself. The intestine is permanently inhabited by bacterial flora which produce many of the B vitamins, and these are in all probability utilized by the body to some extent. During illness or antibiotic administration the intestinal flora could be seriously upset and this could therefore result in the diminution of an important source of our vitamin B intake. Table 3.3 lists the vitamins, the physiological disorders which they prevent, and their recommended intake where known. Our standard three-course meal will supply many of the vitamins of the B complex.

Vitamin C is the water-soluble vitamin which prevents scurvy. This is why it is referred to as the antiscorbutic vitamin and is called ascorbic acid. Apart from its importance in preventing scurvy, vitamin C plays an important role in teeth and bone formation and general bodily repair of wounds. Vitamin C occurs in nearly all fruits and vegetables but the richest sources are rose hips, blackcurrants and citrus fruits. Although pota-

TABLE 3.3. VITAMINS AND RECOMMENDED INTAKE LEVELS

Vitamin	Recommended daily intake
A or Retinol (anti-xerophthalmia)	2500 I.U.s (3000–4000 I.U.s during pregnancy and lactation)
Thiamine (anti-beriberi)	1 mg
Riboflavine	1·5–1·8 mg (higher during pregnancy)
B or { Nicotinic acid (anti-pellagra)	15–18 mg
Pyridoxine (anti-dermatitis in rats)	—
Cobalamin, or B_{12} (anti-pernicious anaemia)	—
C or Ascorbic acid (anti-scurvy)	30–60 mg
D (anti-rachitic)	400 I.U.s (infancy)
E or Tocopherol (anti-sterility)	—

toes contain only about one-hundredth of the amount of vitamin C which is found in rose hips they are still an important source of the vitamin in the United Kingdom and many other countries where a lot of potatoes are eaten. The recommended allowance for vitamin C is between 30 and 60 mg, but an excess of the vitamin will not cause any ill effect. There is no legal requirement for any food in the United Kingdom to contain vitamin C. In Chapter 2 we have thoroughly discussed the extreme sensitivity of vitamin C to cooking temperatures. Great losses are likely to occur, especially during roasting or frying, and this will become much worse if the food is allowed to stand around very long after cooking and before being eaten. In our standard three-course meal the only possible sources of vitamin C would be the potatoes and the cabbage. We can expect very little vitamin C retention in the potato after the very high temperature of roasting so the cabbage is the only constituent of our meal likely to contain any of the vitamin. This too is likely to have lost three-

WHY DO WE NEED FOOD? 47

quarters or more of its vitamin C content by the time the meal is eaten so that we can say that the meal which we have chosen to describe in this chapter would not be adequate to ensure an adequate daily intake of the vitamin. It would therefore be advisable to have an additional course of citrus fruit to meet this requirement.

Vitamin D is a family of chemicals called sterols which prevent the disease of *rickets*, which is a disorder of bone formation, and vitamin D helps the body to absorb the important mineral substances calcium and phosphorus through the wall of the intestine into the bloodstream so that they can be used to form new healthy bones and teeth. We normally obtain our vitamin D by eating the products of animals that contain it, e.g. dairy produce, but it is worth noting that the vitamin D content of milk varies enormously from season to season, and summer milk, for example, may contain twice as much as winter milk. In strong sunlight, as in bright summers, we actually need to eat less vitamin D than at other times because the ultraviolet rays in the sunlight form the vitamin in our skin from steroid substances which are already present. The most important sources of vitamin D in our diet are eggs, milk, cream, butter, margarine and fatty fish. Fish liver oils in particular are sources in which we can expect to find a lot of vitamin D along with vitamin A. Examples of this are, of course, cod-liver oil and halibut-liver oil, but the richest source is tunny-liver oil which contains up to 25 million I.U.s per 100 g! One international unit of vitamin D is extremely small—only 0·025 millionths of a gramme.

Vitamin D is now known to be poisonous in large doses, and symptoms of this are constipation, vomiting and worse, the result sometimes even being fatal. As little as 2000 I.U.s per day in some infants can cause these effects and sometimes only 30,000 I.U.s per day in the case of adults. The recommended intake for infancy is now 400 I.U.s per day in the United Kingdom. By law in the United Kingdom margarine has to be fortified so as to contain 80–100 I.U.s per ounce.

Vitamin E is the antisterility vitamin and consists of a whole family of chemicals called tocopherols. It is present in most vegetables, dairy produce and meat but the richest sources of it are vegetable oils. There is hardly any of the vitamin in fish-liver oils. Intake requirements of vitamin E are not understood, but we probably are able to store it in our bodies to some extent.

Our standard three-course meal probably contains both vitamins D and E from the roast beef, cabbage and the milk that was used in the making of the Yorkshire pudding and custard, and in this respect it is probably therefore nutritionally adequate.

Minerals

Mineral substances in our food consist of a number of metals and non-metals, not chemically combined with carbon. Strictly speaking, therefore, we should include gases such as oxygen and nitrogen within this definition as they exist in the free state in our food and in our bodies. Any substance which becomes chemically combined to carbon is an *organic* substance. Since oxygen and nitrogen are freely available to us in the air we breathe we can consider the mineral substances in our foods separately. Table 2.3 (p. 26) lists the minerals which we are likely to find in our foods under three different physiological headings. We could also, however, divide the minerals into trace elements and others. The trace elements are required only in minute quantities in our food because they are also only present in trace quantities in our bodies. The others, however, are required in much larger quantities in our food because the body contains a lot of them in its normal make up. The essential minerals are iron, calcium, phosphorus, magnesium, iodine, fluorine, sodium and potassium, and we will first of all discuss their importance in the diet.

Most of the iron in the food we eat comes from bread, meat, potatoes, offal and lesser amounts from certain green vegetables. Milk does not contain very much iron and the erroneous idea has grown up among some housewives that the deeper the colour of certain vegetables the more iron they contain; beetroot, for example, is often considered a good source of iron. This idea is quite wrong and beetroot is actually *not* a good source of iron. All flour in the United Kingdom has to be fortified with iron so that it contains at least 1·65 mg per 100 g (see p. 58) and this helps to ensure that we all consume enough of the mineral. The Department of Health and Social Security (1969) recommends an intake of 10–12 mg per day of iron for the majority of adults. The average mixed diet probably contains between 10–50 mg per day. Most people know that iron is needed by the body to make the haemoglobin of our blood. Lack of it leads to the disease of *anaemia*. However, the total amount in our bodies at one time is only 4 g, which is equivalent to one small iron nail.

Milk, cheese and flour products account for over four-fifths of the calcium in average U.K. diets. It is necessary in our diet for bone and teeth formation. Again, by law in the United Kingdom all flour except wholemeal flour and self-raising flour has to be fortified with calcium (as chalk) so that it contains 235–390 mg of chalk per 100 g (see p. 58, Chapter 4) and this helps to ensure that we will receive the recommended daily intake which is normally between 500 and 700 mg.

Phosphorus is also required by the body for teeth and bone formation and we obtain it in our food as phosphate from milk, cheese, eggs, meat and fish. We need 1–2 g per day of this mineral, and more is needed during pregnancy and lactation. Our requirements for calcium and phosphorus would be satisfied by any normal well balanced diet and especially by the standard three-course meal which we have been considering.

Other minerals which we need in considerable amounts in our diet and their recommended daily intakes where known (in parentheses) are: magnesium (0·4 g), iodine (0·15 mg), fluorine (0·5–4 mg), sodium (10–30 g!) and potassium (4 g). Iodine is used in forming a hormone called thyroxine which the body makes in its thyroid gland whereas fluorine is needed for healthy bones and teeth. The reader may know about the controversy which has raged over the past few years about the fluoridation of water supplies; this is discussed further in Chapter 9. Magnesium, sodium and potassium are all metals which are essential and required for complex enzyme and protein reactions within our body cells, but there is more than enough of them in our average diets.

The trace elements which we require in our diet and their recommended daily intakes (in parentheses) are: cobalt (0·045–0·09 g!), copper (0·6–2 mg), zinc, manganese (8 mg), molybdenum and selenium. The last-mentioned metal is toxic if present in anything but trace amounts, and in fact the other trace metals will also be poisonous if we eat too much of them. Zinc in particular has sometimes caused poisoning when acid fruits have been stored in galvanized iron containers. The acid in the fruit dissolved the metal in the container which although mostly iron contained enough zinc to make the consumer very ill. Fever, vomiting and headache are common symptoms of zinc poisoning.

In addition to the above trace elements which are known to be required nutritionally there are many other metals (e.g. the non-essential, non-nutritive, non-toxic elements listed in Table 2.3, p. 26) which are always found in human bodies in trace quantities but for which no essential nutritional role has yet been demonstrated. This does not mean that we may not discover an important role which they might play in trace quantities sometime in the future. Even some of the most highly toxic elements such as arsenic may fit into this category. The trace elements which are required nutritionally are used, like the other minerals which we require to help the body to carry out its complex enzyme and protein reactions and cobalt, for example, actually forms part of the molecule of vitamin B_{12}, which is present in liver and prevents us from suffering from the disease known as pernicious anaemia. All other mineral requirements will be met by well-balanced meals of the type which we have described in this chapter.

Diseases of Excess and Deficiency Caused by Major Food Chemicals

We have mentioned many of the diseases which result from deficiency of one or other vitamin but dietary diseases are just as likely to be caused by an incorrect balance of the major food chemicals. Insufficient food resulting in a completely inadequate Calorie intake would cause us to become thin and emaciated and our bodies would work at very low levels of efficiency. Famine conditions which resulted in these types of conditions would, of course, make us extremely vulnerable to a whole host of different diseases. Even deficiencies of only one class of major food chemical—carbohydrate, fat or protein—might cause some degree of these symptoms because our unbalanced diet would be likely to affect our appetite.

Deficiency of protein (or rather protein of high biological value) in the diet results in the disease known as *kwashiorkor* (the original meaning of the word "kwashiorkor" being "he who has been displaced"). This is found to occur in famine areas, particularly Africa, among children living on vegetable diets. People suffering from kwashiorkor are stunted in growth, have anaemia, swollen bodies and liver damage. Treatment of the disease consists of feeding animal proteins, especially milk. If, on the other hand, we eat too much, the excessive Calories which we consume will be converted into large deposits of fat in our bodies and we will suffer from obesity. This again will result in our bodies working at low levels of efficiency which will make them susceptible to further diseases and disorders. Obesity or overweight will cause an increased strain on the heart which in itself will lower our life expectancies. Furthermore, we will become much more vulnerable to the disease of *coronary thrombosis*. In this disease a fatty deposit builds up on the inside wall of the coronary arteries which surround the heart, this deposit being described as an *atheroma*. This deposit causes a restriction in the flow of blood through the arteries and if a clot of blood happens to get lodged in these arteries it will stop the flow of blood altogether. This will cause a heart attack which might be fatal.

For many years it was thought that since the atheroma consists of a fatty deposit it was liable to be caused by fat in our diet which was therefore to be avoided. This was soon found to be untrue, and in fact as we now know two of the unsaturated fatty acids in our diet—linoleic and linolenic acids (see p. 38 and p. 40)—are actually essential. The latest idea about fat is that saturated fats are likely to cause atheroma more readily than unsaturated ones and we should therefore eat more vegetable fat than animal fat as vegetable fat in general is more likely to contain more of the unsaturated type. On this point it is worth noting that one of the methods of making margarine consists of chemically converting unsaturated vegetable oils to the saturated type in order to make them harder! However, there is much conflicting evidence about the coronary thrombosis-saturated fat relationship and it is by no means certain that the theory is true.

An even newer theory is that of Professor Yudkin who believes that atheroma is not related to saturated fats at all but to common sugar—sucrose! So far evidence to conflict with this theory is lacking but a lot more experimental work needs to be done to prove that it is true. The authors prefer to treat any alarmist views about single articles in our diet with suspicion, believing that coronary thrombosis is a multifactorial disease and not least among its causes are mental worry, stress and general lack of exercise. Furthermore, the eating of well-balanced meals while at the same time avoiding being overweight will go a long way toward ensuring immunity from the disease.

Suggestions for Further Reading

BIRCH, G. G. *et al.* (Ed.) *Health and Food*, Applied Science Publishers, 1972. A Symposium Report.
BIRCH, G. G. and PARKER, K. J. (Eds.) *Vitamin C*, Applied Science Publishers, 1974. A Symposium Report.
BRECKON, W. *You are what you Eat*, B.B.C. Publications, 1976.
DAVIDSON, S., PASSMORE, R. and BROCK, J. F. *Human Nutrition and Dietectics*, Churchill Livingstone, 5th edition 1972.
DEPARTMENT OF HEALTH AND SOCIAL SECURITY. *Recommended Intakes of Nutrients for the U.K.*, HMSO, 1969.
HMSO. *Manual of Nutrition*, HMSO, 7th edn., 1970.
PYKE, M. *Success in Nutrition*, Murray, 1975.
W.H.O. *Handbook of Human Nutritional Requirements*, Geneva, 1974.

CHAPTER 4

From Farm to Table

AN INCREASING proportion of the food we eat has gone through manufacturing processes. The food industry in Britain is indeed a large and growing industry. There are some who feel the urge to do without any processing of food and who wish to go back to nature. But this is no more possible on a large scale than doing without manufactured clothing or houses. We could no more go back to so-called "natural" food than we could rely on skins for clothing or caves for shelter and warmth.

When man was a hunter, as soon as he had finished eating the meat from the last animal he had killed, he had to go and find more, or go hungry. There was no way of keeping the meat from spoilage.

After his nomadic existence, the hunter settled in one place and began to depend more on cultivated crops. He then discovered that while the grain foods stored fairly well, his vegetables, meat and milk would not keep for very long. He did find out that milk could be stored if it was converted into butter and cheese. Later still, he found that root crops could be kept for limited periods and would help out during the lean winter months both for his family and his cattle. It was largely during the nineteenth and early part of the twentieth century that scientists discovered more ways of preserving food of all kinds, particularly meat, milk and vegetables. Food preservers are modern Josephs, evening out the fat and lean years.

In addition to this, preservation of food copes with the problem of the growth of large industrial areas, with huge concentrations of population. The development of new methods of storing food made the Industrial Revolution in Britain possible, and with it the great expansion of population. Far more people could live and work in Britain than her farmers alone could feed, and British people were able to concentrate more on becoming the world's first industrial base while being fed largely by food produced abroad, which was often subjected to various manufacturing processes.

The preservation of food results in a wider variety of foodstuffs being available at different times of the year, and offers an increased choice to the consumer. Stockpiles of food can be more easily built up to deal with emergencies, or for specialized undertakings such as explorations of the South Pole, or for the more hazardous rigours of travel to the moon or outer space. It becomes much easier to satisfy varying appetites, nutritional and quality requirements with the wider variety of food available.

But, of course, manufacture of food does not only concern itself with preservation, or with eliminating the seasons as far as food choice is concerned. A great many new, exciting, attractive and tasty foods are the products of food manufacturing processes. The tough, gristly wheat grain is converted by the magic of the baker and confectioner into attractive, crusty, oven-fresh loaves and gorgeous gateaux which melt in the mouth. Sugar-cane, milk and seaweed are raw materials from which Knickerbocker Glory may be created by the art, craft and science of the ice-cream manufacturer.

It can be thus argued that the introduction and development of food manufacturing processes have played a significant part in raising living standards, helped in industrial progress, lessened food shortages and enriched our lives.

Food processing can be regarded as the conversion of the raw food from the farm into a form suitable for eating. There are many features which are common to most foods in this progress from farm to table.

The first stage—the collecting or harvesting of the food—is primarily the farmer's job, though the food processor or technologist may become involved where the question of quality or ripeness impinges on the efficiency of the process of food conversion. For example, peas which are being cultivated for canning or quick-freezing must be at a particular stage of ripeness in order to produce the best-quality product. A certain degree of liaison is necessary between farmer and manufacturer in order to achieve this end. An employee of the manufacturing firm, the fieldsman, inspects the crop, and may test the tenderness of the peas with a tenderometer, which consists essentially of a pair of mammoth steel jaws, that determines the crushability of the peas.

The raw material, be it milk, peas or meat, is conveyed as rapidly as possible to the site of manufacture so that there is as little deterioration of the raw food as possible. The food must therefore not be allowed to become warm. Meat and milk, for example, are normally conveyed in refrigerated insulated containers.

Many foods have to be cleaned before further processing so that the resulting food is pure, wholesome and free from undesirable impurities and micro-organisms. Apart from earth that one would expect to find on root vegetables, one finds an incredible array of foreign matter in the raw food consignments. Some food manufacturers have a display case which exhibits some remarkable "finds". Stones, tools, nails, pieces of metal, string, wire and pieces of wood are often found as well as the more common stalk, straw, husk, foreign seeds and diseased grain in consignments of wheat. It is very important to remove iron by means of powerful electromagnets in order to protect the machinery—as well as the consumer—from damage. Electronic metal detectors are also commonly used. Grain foods, peas and nuts are sieved, and go through powerful blowing machines to remove loose foreign matter. Many foods such as vegetables and fruits are subjected to prolonged and vigorous washing to remove adherent dirt. The grain of wheat contains a deep groove running along its length. This groove harbours dirt, sand and micro-organisms; and therefore requires even more intensive cleaning. In addition to all the above cleaning processes, the wheat grains are vigorously scrubbed by rotating brushes.

The next stage is often the separation of concentrated nutriment from bulky and indigestible material. Most plant foods are surrounded by protective shells or peel which has to be removed in the course of isolating and extracting the food material itself. The cleaned wheat grain, for example, contains highly nutritious food material inside the multilayered bran, which is largely indigestible. The removal of bran is a long and difficult process, partly because of the groove previously referred to, and partly because of its firm adhesion to the central core of the grain —the endosperm. This will be discussed in more detail later.

Having isolated the nutritious and digestible part of the food the next stage is to make it palatable. Using the grain of wheat as an example, although it would be possible to eat the endosperm it would be rather tasteless, difficult to masticate, and monotonous. Consequently it is ground down to a fine flour. This flour can be put to a very large number of uses. For thousands of years it was made up into a paste with water, rolled out and baked. Even this primitive bread had undergone processing operations, i.e. baking, in order to produce a more tasty food. It is reported that the origin of leavening of bread was the result of an accident in the household of one of the Pharaohs. The royal baker is alleged to have fallen asleep after preparing the usual flat wheaten bread. Hours later he woke up to find that the dough had fermented and risen in the warmth due to the hot Egyptian sun. Instead of throwing it away he baked it, with the result that Pharaoh, in a fit of temper, had the baker beheaded. He was curious enough, however, to sample the offending article. He liked the flavour and texture of the new bread so much that he gave orders for it to be produced regularly. Certainly we must agree that eating a slice of a well-baked bread is pleasanter and tastier than trying to chew grains of wheat. Today an almost unlimited range of flour products tempts us—pastries, biscuits, breakfast cereals, puddings—to name but a few.

This principle—of converting raw foods into "manufactured" foods—has operated over centuries. Whilst a diet of fruit, milk, eggs, vegetables, grain and meat in their raw state may satisfy us nutritionally, a vast range of delectable foods may be produced from these starting materials which make eating a pleasure instead of a chore. Thus milk can be converted into butter, cheese, cream, yoghurt, ice-cream; fruit can be eaten in the form of jam, jelly, fruit drinks and fruit pies.

There is insufficient space to go into the details of manufacture of a comprehensive range of foods in this chapter. Instead, the main principles of a few representative foods—flour and bread, margarine, and jam—will be outlined. These foods have been selected because they represent three different food groups—cereal, fats, and fruit; and, because the type of processing is different in each case.

Flour and Bread Production

Bread is the staple food in Britain and many other countries, and is made almost invariably from wheat flour, yeast, salt and water. Of these, wheat flour is the most important, and it would therefore be profitable to consider how this is produced, and some of its very interesting characteristics.

Flour Production

Flour is obtained by milling wheat which is the most widely cultivated cereal in the world, as it can be grown at the equator as well as the arctic

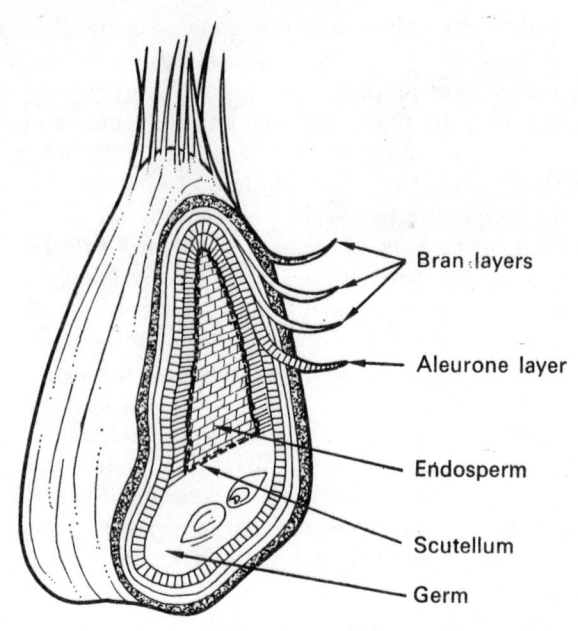

FIG. 4.1. Diagram of a longitudinal section of a grain or berry of wheat.

circle. Its popularity has steadily increased so that it is now grown to a greater extent than rice throughout the world.

A grain of wheat is roughly barrel-shaped, with a longitudinal groove. The outer covering (see Fig. 4.1) or *bran* is tough and indigestible. The next layer, the *aleurone*, is attached to it and contains a high proportion

TABLE 4.1.
PERCENTAGE COMPOSITION OF THE WHEAT GRAIN

Portion of grain	per cent
Bran	8·0
Aleurone	7·0
Endosperm	82·5
Scutellum } germ	1·5
Embryo	1·0

of protein and the vitamin, nicotinic acid. Opposite to the groove and at the lower end lies the *germ*, which includes the *embryo* (the future plant), and attached to this is the *scutellum*, which is especially rich in vitamin B_1. The central part of the grain, comprising 80–85% of the total, is the chalky-white *endosperm*. It is from this that white flour is made.

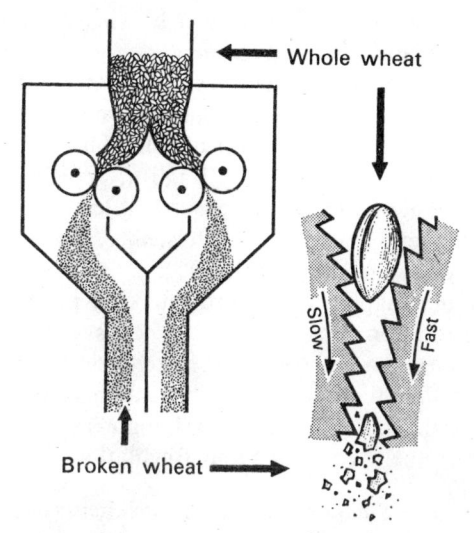

Fig. 4.2. Diagram to show how the grain is sheared by the rollers.

Reference has already been made to the importance and complexity of the cleaning operations. In order to extract the endosperm from the rest of the grain, the wheat is passed through fluted iron rollers which shear the berries open as shown in Fig. 4.2, and then through other rollers which scrape the endosperm off the open skins. The broken endosperm, termed *semolina*, is then freed from broken bran in a machine called a *purifier*, which sifts and blows off the lighter bran.

The purified semolina (also used for puddings) is then passed through a series of smooth iron rollers which gradually reduce the size of the product until they reach the particle size of flour. Flour is in fact produced at each stage of the process in small amounts, and is sieved off from the other material to join the main stream of flour, which has also been passed through very fine sieves.

Flour Treatment

Wheat flour is unique in having the ability to be mixed with water to produce a firm, elastic dough. No other cereal or plant product possesses this property, which is essential to the production of good-quality bread and cakes. The principal feature of the wheat flour which makes this possible is the rather special protein, which, when kneaded with water, produces the strong, cohesive and elastic *gluten*, which gives body to the dough. Different wheats vary in their protein content, and the best breadmaking wheat—Canadian Manitoba—may have as much as 15% protein. The higher protein wheats are best for breadmaking, while those wheats with lower protein contents, such as English, Scottish and Australian wheats, produce doughs which are weaker and less elastic and are more suited to the production of cakes and biscuits. The protein content of these wheats may vary from about 8–10%.

As explained in Chapter 9, for breadmaking purposes the flour is improved by the addition of oxidizing substances such as chlorine dioxide, or potassium bromate. As a result of the exclusion during milling of the aleurone and scutellum there is a loss of the vitamins nicotinic acid and B_1. These, together with iron and calcium carbonate (i.e. chalk) are all added in accordance with the Bread and Flour Regulations at this stage.

TABLE 4.2. BREAD AND FLOUR REGULATIONS (1963)

1. All flour must contain a minimum of

Nutrient	Amount
Vitamin B_1 (thiamine)	0·24 mg per 100 g
Nicotinic acid	1·60 mg per 100 g
Iron	1·65 mg per 100 g

2. All flour other than wholemeal must have added to it

Calcium carbonate	235–390 mg per 100 g

The normal method of aerating the dough is by means of fermentation, involving the use of yeast. It must be remembered that aeration can also be achieved by the use of sodium bicarbonate (baker's soda) and acid, as is used in the making of soda bread. Yeast is a living organism composed of cells each about 1/4000th of an inch, or 0·0001 cm. The word is derived from the Sanskrit word *yas* which means to boil. This relates to the appearance of a sugary solution of any kind to which yeast has been added resulting in lively fermentation.

Though at one time yeast was supplied by breweries from the surplus resulting from the brewing of beer, it is now specially manufactured from selected strains that give adequate gas production and good-flavoured bread. The yeast is normally supplied in compressed form, in small packages, and must be fresh and properly stored to maintain its activity.

Salt or sodium chloride is necessary in breadmaking to bring out the flavour of bread. It also has a slightly stiffening action on the dough, which improves the texture of the bread. Salt, however, does retard the action of the yeast, and sufficient of the latter must be used to allow for this.

Water is absorbed by the flour during mixing to produce the dough; strong flours absorb more than weak flours, but flour absorbs on average about half its weight of water. Not only the amount but also the temperature of the water has to be carefully controlled to ensure that the resulting dough is fermenting at just the right temperature.

Principles of Breadmaking

Three stages are involved in bread production: mixing of the dough, fermentation and baking of the bread. The mixing process enables the protein of the flour to take up the water, with the production of a fairly stiff dough. Fermentation involves the production of gas which aerates, distends and lightens the dough, giving it a cellular structure. The baking process sets or coagulates the gluten and so establishes the final shape of the loaf. It also gives colour and flavour to the bread.

There is about 1% of cane sugar in flour. This is acted on by the enzyme *invertase* (sucrase) in the yeast to produce simpler sugars (invert sugar). A series of enzymes in the yeast, known collectively as *zymase*, then act on the invert sugar to produce alcohol and carbon dioxide (fermentation). The alcohol escapes whilst the carbon dioxide gas blows out the dough. There is not enough sugar in the flour to maintain this fermentation for very long. The major part of the sugar is produced by the action of enzymes called *diastase* in the flour upon the large reserve of starch to produce a sugar called *maltose* or malt sugar. This is split into the simple sugar *glucose* by an enzyme in the yeast. The stage is thus set for a steady production of carbon dioxide gas from this glucose by zymase acting upon it as it is produced. About half a proof gallon of alcohol is made for every sack of flour (280 lb) during fermentation; but, alas, it is practically all lost during baking. If you like your bread freshly baked, you may get about 0·3% of alcohol free of duty with it.

Baking results at first in a speeding up of the fermentation and an increase in volume, but as the temperature rises, it kills off the yeast cells, and destroys the enzymes responsible for fermentation and so gas is no longer produced. As the thermometer climbs, the starch granules (which would give the bread a powdery uncooked flavour and texture) absorb water and are partly gelatinized to smooth out the texture. The gluten is coagulated, giving the bread crumb typical firmness and solidity. The high temperature of the oven browns the crust, and produces some of the delicious flavour of well-baked bread (discussed in Chapter 7).

Breadmaking Methods

1. Straight dough system. This is the conventional English system. A dough is made up by mixing two sacks of flour (560 lb) with 6–8 lb of yeast, about 10 lb of salt, and about 30 gal of water. The yeast will previously have been dispersed in some of the water; and the salt in another portion of water, which may be added later. The temperature of the water is carefully controlled so that the resulting temperature of the mix is about 80°F (27°C). It is common in large bakeries to add about 4 lb of an emulsion containing glyceryl monostearate (GMS) and fat. The object of this is to produce a smoother, softer texture (which facilitates slicing) with more uniform crumb structure, and to counteract the staling process (see Chapter 7). The dough, in large wheeled bowls, is covered to prevent skin formation on the surface, and fermentation is allowed to proceed at the set temperature for a fixed period, usually for 2 to 3 hours. In some bakeries the dough is vigorously beaten, or "knocked back", after two-thirds of the time in order to even out the temperature and improve the mixing.

At the end of this period ("bulk fermentation"), the dough, which will have risen to the top of the bowls, is transferred to a "divider" which cuts it into 1- or 2-lb portions and rolls it into balls, which are dropped into canvas pouches on a travelling belt in a temperature and humidity controlled tunnel for about 10 minutes (first proof). The dough pieces are then mechanically kneaded, given the final shape in a "moulder",

FROM FARM TO TABLE 61

and deposited in tins. This tightens the dough and necessitates a resting period or final proof in another controlled prover for about 45 minutes.

The tins are then passed into the oven, where they are baked at a temperature of 450–500°F (230–260°C) for about 45 minutes. In a small bakery, where manual rather than mechanical methods tend to be used, small static ovens are often employed. Larger bakeries which are more highly mechanized use travelling ovens, in which the dough pieces travel through long tunnels and emerge baked, at the other end. These ovens are fitted with various devices to speed up the baking, such as turbulent jets of hot air, and also with steam jets to produce the glaze on the crust.

2. Chorleywood bread process. This process was devised at the laboratories of the British Baking Industries Research Association in Chorleywood. Its main feature is the replacement of bulk fermentation by intense mechanical energy during the dough mixing stage. This, together with the use of vitamin C (ascorbic acid) as an improver, fat, and a larger amount of yeast and water, gives much the same results as the conventional method in a much shorter time. It is cheaper and it uses less space and labour, and actually gives a higher yield of bread per sack of flour.

With these advantages it is not surprising that it is sweeping the field, and at present the bulk of commercially produced bread is made by this system in Britain. It has meant, of course, that specially designed, though not very elaborate, high-speed mixing plant has to be used for the process.

3. Wholemeal bread. The flour used must consist of the whole of the grain milled down to flour, without any additions or subtractions. The presence of germ and aleurone results in an enzyme system which is too active. If normal fermentation times were used, the dough would become slack and runny, and making good bread from it would be impossible. For this reason the standard methods are modified by using more yeast, and fermenting at a lower temperature for about 1 hour only.

During the baking of bread, there is considerable loss of weight—mostly due to water and alcohol loss—so that the 1 lb of dough produces 14 oz of bread. Most types of bread are required by law to weigh 14 or 28 oz (so called 1- and 2-lb loaves) and it is an offence for this to vary up or down. Loss of weight also occurs during cooling, which may be counteracted to some extent by using damp air currents to cool the bread for 2–3 hours. It is necessary to cool the bread adequately especially if it is to be sliced and wrapped, since warm, over-soft bread would be impossible to cut rapidly and efficiently. On the other hand a thin crust and the use of crumb softeners (GMS) help in this process. Warm bread that is wrapped in waxed paper or placed in a closed van for delivery next morning is liable to develop mould, or even more serious, a disease called "rope". With the latter condition, the crumb liquefies, turns yellow, and has a sickening smell. This is very difficult to eradicate from a bakery once it is established. Adequate cooling, and good hygiene will prevent this.

Bread as a Food

In a recent survey, people were asked to give their opinions regarding the nutritional value of foods. Answers to one question revealed that 2% of the sample interviewed thought that bread "might contain quite a bit" of vitamins; 1% mentioned minerals, 2% mentioned calcium and 4% included protein. Yet the true position is that bread contributes about 16% of the total protein in the average British diet, 11% and 22% respectively of two of the B vitamins (nicotinic acid and vitamin B_1); 13% of the calcium; and about 18% of the iron. In the same survey bread was regarded by most of those questioned simply as a fattening food. In fact the latest figures show that bread contributes about 14% of the total Calories in the diet of this country.

The reason for the high figure for the nutrients mentioned is partly because in spite of a continuing drop in bread consumption we still eat on average about 33 oz of bread per week—corresponding to just under two and a half small loaves. As bread contains quite significant amounts of certain nutrients (10% protein, for example) it is not surprising that it provides such a high proportion of the nutrients in our diet. What is surprising is that it is still rated so low in people's minds after all these years of nutrition education. As far as the nutrients iron, calcium, vitamin B_1 and nicotinic acid are concerned, the high figures quoted are partly due to their being deliberately added to the flour by the miller as discussed earlier.

Wholemeal bread contains slightly more protein than white bread, but the wholemeal protein is of more value to the body (see Chapter 3). It has also more of the vitamins B_1, E and nicotinic acid. On the debit side it is slightly less digestible (so that some of the nutrients are not used), and contains no added calcium or iron. These remarks do not apply to "brown" or "wheatmeal" breads, which are often made from a mixture of white flour and bran; and contain less of the protein and B vitamins than wholemeal bread. In view of this, it is unfortunate that a majority of baker's shops still produce a wheatmeal loaf when a customer asks for wholemeal. If one queries this, the reply is frequently, "Oh, you mean 100% wholemeal!" But, according to the regulations, wholemeal bread must be 100% extraction rate. Germ breads, of which there are several well-known brands, such as Hovis, are made from a mixture of white flour and germ. They therefore are very rich in high-quality protein and vitamins, and are liked for their pleasant nutty flavour. High-protein breads are produced from flour to which has been added a bonus of gluten flour (derived from ordinary flour from which the starch has been washed out) and rank as foods comparable with the high-protein foods in their protein content.

One of the most striking things about bread consumption is that it has been steadily going down since 1945, when it was at its peak. The National Food Survey shows that the average weekly consumption of bread per person has dropped from 51·1 oz in 1956 to 37·9 oz in 1973. Nevertheless, it is still our most important and cheapest staple food, providing the essentials of life at a lower price than any other food. There has been considerable speculation as to the probable reasons for this decline, which is shared by most other countries. As the drop in bread consumption coincides with an increase in the consumption of other foods rich in nutrients, the total nutrients eaten have not changed significantly. In fact, during the war, when bread consumption was considerably higher than it is now, the diet of the nation was at its best. But it seems to be generally agreed that the increase in the standard of living that has taken place among the richer nations has resulted in people spending more on meat, eggs, cheese and fruit, and less on bread. Some allege that another factor is a deterioration in flavour and texture due to the mass production of bread in large-scale modern bakeries. It is probable that like many other social trends the steady drop in consumption of bread may be due to a combination of the above reasons, rather than to any one of them.

Ever since the war the large combines have been steadily buying up small bakeries, with the result that the industry is now dominated by four large groups which between them produce about three-quarters of the bread in the United Kingdom. Because of their large output, they are able to produce bread more cheaply than small bakers. This is made possible by using mechanized methods of storage, movement of ingredients, baking processes and large travelling ovens. The time of baking is reduced, and automatic methods of cooling, slicing and wrapping are used. The sliced, wrapped loaf now accounts for about 90% of all bread sales. As opposed to this the small baker tends to use longer fermentation and baking times in a stationary oven, and therefore produces a more crusty loaf, not usually wrapped. As explained on page 122, the brown colour produced in the crust is caused by sugars combining with protein under the influence of the heat of the oven. This brown colour is accompanied by baked bread flavour and aroma which is drawn into the crust of the loaf during cooling. Shorter baking times of plant-baked bread will therefore result in less of this typical bread flavour. Another factor is texture. The use of GMS (see p. 150), partly to aid in slicing plant-baked bread, gives it a much softer texture. This may be the reason why such bread has been described as "tasteless, with a cotton-wool texture". In a recent survey, it was also alleged that plant-baked bread went mouldy more quickly than other bread. For these reasons it is not surprising that there are still many people who will queue up at the small baker's shop (since the latter cannot afford the high cost of daily delivery), and will also pay more for the bread. The large bakers can undersell their small competitors and they can also deliver the bread. The signs are that the remaining sector of small bakeries will be still further eroded in spite of the considerable minority who are prepared to pay more for and collect bread they like.

Margarine Manufacture

One of the most revolutionary discoveries in the history of food production occurred on 17 July 1869, when Hippolyte Mège-Mouriés, a French chemist, took out letters patent in France and England for an "Invention based on the deductions of modern science, which prove, first, that odoriferous colouring matters volatile and becoming rancid do not pre-exist in the natural fats called suets; second, that they are developed by the action of the organized tissues under the influence of fermentation, of heat, or of chemical agents; third, that the fats of milk called butter are only grease from fat modified, first, by its cellular tissue and afterwards by the organized tissues of the udder."

The instigator of this invention was Napoleon III who offered a prize for the discovery of a cheap butter substitute for the Army, Navy and poorer sections of the population.

Mège-Mouriés' idea was to imitate the cow. He therefore mixed purified cow tallow with milk, water and the cow's own special ingredient in the form of finely minced udder. However, although the initial experiments were not successful, Mège-Mouriés persevered, finding that the udder could be left out after all.

In 1871 two families of butter merchants in a little village in Holland called Oss, unable to meet the demand for butter, began to manufacture the new imitation butter, using Mège's process. These two families were named Jurgens and Van den Bergh, and were quite independent of each other. Butter was so important to the economy of Denmark that margarine was manufactured there in 1870–1 entirely for home consumption, in order to safeguard the export of butter. Denmark, with the highest individual consumption of margarine, became the centre of the margarine-machinery industry. Austria-Hungary and Germany followed suit, and although plenty of margarine was imported into Britain, the first factory was not built here until 1889, at Godley, Manchester.

Mège called his product oleo-margarine—the latter word being derived from the Greek *margarites* meaning pearl—because of its lustrous appearance. Incidentally, since in the Greek root the g is hard like the g in "green", margarine should not be called "marjarine," although this is the popular pronunciation. The product first imported into Britain was renamed "Butterine". This took place during the early part of the "pure food" campaign and the first Margarine Act of 1887 made the word "Margarine" compulsory. It is interesting to note that in some countries there were severe restrictions on margarine—notably in the United States—in the form of taxes and other impositions. Margarine in the United States was not allowed to be coloured until 1950, and even then two States with large dairy-farming interests—Wisconsin and Minnesota—still held out for several years. Margarine without its attractive yellowish colour is bound to lose a good deal of its appeal, and the sales suffered accordingly. It is alleged that butter interests were behind these restrictions.

Nowadays margarine is made from a mixture of liquid oils and solid fats, mostly vegetable, emulsified with soured milk and water. Salt, colour, flavouring and emulsifying agents are usually added. For domestic purposes the margarine must contain the vitamins A and D.

Over 80% of margarine consists of fat. Like butter it is a water-in-oil emulsion (see p. 148). The watery part of margarine is in the form of tiny globules which are completely surrounded by a mixture of liquid and solid fat. The plasticity and spreadability of margarine, like butter, are due to this emulsion.

The main oils and fats used are vegetable in origin and they are palm oil, palm kernel oil, ground nut oil, coconut oil; oils used to a lesser extent are soya bean oil, cottonseed oil and sunflower seed oil. Whale oil has been used to a great extent, but its use has been discontinued. In order to obtain the right texture it is found necessary to use a fairly wide blend of these oils, and to incorporate enough hardened oils (explained later, p. 67). The latter may vary from 20% to as much as 70%.

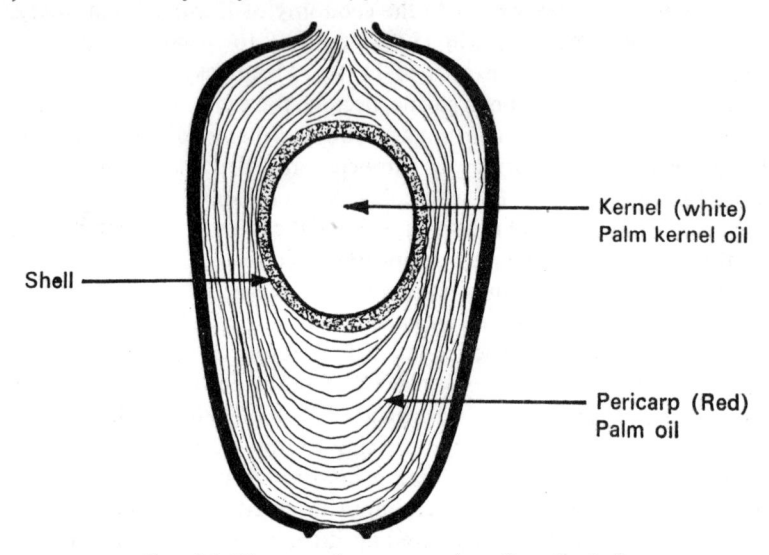

FIG. 4.3. Diagram of a cross-section of a palm fruit.

Palm oil and palm kernel oil both come from the fruit of the oil palm (see Fig. 4.3) which grows mainly in West Africa. Palm oil, a bright orange-red fat, comes from the outer "flesh" and is extracted on the spot; whilst palm kernel oil, a white solid fat, comes from the kernel inside the "nut" of the fruit. The flesh of the coconut is cut up and dried to produce *copra*, from which the oil is extracted. Cottonseed is the seed from which cotton has been removed, and is a rich source of good-quality oil.

The cleaned copra, palm kernel, etc., is crushed, heated in an oven and the melted oil extracted by a powerful screw press. Alternatively, the oil may be dissolved out by solvents, which are distilled off. The crude oil has to be refined if it is to be used for edible purposes. This is carried out firstly by neutralizing any free fatty acid with caustic soda, the resulting soap being centrifuged or run off, and the oil washed and dried. Any undesirable colour is removed by means of carbon or special bleaching earths, and unwanted taints are eliminated by bubbling a fierce stream of super-heated steam through the oil while it is held under a vacuum.

It was explained in Chapter 2 that vegetable fats are in general more unsaturated than animal fats. This unsaturation also confers a low melting point on the fat, so that as a rule the saturated fats are solid whilst the unsaturated fats are liquid, or at any rate rather soft. An unsaturated (soft) fat can be converted into a saturated (hard) fat by combining it with hydrogen. Hardening is carried out by bubbling pure hydrogen gas through the oil in which is suspended very finely divided nickel.

$$\text{Liquid oil} + \text{Hydrogen} \xrightarrow{\text{Nickel catalyst}} \text{Solid fat}$$

The hydrogen is absorbed at the double bonds of the oil to convert it into hard fat, a process that has to be very carefully controlled. It must not be overdone or the consumer will experience the unpleasant sensation of "palate cling"—due to unmelted fat clinging to the palate—as sometimes happens with mutton fat.

Processing

Margarine flavour is primarily due to the use of soured milk. Skimmed milk—either fresh or reconstituted from the dried form—is pasteurized and incubated with special lactic acid-forming bacteria for about 18 hours. This produces the butter-like flavour. In addition other flavouring substances may be added which are normally present in butter. Salt is added to most margarines to the extent of about 1%. This rounds off the flavour but also discourages the growth of moulds and bacteria.

The colour of margarine is commonly attained by using palm oil or extracts of palm oil which are rich in the colouring matter—carotene—though the latter may be used on its own. As a smooth emulsion has to be attained, this is aided by the use of emulsifying agents—one example of which is GMS (glyceryl monostearate), which is derived from ordinary fat. The water content of margarine must not exceed 16%. The law also demands that for domestic use margarine must contain stated amounts of vitamins A and D, with the result that it contains at least as much of these vitamins as butter.

The various oils and melted fats are carefully weighed out, blended and passed to a pre-mixing tank along with the fat-soluble vitamins A and D and colour. The emulsifying agent, soured milk and water containing salt are also added, and the whole tank is warmed and well mixed by paddles to produce a creamy liquid emulsion. To produce the characteristic semi-solid, smooth margarine from this liquid, it is pumped under pressure through a series of tubes which have refrigerated outer jackets, and which contain rapidly revolving shafts fitted with scraper blades. This piece of equipment is called a "Votator". The fat solidifies on the outside walls of the tubes and is rapidly scraped off by the knives, allowing fresh margarine to be solidified and also scraped off. A final tube contains beaters which vigorously knead the margarine to a butter-like texture before it emerges as a solid continuous strip which can be cut and packaged. The Votator has speeded up and simplified margarine manufacture considerably.

Margarine and Butter

Since the days of Mège-Mouriés great strides have been made in perfecting the modern margarine, which can now, by using scientific techniques, be tailor-made to satisfy different requirements. Special grades are made for summer and winter, tropical countries, for cake-making and for pastries. In some ways the texture can be an improvement on that of butter, and its content of Calories, vitamins A and D are at least as high as those of butter. Nevertheless, in spite of these facts and the relative cheapness of margarine, the average consumption of butter per week is nearly twice that of margarine. The consumption of butter since 1962 has been fairly steady, whilst that of margarine has been falling since then at an average rate of about 2% per annum. This may well be related to the rising standard of living. Since most people probably regard margarine as a substitute for butter, and not as having any special merit of its own (except perhaps for cake-making), they buy butter if they can afford it. It is still fairly cheap compared with food prices as a whole.

The Manufacture of Jam

The first sweet spread used was almost certainly honey, but a fruity spread is reported by Pliny to have been used by both the Greeks and the Romans, called by the latter "de fructum". It was obtained by boiling down grapes, but was commonly mixed with wine (!) or milk to produce a sweet dish. Conserves, probably made with quinces and sugar, were referred to in a book published in 1310. The word "marmalade" is said to be derived from the Portuguese word *Marmelo* — a quince, and there are accounts of its use in the sixteenth century.

Fruits other than quinces and oranges were used for making marmalade, but when other fruits were used, the product became known as "jam", a word which is alleged to be derived from the French *J'aime* and was first referred to in 1730. Others say it comes from the Arabian word *Jamad* for preserved fruit.

Due to the high price of fruit and sugar, jam was a luxury for many years. But in some quarters it was eaten for its alleged medicinal qualities, particularly for those suffering from "coughs, colds, or shortness of breath". Home-made jams and marmalade steadily gained in popularity, but it was not until the early part of the nineteenth century that it was made commercially. The cheapening of sugar by reduction of the heavy duty in 1874 led to a rapid increase in manufacture, and Britain became jam-makers with world-wide sales.

Jam can be described as a preparation made by boiling fruit with sugar to produce a consistency firm enough to spread on bread and capable of being transported without flow taking place. Jams are eaten primarily for their pleasant flavour, hence the type of fruit is important. So also are the colour and freshness of the fruit. All fruits contain a carbohydrate called "pectin" (see Chapter 2) which gives the fruit its texture. It is above all the pectin in the fruit which, along with the fruit acid and added sugar, produce the characteristic "set" or "gel" of jam. A jam therefore can be regarded as consisting of fruit tissues embedded in a firm pectin–sugar–acid gel.

Composition of fruits. As fruits are the major constituent in jam, it is worth-while looking briefly at their composition. They contain between 80% and 90% water. As jam contains only about 30% of water, it will be seen that a good deal of water must inevitably be boiled off. Other components are sugar, fruit acids (responsible for the sharp taste), pectin, fibrous matter including cellulose, and a variety of minor ingredients

TABLE 4.3. AVERAGE COMPOSITION OF FRESH FRUIT

Component	Normal range	Typical example	Fruits with low content		Fruits with high content	
	%		%		%	
Water	80–90	apples apricots	bananas	70	melons	94
Protein	0·3–0·9	oranges plums	pears	0·2	blackberries	1·3
Sugar	3–10	loganberries pineapples	lemons	1·4	bananas	19
Pectin	0·5–1	apples gooseberries	strawberries	0·3	oranges	1·3
Calories per 100 g	17–40	blackberries gooseberries pears oranges plums strawberries	lemons (juice) lemon (whole) rhubarb	7 15 6	bananas grapes	74 60

which nevertheless are important, such as flavouring materials, colouring matter, vitamins (especially vitamin C), minerals and a very small amount of protein.

As pectin is the essential component of the final jelly, the jam manufacturers must know if there is enough in the fruit to make the jam set. Many a housewife knows to her cost that home-made strawberry jam is sometimes more suitable for pouring than for spreading on bread. This is because strawberries are very low in pectin content. The manufacturer would not sell his jam if it did not have a good set. He therefore adds pectin to those fruits which are inclined to be poor sources of pectin. This is just what the housewife does when she adds one of the marketed brands of pectin, though she can produce the same result by combining a high pectin fruit—say apple—with a low pectin fruit. Commercially, pectin is derived either from apples or from peel of citrus fruit and it is marketed in the form of free-flowing powder or as a syrup. Fruit contains most pectin and is best for making jam just before it reaches ideal eating quality, when it can be transported easily without too much damage, and will also stand up to the boiling process without breaking down completely. The fruit will need to be washed and graded, and prepared for the boiling process: apples must be peeled and cored, strawberries must have their plugs removed and be lightly crushed, gooseberries must be "topped and tailed", blackcurrants must be "strigged" (i.e. stalks removed). Cherries can be destoned by a stoning machine which neatly pops out the stone individually. For most stone fruits this is not possible, and it is necessary to boil the fruit (using steam vats) until it is soft enough to pass through a brushing machine, which brushes the fruit pulp through a sieve, the holes of which are just too small to allow the stones to go through.

For seedless jams the same principle applies as above for all fruits, but the sieve holes are very fine. Such jams are used particularly in the bakery trade, e.g. for Swiss Rolls, and for boiled sweet centres.

Bitter oranges for marmalade come mainly from Spain and Sicily, and are shipped when still under-ripe, arriving in Britain practically ripe. Apricots, peaches and pineapples are normally imported as slices, halves or broken up still further, in cans, already cooked. Soft and stone fruits are mostly home-grown, but home-grown strawberries are often insufficient and we have to import them preserved with sulphur dioxide.

Since the fruit season is highly concentrated in Britain, it is necessary to store much of the fruit in order to spread the manufacture of jam over the year. This is done in three ways: by sterilization, freezing, or chemical preservation. Of these the commonest method of storing fruit, usually in the pulp form, is with preservative. The fruit is usually cooked (not strawberries or raspberries), sieved, if necessary, and packed into barrels to which is added a solution of sulphur dioxide, whose strength is limited by law. This will keep for many months, and during the jam boiling process practically all the sulphur dioxide is lost. The law insists that there shall not be more than 100 p.p.m. of sulphur dioxide in the finished jam.

Sugar is the major ingredient in jam. For a satisfactory set, the sugar content must be about two-thirds of the whole. This is also necessary to discourage moulds and yeasts which may cause fermentation. In fact, sugar content is controlled by law at 65% for a sealed product, and 68·5% for a non-hermetically sealed jar. Any good quality sugar is used, whether cane or beet. During the boiling of the jam the acid present converts some of the sucrose into invert sugar, but if this conversion is insufficient the jam will crystallize, because sucrose is less soluble than invert sugar.

This is the reason why home-made jam often crystallizes. To overcome this, the manufacturer adds invert syrup, and the final invert sugar content is checked by analysis.

It will be seen that the law is very fussy about the quality of jam as in addition to sugar and sulphur dioxide standards, there are regulations which provide for a minimum fruit content of the stated fruit. The list covers all jams as well as marmalade, and some examples are shown below in Table 4.4.

TABLE 4.4. SOME EXAMPLES OF MINIMUM PERMITTED FRUIT CONTENT

Type of jam	Minimum fruit content (%)
Marmalade	20
Blackcurrant	25
Gooseberry	30
Damson	35
Strawberry	38
Blackberry	38
Plum	40

Boiling of the jam. Most fruits, other than strawberry and raspberry, need to be softened by boiling first of all. The calculated amount of fruit, or pulp, to comply with the above regulations is weighed into the stainless-steel boiling pan (which is steam-jacketed) and to this is added the correct weight of sugar (possibly in the form of syrup), water, pectin, acid (if required in the recipe). The steam is then turned on. A large, robust metal-clad thermometer is the main indicator for the completion of the boil, which is reached when enough water has been boiled away to produce a concentration of 65–70% sugar, and the pectin–sugar–acid system is formed. When the temperature approaches 220°F (105°C) a large metal spoon (called a "skimmer") is dipped into the jam. If on holding it up the jam flakes off the skimmer it is regarded as having set. But the final point is determined by measuring the dissolved sugar using an accurate instrument. Both scientific control and judgment are required to assess the end-point of the boil.

The jam is poured into a water-cooled trough, in which the temperature is rapidly reduced to about 180–190°F (82–88°C) and filled out into the jars or cans. Too high a filling temperature may result in fruit floating to the top after filling. The jars are capped while still hot, which results in the formation of a partial vacuum after cooling. The jars are immediately inverted to sterilize the tops, and cooled as quickly as possible to prevent further inversion of the sugar (which might produce another type of sugar crystallization) and to prevent browning of the jam.

Although Britain is the "home country" as far as jam manufacture is concerned, it is interesting to note that there is a steady decline in the amount of jam purchased. Thus the amount of preserves and syrups consumed averaged 3·2 oz per person each week in 1960; but by 1973 this had dropped to 2·1 oz.

People eat jam because of its sweet and sharp flavour. They like it on bread with which it blends very well. It is true that this is yet another example of pandering to our sweet tooth, and the point has been made that the consumption of sugary foods without other nutrients tends to lower the relative amount of proteins and vitamins in the diet. This is not altogether true in the case of jam because most of the vitamin C in the original fruit is still there. The jams containing most vitamin C are blackcurrant and strawberry jam, and marmalade. Nevertheless it must still be remembered that with 65–70% of sugar, jam is a food of fairly high calorific value. It is an interesting thought that the traditional teatime jam spread on bread-and-butter provides us with Calories, protein, vitamins A, B_1, nicotinic acid, C and D, and the minerals calcium and iron.

Suggestions for Further Reading

CHIVERS AND SONS LTD. *The Manufacture of Jams, Allied Preserves and Table Jellies*, 1960.
KENT, N. L. *Technology of Cereals* (with special reference to wheat), Pergamon, 2nd edn., 1975.
MOORE, E. *Margarine and Cooking Fats*, Unilever Educational Booklet, 1971.
MCCANCE, R. A. and WIDDOWSON, E. M. *Breads, White and Brown: their place in Thought and Social History*, Pitman, 1956.
PYKE, M. *Food Science and Technology*, Murray, 3rd ed., 1970. The processing of all major foods is described in an interesting and clear manner.
PYKE, M. *Technological Eating*, Murray, 1972.
RAUCH, G. H. *Jam Manufacture*, Leonard Hill, 2nd ed., 1965.
REDMAYNE, P. *Britain's Food*, Murray, 1963.
TAYLOR, R. J. *Facts about Margarine*, Van den Berghs Ltd., 1969.

CHAPTER 5

Drink

ALTHOUGH it is possible to live for many days without food it is impossible to live long without drink because our bodies—unlike the camel's—do not have any reserve supply. The essential component of any drink is the water that it contains; other components of a drink, such as stimulants or flavouring agents, may perform some useful functions but they are not essential to the proper functioning of the body. In this chapter we shall start by considering water itself and then go on to other types of drink in which water is just one of several constituents.

Water

Water is both the most common and the most peculiar liquid that exists. The first part of this statement will be readily accepted by most people and it is illustrated by the fact that non-chemists, to whom chemical formulae are utterly mysterious, take a certain pride in being able to quote the formula of water as H_2O. The peculiarity of water may not be so obvious because it is masked by its ubiquity which causes its presence, like that of air, to be taken for granted. In reality, however, it is a most extraordinary liquid; it is colourless, odourless and tasteless and, under normal atmospheric conditions, boils at 100°C and freezes at 0°C. These facts are well known and cause no surprise; yet because water has such a low molecular weight it is odd that it should be a liquid at all. Compounds such as hydrogen sulphide, H_2S, which have a similar formula, are gases, and it is therefore to be expected that water should be a gas. The reason why water is a liquid is that the individual molecules are linked together into groups containing several molecules. The linkage is brought about by weak electrostatic attractions—called hydrogen bonds—between neighbouring water molecules.

The peculiar properties of water make it uniquely suited to the vast number of purposes for which it is used, including the support of life itself. As we have already mentioned it is essential to the proper functioning of the body, and indeed the body is about two-thirds water, all the organs, tissues and fluids containing water as an essential constituent. Water is one of the best solvents known and this enables it to act as an effective transport system for the body and to transport nutrients to where they are required. During life the body is continually losing water —in the urine, as sweat and as water vapour—and this water must be replaced if life is to continue. Water is supplied not only as drink, but also as solid food and from reactions taking place within the body, though of these drink is the more important.

The amount of water, or of beverages containing water, that a person drinks is largely a matter of personal preference though on average a person living a sedentary existence in a temperate climate drinks about a litre per day. A much larger quantity may be drunk without harm, however, because any excess is promptly removed from the blood by the kidneys and excreted as urine. Moreover, it is immaterial whether the water is taken before, during or after meals.

The water we drink must be free from contamination, and to ensure that this is so, natural water required for human consumption must be carefully purified before it is used. In addition to small quantities of dust and dissolved gases present in rainwater, water stored in reservoirs contains impurities from vegetation which make it a natural breeding ground for bacteria. In the past bacteria present in water supplies have been responsible for such diseases as typhoid fever, jaundice and cholera. In order to destroy such bacteria water is sterilized by adding about 1 part of chlorine to 2,000,000 parts of water.

Soft Drinks

Soft drinks provide water in a pleasant and acceptable form though they vary widely in quality from preserved fruit juices with a useful vitamin content to artificial carbonated drinks which may contain little or no fruit, and whose nutrient content may be negligible.

Fruit juices may be preserved by the addition of sulphur dioxide or benzoic acid though in practice most fruit juices do not contain any preservative. From a nutritional point of view they are valuable for the vitamin C which they contain. Blackcurrant juice, orange juice and rose hip syrup are all rich sources of vitamin C and are used as convenient sources of this vitamin for babies and young children. A glass of orange juice, for example, contains at least a day's supply of vitamin C and often a good deal more.

A recent survey carried out by the Consumer Council shows that many people are confused by the many different types of fruit drink available such as squashes, cordials and fruit drinks and it may be helpful to explain how they differ from each other. Fruit squashes have a higher nutritional value than other fruit drinks which are diluted with water before consumption, and by law at least 25% of the undiluted drink must be fruit juice. At present there is an increasing trend towards comminuted drinks which utilize the whole fruit. Such drinks, called fruit drinks, are made by liquidizing the whole fruit and at least 10% of the volume of the undiluted drink must be whole fruit. A fruit cordial is simply a fruit squash which contains no solid matter and is perfectly clear. The main differences between fruit juices, squashes and drinks are shown in Table 5.1.

TABLE 5.1. THE AVERAGE CONTENTS OF FRUIT DRINKS AS ACTUALLY DRUNK

	Fruit juice	Fruit squash	Fruit drink
Amount	$\frac{1}{2}$ pt juice	$\frac{1}{2}$ pt diluted drink	$\frac{1}{2}$ pt diluted drink
Added water	None	95%	98%
Fruit content	100% fruit juice	5% fruit juice	2% whole fruit
Added sugar	1 oz	$\frac{1}{2}$ oz	$\frac{1}{2}$ oz
Vitamin C*	100 mg	3 mg	3 mg
Preservatives	None	Present	Present
Added colour	None	Present	Present
Added flavour	None	Present	Present
Artificial sweetener	None	Present	Present

* Figures for vitamin C refer to orange fruit drinks.

Some drinks—for example, orangeade or an orange-flavoured drink—do not necessarily contain any fruit at all, and the nutritional value of such drinks is no more than the sugar they contain. As an aid to selling, some fruit drinks contain added glucose. This is not significant, however, because whether glucose or sucrose is used the result is similar because the latter is converted into glucose and fructose by the fruit acids present,

The best-quality carbonated fruit drinks are made in a similar way to fruit squashes, except that they are charged with carbon dioxide. It is to be regretted, however, that in many such drinks the natural fruit is replaced by synthetic flavourings together with citric or other acid, and natural colour is replaced by synthetic colour. From a nutritional aspect these products are of no more value than sweetened water.

Mildly Stimulating Beverages

The stimulating effect of such beverages as tea, coffee, cocoa and cola drinks is due to the presence of alkaloids, the most important of which is *caffeine*. Caffeine is a drug which stimulates the nervous system and prevents fatigue. It is a very mild drug—so much so that although most people in Western countries are accustomed to it they do not become addicted—and even if large amounts of beverages containing caffeine are consumed the result is nothing worse than a bout of sleeplessness. No permanent harmful effects can be attributed to the intake of such beverages, even when many cupfuls are consumed.

Apart from water and milk, tea is the world's most popular beverage and Britons drink more than anyone else. The average annual consumption of tea in Britain is about 10 lb per person which corresponds to about 2500 cups of tea! Apart from its action as a stimulant, tea is prized for its fragrant aroma and delicate flavour which are contributed by a very small amount—about 0·01%—of essential oils containing large numbers of volatile components. The leaves also contain appreciable quantities of tannin which impart to the beverage a bitter taste.

When boiling water is added to the familiar black tea leaves—which are produced by drying and fermenting the natural green tea—the soluble components of the leaf are extracted. The desired objective in making tea is to extract the maximum amount of caffeine and essential oils and the minimum amount of tannin. This may be achieved by allowing the infusion to "brew" for about 5 minutes. After this period further extraction of caffeine is slow, volatile essential oils escape and bitterness increases.

Several attempts have been made to manufacture an "instant" tea by extracting the water-soluble components, removing the volatile constituents, concentrating the solution remaining which is then dried, usually by vacuum drying, and reincorporating the volatile constituents. The resulting powder is converted to tea simply by adding hot water. "Instant" tea has not as yet gained much popularity, but considerable efforts are being made to improve the product and exploit it commercially.

Although the consumption of coffee in Britain is lower than that in any other major Western European country, it is nevertheless three times as big as it was pre-war. The growth of coffee bars bears witness to coffee's present popularity, a popularity which has been encouraged by the advent of "instant" coffee which now accounts for more than half the total consumption.

Coffee beans, which are seeds of the bright-red fruit of the evergreen coffee shrub, are roasted before use and this develops flavour and makes them more brittle and therefore easier to grind. After grinding, the flavour and aroma of coffee diminish rapidly although ground coffee can be kept fresh almost indefinitely if it is stored in an airtight tin under vacuum.

When very hot water is added to ground coffee, volatile aroma constituents are released and caffeine is rapidly extracted. The optimum extraction time is about 2 minutes as this allows 80% caffeine to be extracted while limiting the extraction of substances that contribute to bitterness. Coffee produced in this way and drunk with milk contains about twice as much caffeine as a cup of tea.

In many countries coffee is very expensive and it may be adulterated by addition of cheap materials such as chicory, malted cereals and dried figs. In France roasted chicory is frequently added to coffee and many people prefer this mixture to pure coffee. Although roasted chicory contains no caffeine, it does contain caramel and it adds both colour and flavour to the beverage.

In making "instant" coffee the aim is to extract the water-soluble components of roasted coffee beans and to retain the flavour and aroma constituents. In most processes the concentrated liquid extract is spray-dried by allowing a fine spray to pass through a current of hot air, although more recently freeze-drying (see p. 99) has been introduced, for example in the production of Maxwell House and "granular" Nescafé. "Instant" coffee made by modern processes retains most of the flavour and aroma of the roasted beans.

The nutrient content of tea and coffee—apart from the milk and sugar that may be added—is extremely small. Both contain small quantities of B vitamins and, because of the large amount of tea that we drink, tea supplies us with useful amounts of the vitamin riboflavine providing us with about 6% of our intake of this vitamin. Cocoa powder, on the other hand, has a higher nutrient content than tea and coffee and contains roughly a fifth protein, a quarter fat and a third carbohydrate. However, because cocoa as consumed is mainly water and because consumption is small it makes a negligible contribution to our total nutrient intake. The main attraction of cocoa, which is made from cocoa beans by fermentation, roasting and other processes, is due to its stimulating effect. Cocoa acts as a mild stimulant, because, although it contains very little caffeine, it contains about 2% of the alkaloid *theobromine*.

Alcoholic Beverages

The basis of all alcoholic drinks, *ethyl alcohol* or simply alcohol, is a very simple substance containing only carbon, hydrogen and oxygen. In the body it acts in two quite distinct ways. On the one hand, it is a food which is broken down in the body to give energy; on the other hand, it is a drug which affects the central nervous system. As a source of Calories alcohol has a higher Calorific value than either carbohydrate or protein and as it can be absorbed by the body without prior digestion this energy is rapidly made available to the body. As a drug the effect of alcohol on the body varies from mild stimulation, when a small amount is consumed, to loss of co-ordination and even death when large amounts are taken.

Alcoholic drinks are judged in terms of flavour and stimulant effect and hardly at all as a source of Calories. It is interesting to note, however, that the Calorific value of wine is about the same as that of milk and that beer drunk in large quantities can be fattening. There are three main classes of alcoholic beverages, namely wines, beers and spirits, and though these differ both in their method of manufacture and in their character they all share one common characteristic—they are made by the process of fermentation. The essential step in all fermentation processes is the conversion of glucose into alcohol which we can represent:

$$\text{Glucose} \xrightarrow{\text{zymase enzymes}} \text{Alcohol} + \text{Carbon dioxide} + \text{Energy}.$$

It is common knowledge that when you dissolve glucose or any other sugar in water you simply get a sweet-tasting solution; no chemical reaction whatsoever occurs. We may well ask, then, what agents cause glucose to break down during fermentation. The answer is that they are the same sort of agents that cause food to be broken down in the body during digestion, namely enzymes. One of the earliest known sources of enzymes was yeast and this explains how the word arose because it means literally "in yeast". It is in fact the enzymes present in yeast that enable fermentation to take place. Although the breakdown of glucose to alcohol represented above may appear simple, it is in reality a complex process involving twelve distinct stages, each stage being controlled or catalysed by a different enzyme, the whole collection of enzymes being known as the zymase complex.

In making different alcoholic drinks many different starting materials are used but they all have one common feature; they are carbohydrates. As we saw in Chapter 2, glucose consists of a single unit whereas sucrose and other disaccharides contain two units and starch contains many units. If starch is the starting material, as it is when potatoes, grain or rice are used, its many glucose units must be split up into single ones before the final stage of fermentation can proceed. It is the enzymes present in malt which enable starch to be broken down to maltose which is then broken down to glucose by a yeast enzyme. If sucrose is the starting material, as it is when molasses is used, other enzymes in yeast break it down into fructose and glucose which are both converted into alcohol by the zymase complex.

Beer

Considering the popularity and antiquity of beer it is rather surprising that so much confusion exists as to exactly what it is and what the terms beer, ale, stout and lager imply. The term beer is normally applied to a beverage made by fermentation of malted barley, and the essential materials used in its manufacture are water, malted barley, hops and yeast. Although beer has been made for several thousand years, during which the principles involved have changed very little, yet what was once an art has, in the last hundred years, become a highly organized and profitable science.

The starting material for making beer is malt which is obtained by steeping barley in water and, after removing it from the water, drying it very carefully. The details of beer manufacture are complex but the essentials can be simply explained. Malt is "mashed" by adding hot water and this extracts the soluble material from the malt. During malting and mashing, starch is broken down into maltose and this is extracted into the liquor during mashing. The liquor resulting from mashing, known as "wort", is boiled with hops and this extracts flavouring material from the hops, destroys the enzymes present and sterilizes (and concentrates) the "wort". After addition of yeast to the wort, fermentation commences and it is allowed to continue for several days during which time the maltose is broken down into glucose which is then converted into alcohol as described earlier.

The crude beer thus produced contains yeast which is removed by allowing the beer to stand until the yeast has settled out. During this time the beer matures and flavour and bouquet are developed. The maturing process varies from only a few days for mild- or low-strength beers to several months for strong beers. Bottled (or canned) beer is pasteurized and carbon dioxide under pressure is introduced during bottling. Present fashion demands that bottled beer be crystal clear and sparkling, and to achieve this it is carefully filtered before being bottled.

Although the principles of beer manufacture are simple, the details vary a great deal and result in the production of a wide and confusing variety of beers. The main source of confusion concerns the use of the terms beer and ale because this implies that there is a distinction between them whereas in fact there is none. Table 5.2 gives a rough classification of the main types of beer, and shows how the alcohol and Calorie content vary. Mild ales are the weakest—and cheapest—and are inferior in that they are matured for only a few days. Bitter ales have more flavour both because they are allowed to mature longer than mild ales and because additional hops are added at the start of the maturing period. Stout is

TABLE 5.2. DIFFERENT TYPES OF BEER

Type	Example	Alcohol content (g/100 ml)	Calorific value (Cal/100ml)
Light beers	Bitter	3.1	31
	Pale ale	3.3	32
Dark beers	Brown ale	2.2	28
	Mild ale	2.6	25
	Stout	2.9	37
Strong beers	Stout, extra	4.3	39
	Strong ale	6.6	73

characterized by a dark colour and often by a relatively high alcohol content. It is made from special malt mixtures which are heated to a sufficiently high temperature to produce some caramel which imparts a dark brown colour to the liquor. The alcohol content and Calorific value of strong beers is relatively high, the former rising to about 10% and the latter being similar to that of milk or potatoes. Lagers differ from other beers in the way that fermentation is carried out and also in the fact that they are matured at a low temperature for several months. Although lagers are commonly supposed to be a pale coloured type of beer, some are, in fact, quite dark in colour. The alcohol content of lager is 3–4%.

Wine

Whereas beer is a synthetic product in that it can only be made when the essential ingredients are brought together, wine is a natural product in that all the necessary ingredients are present in grapes. Strictly speaking, wine is the product of the vine, though in a more general sense the term is often extended to include all fermented liquors obtained from fruit and vegetables. In what follows we shall confine ourselves to grape wines.

Grapes ferment naturally because they contain all the essential ingredients, namely sugar, water, and yeast, the first two being present in the juice and the last on the skin. Different types of wine have their own special character, however, because grapes grown in different regions differ slightly in composition—particularly with respect to their volatile components which contribute to flavour and bouquet—and because different regions have evolved their own techniques of wine-making. Although the art of wine-making is an ancient one, modern methods of production are carefully controlled, being the outcome of much research. The essential stages in wine-making are pressing, fermentation, casking and bottling.

During pressing, the juice is extracted from grapes and at the same time yeasts and other micro-organisms from the skin pass into the juice. Many thousands of different types of yeast may be present on a single type of grape and because many of these are "wild" yeasts that would produce poor-quality wine, sulphur dioxide is added to the juice in such quantity that all but the stronger wine yeasts are destroyed. During fermentation which follows, glucose and fructose present in the juice are converted into alcohol. If fermentation continues until all the sugars are used up the resulting wine will be dry, whereas if it is stopped while some sugar remains it will be sweet. In any case yeasts cannot tolerate an alcohol content greater than about 16%, so that natural wines cannot contain more alcohol than this, and in general they contain about 10%.

After fermentation, wine is transferred to casks where it may remain for anything up to 5 years; during this time sediment is occasionally removed and the wine matures as a result of slow chemical changes which contribute to flavour and bouquet. After bottling maturing continues, the optimum time in bottle being dependent on the wine—for a vintage champagne this period may be as long as 20 years.

There are a bewildering and fascinating array of different wines, each being named by reference to its place of origin; some of the most renowned of these wines are given below. These wines differ mainly according to whether they are red or white, natural or fortified, still or sparkling. It is a popular fallacy that the colour of a wine depends on the colour of the grapes from which it is made; in fact white wines may easily be made from black grapes. The colour of grapes depends upon pigment which lies just under the skin and as only the juice is used in making white wine, the colour of the grape used is immaterial. In making red wines, however, both juice and skin are used, the colour of the grapes being extracted from the skin during fermentation.

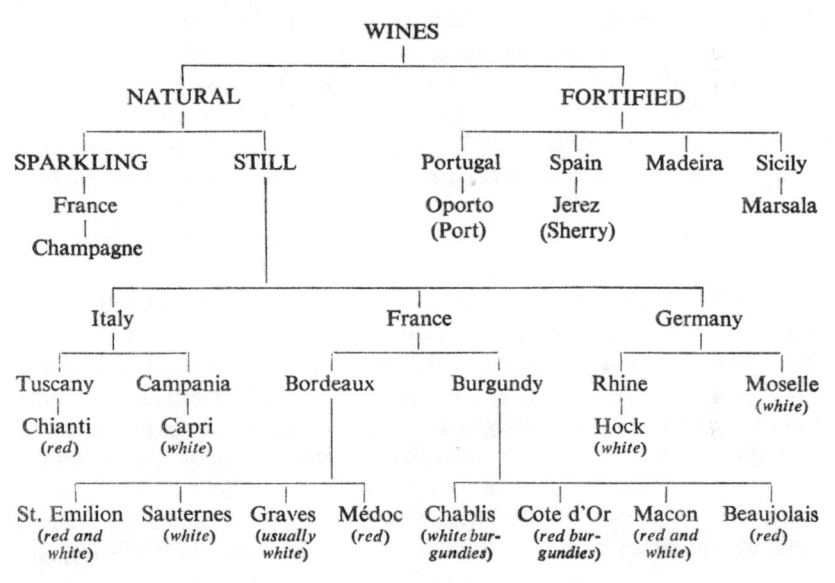

```
                              WINES
                ┌───────────────┴───────────────┐
             NATURAL                         FORTIFIED
         ┌──────┴──────┐        ┌──────┬──────┬──────┐
     SPARKLING       STILL   Portugal  Spain  Madeira  Sicily
         │             │        │       │              │
      France           │      Oporto   Jerez         Marsala
         │             │      (Port)  (Sherry)
    Champagne          │
                       │
         ┌─────────────┼─────────────┐
       Italy         France        Germany
    ┌────┴────┐   ┌────┴────┐   ┌────┴────┐
  Tuscany  Campania Bordeaux Burgundy Rhine   Moselle
    │        │                        │      (white)
  Chianti  Capri                    Hock
   (red)  (white)                  (white)

  ┌────┬────┬────┬────┐   ┌────┬────┬────┐
St. Emilion Sauternes Graves Médoc Chablis Cote d'Or Macon Beaujolais
(red and  (white)  (usually (red) (white bur- (red bur- (red and (red)
 white)            white)         gundies)   gundies)  white)
```

Fortified wines—of which the best known are port and sherry—differ from natural ones in that extra alcohol is added to give them a higher alcohol content than natural wines. Port, which comes from Oporto in Portugal, is made by adding brandy to wine before fermentation is complete. Some people's enthusiasm for this wine wanes considerably when they discover that the initial pressing of the grapes is traditionally carried out by bare-footed peasants! Genuine sherry is made from a special variety of grapes which is grown near Jerez in Southern Spain. Both sherry and port keep well because they have an alcohol content of about 20% which is sufficiently high to kill micro-organisms that attack natural wines.

Sparkling wines, of which champagne is pre-eminent, are made by allowing a secondary fermentation to occur after bottling. The carbon dioxide generated is stored within the liquid under its own pressure, and though most of it is lost when the cork is drawn, enough remains to give the wine a "sparkle" and its well-known "bubbliness".

Spirits and Liqueurs

Spirits are made by distilling fermented liquors. Thus brandy is made by distilling wine, rum from fermented molasses and whisky from fermented grain. Such distilled liquors have a high alcohol content, usually about 40%, and thus have excellent keeping qualities. After being distilled they are usually allowed to mature; for example, whisky is matured in wooden casks when it loses its raw fiery nature and becomes smooth and mellow. The best whiskies are allowed to mature for at least 5 years, and malt whisky does not reach its prime for 15 years, after which it starts to deteriorate.

The essential stage in making spirits is distillation, in which dilute alcoholic liquors are concentrated. The simplest way of doing this is to heat the liquor and convert it into vapour. As alcohol has a lower boiling point than water the proportion of alcohol to water is higher in the vapour phase than in the liquid. If the vapour is led away and cooled until it liquefies, the liquid formed—known as the distillate—is at first richer in alcohol than the original liquor, though, as heating is continued the alcohol content of the distillate falls. Obviously, if distillation is stopped before all the liquor has distilled, the distillate will be richer in alcohol than the original mixture. Such a simple distillation is commonly carried out on a small scale in laboratories (though it is illegal to make spirits in this way), and in the manufacture of spirits a similar, though scaled-up process, is carried out in pot stills.

If a very concentrated alcoholic liquor is required, distillation in a pot still has to be repeated a number of times. To overcome this disadvantage a continuous still has been developed in which many separate distillations are carried out continuously in the same still. Although such continuous stills are much more efficient and much quicker than pot stills, the latter are nevertheless used extensively for making the finest brandies, whiskies and other renowned spirits. This is because the pot still allows many of the volatile components which contribute character and subtle flavours to the drink to pass over with the alcohol into the distillate. The best brandies, for example, which come from the region around Cognac in France, are distilled twice in pot stills in order to achieve the desired alcohol content together with the desired flavouring materials.

Whereas the subtle flavours of fine whiskies and brandies result from the distillation process, those of spirits such as gin are added after distillation is complete. For drinks such as this a colourless, tasteless spirit is required and this can be achieved using continuous stills. This concentrated spirit—known as silent spirit—can be made from any fermentable material, though cereals are usually used because they are cheap. Vodka is the "purest" spirit in that almost all traces of flavour and colour are removed during distillation. Gin, on the other hand, is made from diluted silent spirit to which certain plant essences are added. The exact recipe is kept secret but it is well known that juniper berries are an important constituent. This mixture is redistilled in a pot still and diluted to the desired alcohol content.

Even in this scientific age the making of spirits remains much of a craft and something of a mystery. Much of their character is attributed to strange details of manufacture. Thus the characteristic flavour of malt whisky is said to owe much to the fumes from the peat fires used to dry the malt, whereas fine brandies are said to owe something to the oak casks in which they are allowed to mature for as long as 20 years.

Liqueurs, to an even greater extent than spirits, are surrounded by an aura of mystery and romance. They are made by steeping herbs in silent spirit, and the resulting liquor is often distilled. The recipes of most liqueurs are closely guarded secrets, and in some cases—for example, Benedictine—it remains the property of the monastery which conceived it. It is said that the complex recipe of Benedictine, which has been made for over 400 years, is completely known to only three people at any one time. Many flavouring agents are used including honey, herbs, fruit skins and certain seashore plants. Even those liqueurs which do not have a monastic origin often have a romantic background. For example, the recipe of the renowned Scots liqueur Drambuie, literally "the drink that satisfies", is associated with Bonny Prince Charlie. The secret recipe, which is based on whisky and honey, is said to have been divulged by the fleeing Prince as a token of gratitude for the help he received in escaping to the island of Skye after the military disasters of 1745.

Suggestions for Further Reading

AUSTIN, A. *The Science of Wine*, University of London Press, 1968.
BRAVERY, H. E. *The Simple Science of Wine and Beer Making*, Macdonald, 1969.
CARR, J. G. *Biological Principles in Fermentation*, Heinemann, 1968. A concise and simple account of the fermentation of alcoholic drinks.
JOHNSON, H. *Wine*, Sphere Books, 1968.
MARRISON, L. W. *Wines and Spirits,* Penguin Books, 2nd edn., 1968. An authoritative but readable book.
TAYLOR, R. J. *Water*, Unilever Educational Booklet, 1966.

CHAPTER 6

Food Poisoning and the Preservation of Food

> ... It shall be eaten the same day we offer it, and on the morrow: and if aught remain until the third day, it shall be burnt with fire. And if it be eaten at all on the third day, it is an abomination; it shall not be accepted: ...
> Leviticus 19:6

EVEN in the time of Moses it appeared to be well understood that food could spoil if it was kept for too long and the above record is full of many similar exhortations about food and hygiene. Food poisoning and spoilage have been known by man as long as records have been kept, but unfortunately all historical descriptions of food poisoning are based on the belief that the symptoms were caused by poisonous chemicals. Until the nineteenth century people knew nothing about the existence of germs, and it is therefore clear from what we now know, that many of the cases of chemical poisoning mentioned in historical accounts were in fact caused by eating food contaminated by micro-organisms. There were no doubt many cases of genuine chemical poisoning also observed in the past, especially in the Middle Ages as, for example, when people began to add chemical compounds of lead to their food (sugar of lead) for sweetening purposes. As we now know lead is a very deadly poison so that its use as a "mediaeval food additive" almost inevitably resulted in fatal consequences. Many other metals which found their way into food such as beryllium compounds (sugar of beryl) were also used for sweetening purposes and predictably led to death or at least serious illness. Metal poisonings such as these are doubly dangerous because the poisons are *cumulative*. This means that the body gradually builds them up in its tissues and may not exhibit symptoms of the poisoning until several meals have been eaten over several years and the amount of metal in the body tissues reaches a certain level. At this point hair and teeth might start dropping out and vomiting, diarrhoea and headache might set in.

"Ptomaine poisoning" was used and still is used by the popular press to describe food poisoning. However, ptomaines are actually chemical compounds which are formed in putrefying tissues and do *not* cause food poisoning symptoms, and generally foods which do not appear to be spoiled or putrefied in any way are more likely to cause dangerous poisoning symptoms than spoiled or putrefied ones.

We now know that nearly all cases of food poisoning are caused by germs which grow actively in the food. The study of germs is called *bacteriology* after the Greek word *bactron* meaning rod, because the first person to observe them was a Dutchman called Van Lowenhoek who was not a professional scientist but whose hobby was making microscopes. He first saw them in 1675 but did not realize their universal importance in causing disease and food spoilage.

The first man to realize the tremendous importance of germs was the famous chemical microbiologist Louis Pasteur, who lived in the nineteenth century. Pasteur discovered that germs or bacteria are everywhere —in the soil, water, dust or air—and could contaminate a food causing poisoning or spoilage or could invade a wood causing infection and sepsis. About this time scientists were coming to the realization that bacteria were often observed in infected tissue, but believed that they were "spontaneously generated" by the diseased tissue! In other words, they believed that the diseased tissue caused the bacteria to be born of itself. Pasteur showed that the infection in a wound is actually caused by bacteria, brought in from outside, and that spoilage of food or drink could be caused by bacteria from the environment which invade the food or drink and then multiply inside them. He was also able to show that if a particular food product was sterilized by heating, living bacteria would not appear in the food unless they came from outside, either from the air, the hands, or some other infected material.

Between the latter part of the nineteenth century and the early part of this century two of the micro-organisms which actually caused food poisoning were discovered. These were *Salmonella*, named after its discoverer Dr. Salmon, and *Staphylococcus*. The process of milk *pasteurization* was gradually introduced. In other words the milk was subjected to a partial heat treatment to kill harmful (pathogenic) micro-organisms. However, even up to a few years ago many people in country districts still drank raw (unpasteurized) milk, causing epidemics of sore throat, scarlet fever, dysentery, typhoid and paratyphoid fever.

In the nineteenth century it was discovered that outbreaks of disease

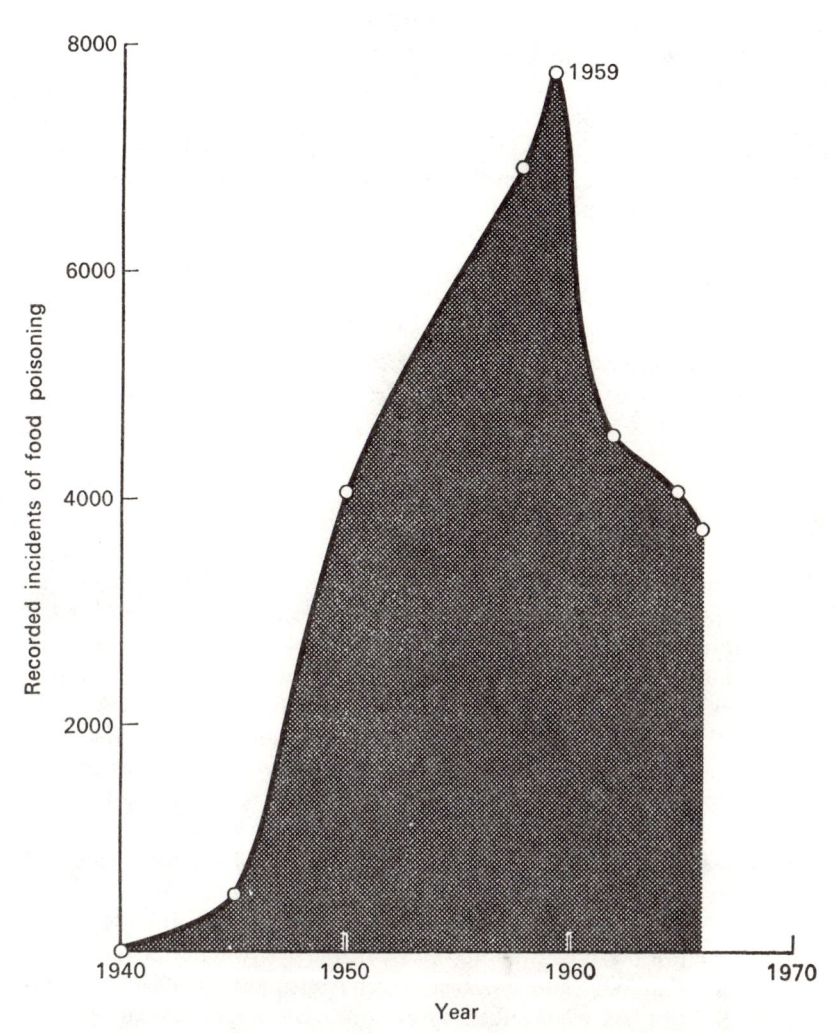

FIG. 6.1. Recorded incidents of food poisoning in England and Wales from 1940 to 1966, showing a peak in 1959 followed by a decline since then.

could often be traced to common infected sources of drinking water. This resulted in the gradual chlorination of drinking water supplies so that we can now say with some confidence that water-borne infection has been virtually eliminated in many countries. Similarly, canned heat-sterilized foods have been made safe from pathogens, but open pack solid foods still create difficulties in this respect. Now chemical preservatives have completely solved the problem.

Probably it was the increased availability of open pack solid food (e.g. cream cakes) in cafes and snack bars, during the first half of this century, which caused a high proportion of the reported cases of poisoning. This has been largely due to a general lack of understanding about how to control and prevent the growth of pathogenic micro-organisms in such foods. Figure 6.1 shows the sharp rise in reported cases of food poisoning recorded since 1940. The number of reported cases declined somewhat by 1966, but in 1972-3 showed signs of a rise back toward the 1959 peak.

Bacteria and Food Poisoning

Bacteria are organisms of extremely small size and variable shape. They are minute single-celled plants which are found everywhere in the world—e.g. soil, water, dust, or air—and there are thousands of different types. Although in this chapter we are concentrating our attention on a harmful aspect of bacteria we should not be misled into thinking that all bacteria are harmful. Some perform many useful functions, being able for example to turn decaying vegetable matter into manure. Some bacteria which live in the human intestine are able to make certain vitamins of the B complex and thus provide us with an essential set of nutrients. Some bacteria are used commercially in food manufacture—cheese-making for example—and in fact only a very small proportion of the total bacterial population causes disease of man and animals.

Bacteria are so minute that they cannot be seen by the naked eye and it may therefore be impossible to tell by inspection when food is dangerously contaminated. The bacteria which cause the *spoilage* of food are usually harmless when taken by mouth. The dangerous bacteria, or *pathogens*, are those which harm man but do not usually change the appearance, taste or smell of food.

Bacteria may be as small as 1/1000th of a millimetre! This means that clusters of a thousand or more of them are only just visible to the naked

FOOD POISONING AND THE PRESERVATION OF FOOD   91

eye. They are classified according to their shape and may be either round *(coccus)*, straight or rod shaped *(bacterium* or *bacillus)* or spiral *(spirochaete)*.

Although bacteria are only single plant cells, they are often mobile and able to swim about in watery fluids by means of tiny hairlike processes which protrude from around the bacterial cell. However, when conditions are unfavourable for growth, particularly when there is a shortage of water, some bacteria can produce resting bodies which are called *spores*. Spores form within the bacterial cell which afterwards disintegrates gradually releasing the spores. The spores remain inactive until conditions for growth again become favourable when normal vegetative bacterial cells are gradually regenerated from them. The spores are extremely resistant to unfavourable conditions and can thus withstand high temperatures for long periods. Commercial methods for the *sterilization* of canned foods are therefore based on the time and temperature required to kill spores, which of course varies from one species of micro-organism to another. Some of the sporing bacteria, when allowed to multiply in foodstuffs, may be responsible for ordinary spoilage, decomposing the food with the production of gas. Others such as the organism *Clostridium botulinum* cause food poisoning by the formation of poisonous substances or *toxins* in the food.

A bacterial cell multiplies by simple division into two, and under favourable conditions this will occur every 20 to 30 minutes. Thus one cell could become 2000 million cells after 12 hours of continuous growth! When bacteria are encouraged to grow on a suitable culture medium such as meat broth each cell will divide into two every 20 minutes, so that overnight a small heap of bacteria consisting of many million cells is formed. This is called a colony.

Most bacteria require air to live actively and are therefore called *aerobes;* others can multiply only in the absence of oxygen and are called *anaerobes*. Amongst the latter type are the various spore forming organisms causing *botulism*, such as *Clostridium botulinum*. These organisms flourish under the conditions found at the bottom of large containers filled with stew at room temperatures, and keeping food like this for periods of time is therefore an extremely bad practice.

The symptoms of food poisoning—headache, vomiting and diarrhoea— are caused by the food poisoning organisms multiplying in sufficient numbers either in the food or in the body to produce enough toxin to cause ill effect. Since the poisoning could be caused by a number of different types of organism it is important to be able to diagnose the cause of illness from a knowledge of the incubation period (time taken for symptoms to appear following ingestion of poisoned food) and duration of symptoms. Table 6.1 lists these two time intervals for four of the organisms most commonly involved in outbreaks of food poisoning.

TABLE 6.1. ORGANISMS COMMONLY INVOLVED IN FOOD POISONING

Organism	Incubation period	Duration of symptoms
Salmonella	12–36 hours	1–8 days
Staphylococcus	2–6 hours	6–24 hours
Clostridium welchii	8–22 hours	12–24 hours
Clostridium botulinum	24–72 hours	Death in 24 hours to 8 days or convalescence over 8 months

The four organisms listed in Table 6.1, and in fact all pathogenic organisms, grow best at about the temperature of the body (i.e. 98·6°F or 37°C) although the majority of them will multiply between 20°C and 43°C (i.e. 68°F and 109°F). Extreme cold will *not* kill bacteria but it will prevent them from growing and this is the reason for the storage of susceptible foods at low temperatures. Refrigeration prevents not only the spoilage of food, but also the danger of proliferation of harmful bacteria.

Above 40°C (104°F) the growth of bacteria falls off very rapidly and in general it ceases above 45°C (113°F). Non-sporing bacteria are *killed* at temperatures above 60°C (140°C) but the length of time needed to kill them when held at this temperature varies from species to species. For example, to make milk safe to drink (i.e. free from harmful bacteria) it may be held at 62·8°C (145°F) for 30 minutes.

Consideration of the information contained in the last two paragraphs will make it clear to the reader that the best way to avoid food poisoning from stored (unsterilized) foods is to ensure that the storage temperature is not within the range in which harmful bacteria will grow. Thus if foods are kept below about 10°C or above about 65°C there should be little danger of toxins being produced through the proliferation of harmful organisms. In the United Kingdom consumers have a built-in safeguard against some types of food poisoning through the Food Hygiene Regulations which make it an offence to keep certain open food packs for consumption on the premises at a temperature between 10°C (50°F) and 62·8°C (145°F).

Nowadays most housewives know enough elementary hygiene to avoid causing food poisoning in the home. Lack of proper attention to clean food handling and sensible hygienic precautions (e.g. hand-washing after visiting the toilet) can not only lead to an illness within the family but possibly also to recurring bouts of symptoms as the organism is passed from one member of the family to another. This type of effect is frequent with *salmonella* poisoning. People who handle food with boils or septic wounds on their hands are liable to transmit infection by means of the organism *staphylococcus*. There have been reports of it occurring within the food industry and entire factories have had to close down for periods of time as a result. Usually these outbreaks of food poisoning have been traced to an infection on the hands of one single operative. *Staphylococcus* organisms usually produce ill effects by means of toxins which act on the stomach and intestines. The organisms themselves do not usually survive for long once ingested and will not reach the bloodstream. *Salmonella*, on the other hand, might either infect the stomach and intestine alone or pass through the wall of the intestine into the bloodstream where they may survive for a while longer.

The anaerobic organisms *Clostridium welchii* always grow in non-acidic foods such as meat and vegetables. They do not grow in fruit and, because of the acidity of the stomach, they do not survive after eating. However, these organisms produce toxins which act on the stomach and intestine causing violent sickness. *Clostridium botulinum* is by far the more dangerous of the two and poisoning caused by this organism is frequently fatal, due to the powerful botulinus toxin which it produces in the food. This toxin is the most poisonous substance known and as little as one-hundred-thousandth of a gramme may cause death in man. In this type of food poisoning it is important to diagnose the cause as rapidly as possible so that the appropriate antitoxin may be administered. However, this is made difficult by the long period of incubation before symptoms appear. These usually start as tiredness, headache and dizziness, then diarrhoea followed by constipation, and finally paralysis of the eye and neck muscles and respiratory centres. Fortunately botulinus toxin is sensitive to heat, but boiling of foods for several hours is necessary to ensure its destruction.

Boiling kills all living cells so that bacteria will only survive a few seconds if subjected to boiling water. However, bacterial spores are far more resistant and boiling for 5 or more hours is necessary to destroy them. To kill spores in a shorter time than this, temperatures well above boiling must be used.

Bacteria will not multiply if they are kept without water and there must be at least 15% water in any foodstuff for normal bacterial growth. Dehydration, however, does not kill bacteria and they may survive for long periods, finally reviving when water is added to them.

Food Spoilage by Bacteria, Yeasts, Moulds, and Fungi

As well as bacteria, yeasts, moulds, and fungi can cause the *spoilage* of food by growing in it and altering its chemical composition. Foods which humans eat are also often a lush pasture for micro-organisms which "consume" the chemical components of the food and replace them with other chemicals which alter the colour, flavour, odour, and texture of the food. These changes may cause the food to lose nutritional value, or to become unpleasant or even positively harmful to the consumer. These changes are collectively referred to as spoilage and it is the business of modern food technology (either in the home or in the industry) to keep this to a minimum.

For many foods "spoilage" could be said to be a matter of taste. The hanging of game, for example, until a strong flavour develops is in reality a controlled type of spoilage by micro-organisms and may be acceptable to some people but not others. The Eskimoes bury fish to produce a malodorous product called "titmuck" which is semi-liquid in appearance and would not be eaten by most British or American people, and would most certainly be labelled as spoiled. It is therefore difficult to say whether such foods are or are not fit for human consumption.

Because spoilage organisms only grow in and spoil foods from which they themselves can derive nutritional value it is possible from a study of the organisms concerned to predict which foods are likely to be spoiled and under what conditions. For example, we now know that a certain amount of water (15%) is necessary in high concentration before an organism can grow in a food. Furthermore, organisms can only grow in foods of low sugar content because sugar acts as a preservative by rendering much of the water present unavailable to the organism. A good source of energy in the food (often carbohydrate) is yet another essential requirement for the growth of organisms to take place, and nitrogen (and possibly oxygen) and minerals must also be supplied. Even when all these conditions are fulfilled the organisms will not grow unless the acidity of the food suits their particular needs. Thus although moulds can grow over a wide range of acidities, yeasts require a very narrow range of acidity in which to grow and bacteria normally only grow in foods near neutrality.

Let us now consider a few examples of foodstuffs in relation to their tendency to spoil. Generally these can be divided into three classes —stable foods, semi-perishable foods, and perishable foods—so we will choose examples from each class. Sugar and chocolate are examples of stable foods which do not spoil microbiologically due to the fact that they are free of water. It is true that chocolate can suffer from a defect called "bloom" if it is subjected to hot or damp conditions, but this is entirely a physical effect and in no way causes the chocolate to become unwholesome even if it is unsightly. Flour is another food which under dry conditions does not suffer from microbiological spoilage. Among the semi-perishable foods we could classify potatoes and some varieties of apples. Potatoes, if they are not bruised or damaged in any way, and are stored at the right temperatures and humidity, will keep for many months, and the same thing applies to apples. Many other fruits, however, suffer from the growth of yeasts and moulds on their surface which not only make the fruit too unsightly to eat but immediately begin to ferment the juices in the fruit forming alcohol and possibly other more harmful chemicals. Yeasts and moulds are usually already present on the surface of fruits before they are picked and will rapidly spoil some varieties, such as strawberries, if they are kept for a few days after picking. Yeasts and moulds are able to use the carbohydrate in fruit as an extremely useful food for their own growth, and in this respect it might be asked why it is that jams and jellies, which we make by boiling fruit with a lot of carbohydrate (sugar), do not also suffer from mould growth at the surface. The answer is that most recipes which we use to make these products ensure that there is so much sugar present (about 70%) in the finished product that its "natural" preservative action prevents the growth of yeasts and moulds. If the reader has spent much time making home-made jam, he or she may have noticed that some batches do actually grow mould on the surface if they are left exposed to the air for some time. This is because they do not contain enough sugar due to the recipe not being correctly followed. There is a law in the United Kingdom requiring all manufactured jams, jellies and preserves to contain at least 68·5% soluble solids as sugar unless they are packed in hermetically sealed containers to prevent the access of micro-organisms. Bacteria will not normally grow in jams due to the natural acidity of the fruit.

One of the foods most susceptible to spoilage is meat, which can easily be contaminated with organisms from soil, dust or dung, and which should therefore be kept refrigerated. This will not, however, stop the growth of *psychrophilic* (cold-loving) organisms such as the mould *Cladosporium herbarum*, which is able to grow at refrigerator temperatures and cause discoloration, especially blackening of carcass meat with accompanying distasteful odours and taints. It may not always be possible for a consumer to tell whether fresh meat comes from a diseased animal. However, this risk is overcome in the United Kingdom by qualified inspectors who examine animals slaughtered for food before and after death, and only the satisfactory meat is released for human consumption. Fish is just as susceptible to spoilage as meat. Sometimes fish become contaminated with luminous organisms which cause them to glow in the dark.

Perhaps our most important foodstuff is milk, because it not only provides most of us with the dietary calcium and many of the vitamins which we need, but is actually the major foodstuff of infants. It is therefore important that we guard it as carefully as possible from contamination by micro-organisms, and this is done largely by pasteurization. Pasteurization is carried out to destroy micro-organisms which collect in the milk before it is capped in bottles. On leaving the mammary glands milk is sterile; it becomes progressively contaminated on passing down the ducts of the udder. Even before it reaches the exterior of the teats it therefore acquires a bacterial count of at least 500 organisms per millilitre. Milk has a certain natural bacteriostatic property but if heavily contaminated with bacteria, yeasts or moulds this will not be enough to prevent them multiplying. The milk will then turn sour, form clots and putrefy with gas production.

Eggs may be contaminated with the organism *Salmonella* even before they are laid. There is a delicate film or cuticle on the surface of eggs which normally prevents micro-organisms from getting into the egg through the pores in the shell. If this is removed in any way—e.g. by water or mechanical agitation—the egg may be invaded by micro-organisms and will not keep well. For this reason eggs should not be washed if intended for storage.

A more specific spoilage organism is *Bacillus mesentericus* which has the peculiar effect of being able to cause the condition known as "ropiness" in bread. The spores of the organism survive the baking process and germinate in moist bread during storage producing a characteristic slimy texture. Another special example is the mould *Aspergillus flavus* which grows on stale peanuts or peanut meal producing a poisonous substance called *aflatoxin*. This toxin is able to cause cancer of the liver in animals but there is no evidence to show that it does so in man.

There are many more examples of food spoilage caused by micro-organisms which are well understood, but it would take a book much larger than this to recount them.

Ways of Preserving Food

As food technology progresses more methods of treating foods to avoid spoilage and poisoning become known and several of these are now used by the food industry.

Let us first of all look at *pasteurization* which was discovered by Louis Pasteur in the nineteenth century and used as a means for destroying organisms in wine. Now it is used mainly to destroy harmful organisms in milk and nearly all milk supplies in the United Kingdom are treated this way. In the pasteurization process milk is usually heated to 62·8°C (145°F) and held at this temperature for 30 minutes. But a newer variation of this is the high-temperature short-time process (HTST) in which the milk is heated to 71·7°C (161°F) for 15 seconds and achieves the same results. Pasteurization kills most non-sporing organisms including all non-sporing pathogens thus rendering milk safe for human consumption and extending its shelf life. Most of the organisms which ferment milk sugar (lactose) are destroyed in the pasteurization process and as a result milk treated in this way does not readily go sour, but may instead become putrid due to the action of proteolytic spore-bearing organisms which are not killed by pasteurization. It should be emphasized here, therefore, that pasteurized milk is not sterile, and refrigeration is therefore essential for keeping it in good condition. So-called "sterilized milk" is held in bottles at 100°C and sealed, but in fact it is not really totally sterile and will not therefore keep indefinitely.

Since most housewives nowadays own their own refrigerator it might be thought that refrigeration would be the best understood method of preservation of food. However, it is usually the case that the fundamental microbiological facts of refrigerated food storage are *not* understood by most people. Cold storage (e.g. 0–10°C) in a domestic refrigerator will not kill organisms but will keep their growth rate low. Perishable foods will remain edible for days or even weeks in a domestic refrigerator, but will not be indefinitely preserved. Some organisms are able to multiply, although slowly, even at freezing point or below. Even near −20°C "Black Spot" may appear on frozen meat due to yeasts and moulds. Below −20°C, however, most foods remain practically unchanged for weeks or months, and most modern refrigerators have a star rating inscribed on their deep-freeze compartment. One star means that frozen food packs will keep for one week; two stars indicates one month, and three stars indicates three months maximum storage time. Canned sterilized food will keep a lot longer than this, of course, and some typical examples are canned milk (1 year), canned vegetables (2 years) and canned fish or meat (5 years). However, if cans become dented, rusted, swollen or leaky they should be immediately discarded.

When foods are frozen for storage purposes the main problem is that water present in the food turns to ice crystals which are able to damage the structure of the food, especially if they become too large. In this respect the rate of freezing is important. Slow freezing produces large ice crystals which disrupt the food structure, causing separation of the tissue fluids, which are then lost when the food thaws. Rapid freezing produces only small ice crystals and almost no separation of tissue fluids results, thus eliminating loss of these upon thawing. This is of particular importance in retaining the nutritional value of carcass meat, since rapid freezing eliminates the so-called "drip" from thawed meats. Frozen foods once thawed are subject to rapid deterioration by microbes present in them and therefore should be used without delay. Refreezing should never be practised since micro-organisms which will have increased in number during the thawed period will be preserved in the food together with any toxic products of their metabolism. One is reminded of the unfortunate young man from Pendrick:

> There was a young man from Pendrick,
> Who at food from the fridge liked to pick,
> He'd munch it and chew it
> Each time he withdrew it,
> And now he is feeling quite sick.

To preserve foods for long periods in good condition the best technique is to freeze them quickly to $-26°C$ and keep them at this temperature. In this way, many foods (e.g. meat, fish, fruit, and vegetables) are kept in a condition nearer to freshness in terms of flavour, odour, colour, general palatability, and nutritional value, than by any other method of preservation.

Dehydration or drying is one of the oldest methods of preserving foods. It has been used successfully for preserving fruits (e.g. raisins, apricots and apples), vegetables, milk, eggs, fish, and meat. Although micro-organisms cannot multiply in the absence of water and cannot survive indefinitely in the dehydrated state, they may survive in dried foods for many years. Surviving micro-organisms multiply again and bring about spoilage of foods when these become wet. Dry foods must therefore be kept away from humid atmospheres.

Both freezing and drying are modern methods of food preservation which are used commercially. A more recent technique, however, is freeze-drying or drying from the frozen state. In this technique foodstuffs are first frozen, then subjected to a very high vacuum which removes all the water from them without thawing. This is the same effect as we may observe on cold days on hanging out the washing. While still very wet the washing on the line may freeze and then dry in the frozen state as the wind blows it. When we come to collect it, it is still very stiff but free of water. In the case of foods this method of processing has the advantage that it removes water without the concentration effect which normally occurs during evaporation. In other words, the molecules of the chemicals in the food (carbohydrates, fats, proteins and vitamins) are not forced into close proximity as they are in conventional drying procedures, and therefore do not react with each other to cause changes in the palatability and nutritional value of the food. The texture and flavour of freeze-dried foods is therefore of a high standard. Freeze-drying is already being used commercially, especially for the production of meat and fish used in the preparation of instant foods such as prawn, chicken, and beef curries.

Canning or bottling are methods of heat-treating foods in containers, to remove all harmful organisms, after which the food is sealed in the container. Although the idea of heating food in sealed containers was probably known in the early eighteenth century or before, it was a Frenchman called Nicolas Appert who first developed the process with clear instructions about how to carry it out. He has since been called the "Father of Canning" as a result of his pioneering experiments which he performed between about 1795 and 1810. Appert started his work on canning in response to the offer of a prize by the French government for a published method for preserving food for Napoleon's army. In 1809 he won the prize of 12,000 francs for a treatise which he published soon afterwards called *The Book for All Households; or the Art of Preserving Animal and Vegetable Substances for Many Years.* Nothing was known about the relationship of micro-organisms and spoilage at the time that Appert did this work; but some of the directions which he gave are still applicable today.

Canning and bottling involve achieving near sterility although this is impossible to produce completely owing to the resistance of spores. The aim of the canner or bottler is to destroy all pathogenic organisms, of which *Clostridium botulinum* is the most resistant, and as many spoilage organisms as possible without causing deterioration of the food. The "commercial sterility" which is achieved in the food industry today usually preserves the product from spoilage under ordinary market conditions. The few organisms which survive are mostly spore-bearing thermophiles (i.e. heat-loving organisms), and these do not germinate if the food is held at normal storage temperatures.

Acid foods are much more easily canned or bottled than non-acid ones. Fruits, for example, can be processed at 100°C or less while non-acid foods such as meats or vegetables require steam pressure treatment. In acid foods even if *Clostridium botulinum* is not destroyed it is prevented from growing and producing its toxin. Hence, home bottling of acid fruits is usually satisfactory but similar processing of meat or vegetables may be highly dangerous. In the food industry some foods which would be ruined by long processing are artificially acidified to reduce the processing time and temperature. Cans which contain micro-organisms that survived the heat treatment may evolve gas (e.g. hydrogen) and swell, and if the swelling becomes very great the can may burst or explode. On the other hand, the surviving organisms may be of a type which does not produce gas but simply turns the contents of the can sour, while allowing the can to retain its shape. Yeasts may survive heat treatment and spoil sugary foods such as canned fruit syrups. Moulds, on the other hand, are not usually much of a problem to canners as they rarely survive the heat treatment.

The Chemical Preservation of Foods

Chemical preservatives can be defined as substances which are added to foods to prevent spoilage. This includes traditional "natural" preservatives such as sugar, salt, etc., and antibiotics as well as synthetic preservatives but not the antioxidants. The latter are a special class of chemicals designed only to prevent oxidation of fatty foods. Table 6.2 lists some of the types of preservatives which we can nowadays expect to find in foods.

TABLE 6.2. PRESERVATIVES USED IN FOODS

Traditional preservatives	Synthetic preservatives	Antibiotics
Sugar (jam)	Acetic acid (pickles)	Chlortetracycline (fish)
Nitrites ⎱ (ham, cured Nitrates ⎰ meat)	Benzoic acid and benzoates (coffee essence)	Oxytetracycline (fish) Nisin (cream)
Salt (ham, cured meat)	Methyl or propyl para-hydroxybenzoates (drinking chocolate)	Subtilin
Products of smoking (kippers)	Sorbic acid or sorbates (marzipan)	
Alcohol (wine)	Propionic acid or propionates (bread)	
	Orthophenyl phenol (citrus fruits)	
	Diphenyl (citrus fruits)	
	Sulphur dioxide or sulphites (sausages)	

The first column in Table 6.2 contains those chemical preservatives which have been known to man for many years as useful agents for the preservation of food. Column 2 does not contain all known chemical preservatives which have been prepared synthetically, but lists only those which are permitted in the United Kingdom. Acetic acid, however, which is usually present in foods as vinegar, is really also a traditional preservative as its usefulness in this direction has long been recognized. Column 3 lists four antibiotics (i.e. chemicals which actually kill certain micro-organisms) which may be present in foods. In the United Kingdom only *specified* synthetic preservatives are allowed in *specified* foods in *specified* quantities which vary between 3 and 3000 p.p.m. of the total food weight. There is, of course, no legal restriction on the use of naturally occurring or "traditional" preservatives in foods except for the general proviso of the Food and Drugs Act (1955) that food should be "... of the nature and quality demanded by the purchaser". Let us now consider the different types of chemical in Table 6.2 in relation to their function in food.

First of all not many people would object to sugar as a preservative in food and still fewer would object to alcohol: incidentally, if there were not enough sugar in some foods to preserve them the sugar itself would be converted into alcohol by the action of yeasts. Although many people may subscribe to the opinion that naturally occurring substances like these, since they have been known and used for so long, *must* be safe to eat, it is worth noting that some of these substances have already been shown by modern science to have toxic properties. Nitrates and nitrites are used in the curing of meats (e.g. bacon, ham, and luncheon meat) but this has now been controlled because nitrites in excess are able to cause damage to the bloodstream by acting on the haemoglobin of the blood. Nitrates are also a danger in excess because some people are able to convert them into nitrites by the action of micro-organisms which are present in the intestine. There has been a report published of babies who died as a result of ingesting water (in Norfolk) containing only 30 p.p.m. of nitrate. Although they are traditional preservatives, nitrates and nitrites are now treated as synthetic chemical preservatives in the United Kingdom by the 1962 Preservatives in Food Regulations. Smoking is as old as the hills as a method of food preservation, but it is important to realize that the exposure of a food substance to wood smoking in the way this is traditionally carried out causes many toxic chemicals such as phenol to be absorbed into the food. These substances would certainly not be permitted for use in foods by the Preservatives in Food Regulations.

Probably the commonest preservative in column 2 of Table 6.2 is acetic acid, which is used in the form of vinegar in foods such as pickles and sauces. While acetic acid is *not* classified as a preservative according to the regulations now in force in the United Kingdom, all the other acids in column 2 of Table 6.2 are. This simply means that there are no restrictions in quantity or types of food permitted to contain acetic acid as there are with the other acids. Among the latter the acidic gas sulphur dioxide is the commonest preservative. For example, it is used for preserving soft drinks and sausages. It not only preserves food well against microbial spoilage, but also conserves the vitamin C content of food and drinks in which it is used. Unfortunately, however, it causes the breakdown of vitamin B_1 (thiamine) so that foods containing sulphur dioxide may not be good sources of this vitamin. Benzoic acid is also commonly used as a preservative in soft drinks and coffee essences but it is not as widely used as sulphur dioxide. Benzoic acid also has the advantage of being flavourless, whereas sulphur dioxide leaves an unmistakable taste in the mouth, which makes it detectable to many people at extremely small concentrations. Nevertheless, sulphur dioxide is used extensively by the food industry; fruit pulps, for example, being "sulphited" prior to jam manufacture to preserve quality, most of the preservative being subsequently lost during the boiling process. Propionic acid, which is used specifically to prevent "ropiness" in bread, and the other preservatives mentioned in column 2 of Table 6.2 are employed much less frequently than sulphur dioxide for the commercial preservation of food, their use being confined to restricted classes of commodity.

Finally the third column of Table 6.2 contains the antibiotics which may be found as food preservatives on the market today. Chlortetracycline (aureomycin) and oxytetracycline (terramycin) are allowed in raw fish because they are used in the ice in which the fish are placed after catching before being transported to the retailer. Subtilin is not allowed in foods in the United Kingdom, but nisin is an antibiotic which is produced by the bacterium *Streptococcus lactis* which is used in cheese manufacture and is therefore present naturally in these products. However, it is also intentionally added to many canned foods and meat and fish pastes to aid in their preservation. There is no legal restriction about the quantity of nisin in foods in the United Kingdom and it is therefore very useful in the preservation of highly perishable foods such as clotted cream. Milk, however, is not allowed to contain any chemical preservative, antibiotic, antioxidant or other additive.

There has always been a certain amount of public concern about the use of "synthetic chemicals" in our food, but this has often been founded on lack of understanding of the facts. Synthetic food preservatives are pure, stringently tested substances, the possible bodily effects of which are considered in great detail by expert and informed opinion before they are released for use in foods. It is true that adulterants may also be present in our foods and steps are constantly taken by responsible bodies to guard against and control such possibilities. For example, penicillin (which is not allowed in foods in the United Kingdom) may be present in milk after cattle have been treated with it for veterinary purposes and may be a danger to people who have already been sensitized by treatment with it. The Milk Marketing Board carries out regular surveys on this type of problem, and steps are taken to prevent their occurrence.

Conclusion

Finally, a word should be said about the general nutritional adequacy of all our food nowadays subject to all the different technological and chemical methods of preservation which have been outlined in this chapter. The nutritional value of modern processed and preserved foods is now probably greater than it has ever been before, and the major food chemicals (carbohydrates, fats and proteins) are kept in a fresh, palatable and nutritionally satisfactory state. Minerals are, of course, completely unaffected either by heat processing or by chemical preservation. Generally, therefore, any question about the nutritional adequacy of processed foods must be confined to the area of vitamins. Vitamins, with the one exception of vitamin B_1 (thiamine) which is destroyed by sulphur dioxide, are completely unaffected by the presence of preservatives in foods. They are, however, damaged by heat, and vitamin C (ascorbic acid) is the most sensitive in this respect. Modern processing methods have now advanced to the stage where the loss of this or any other vitamin can be minimized so that vitamin deficiency in processed foods (if any exists) is almost certainly the result of bad domestic handling, e.g. exposure of foods to air and metal containers at room temperature for long periods, or over-roasting, over-boiling or soaking of foods for long periods. If proper attention is paid to home cooking methods, consumers can rest assured that commercially processed and preserved foods are little—if at all—inferior to fresh ones.

Suggestions for Further Reading

CHRISTIE, A. B. and CHRISTIE, M. C. *Food Hygiene and Food Hazards*, Faber and Faber, 1971.
FORD, B. J. *Food Microbiology*, Northwood, 1970. A useful elementary review.
HERSOM, A. C. and HULLAND, E. D. *Canned Foods: an Introduction to their Microbiology*, Churchill, 1969.
HOBBS, B. *Food Poisoning and Food Hygiene*, Edward Arnold, 3rd edn., 1974
LEACH, M. (Ed.) *Freezer Facts*, Forbes Publications, 1975.
MINISTRY OF AGRICULTURE, *Domestic Preservation of Fruit and Vegetables*, HMSO, 11th edn., 1966.
MOORE, E. *Food Preservation*, Unilever Educational Booklet, 1969. An elementary but well-presented account.
ROGERS, J. L. and BINSTED R. *Quick-Frozen Foods*, Food Trade Press, 1972.
SPENCER, M. *The Chemical Preservation of Food*, Food Trade Review, 1960, *30*. Nos. 2 and 4.
TAYLOR, J. (Ed.) *Bacterial Food Poisoning*, Royal Society of Health, 1969.

CHAPTER 7

Changes in Food During Storage and Preparation

IN THE previous chapter the emphasis was on changes which take place in foods which involve micro-organisms, and the methods used to protect foods from such spoilage. In this chapter we shall consider chemical and physical changes which occur during the storage and preparation of food, other than those which are primarily microbiological in nature.

Most fresh foods cannot be held in the larder for very long without undergoing spoilage. Apart from invasion by moulds, yeasts, or bacteria, this may be due to enzymes present in the food, or may be caused by other chemical processes. Such enzymic or non-enzymic activity may affect the texture, flavour or the colour of the food; and it may lower its nutritional value.

The importance of keeping foods dry. Many chemical reactions cannot take place in the absence of water, and enzymes in particular require an aqueous medium. Consequently one way of keeping foods in an edible condition is to dehydrate them. Although the drying of food is a commercial process (see previous chapter), this is occasionally practised in the kitchen: thus the housewife can make her own apple rings by threading them on sticks and drying them slowly in a cool oven. Similarly, quartered pears, and small, whole plums can be successfully dried. Runner beans can be dried if they are small, or sliced if they are large, but must be blanched (to destroy the enzymes) and spread on trays in an oven that is slowly allowed to warm up from about 120°F to 160°F (50°C to 70°C) when the beans should become crisp and rather brittle. Many herbs and mushrooms can be preserved by drying in a similar manner, but the temperature should not exceed 130°F (55°C). All dry foods will tend to pick up water in a moist atmosphere. In addition to dehydrated foods, this includes such foods as flour, cereals, pulses and spices. These foods must be kept under dry and preferably cool conditions to prevent the enzymes from affecting the quality of the food. Jars with snug-fitting lids, tins with snap closures,

CHANGES IN FOOD 107

cartons with heavily waxed bags (those used for corn flakes, for example) may be used to keep such foods from attracting moisture. In a damp atmosphere jam will be hygroscopic and may grow mould on the surface if it is not hermetically sealed.

Temperature has a considerable influence on the rate of all chemical reactions, which are slow at low temperatures and increase as the temperature rises. The activity of enzymes also slows down considerably under

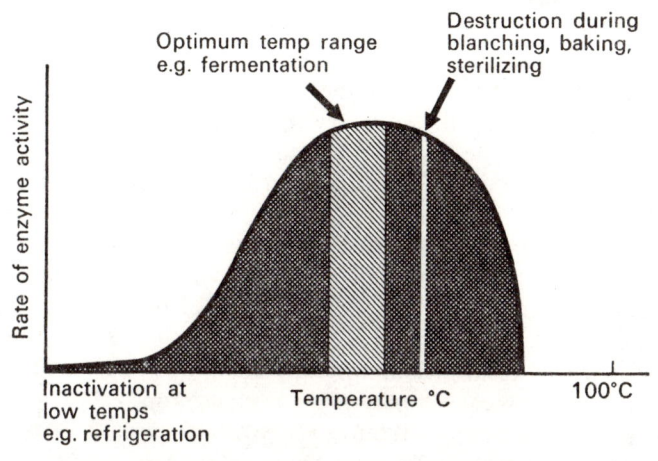

FIG. 7.1. Effect of temperature on the activity of enzymes.

cold conditions, but at temperatures between 150°F (65°C) and the boiling point of water, enzymes are normally destroyed, as explained in Chapter 2. Use is made of these two ends of the scale to cut down spoilage—by keeping foods cold, or by destroying the enzymes with very hot water. This is illustrated in Fig. 7.1.

The use of refrigerators. A domestic refrigerator is normally maintained at a temperature which varies between 40°F and 50°F (4°C and 10°C). It consists essentially of a metal cabinet with a very thick insulated lining —which may be as much as 4 inches thick and a freezing unit which may be operated by gas or electricity. Most refrigerators have a thermostat which can be adjusted to give temperatures outside the usual range. With a dial reading from 1 to 10, a reading of number 3 or 4 should usually give the desired 45°F (7°C) (approximately), but will need to be raised in warm weather, in a hot kitchen, or if needed to make or keep ice-cream. It should be emphasized that a refrigerator is extremely useful the whole year round, not just in the summer. With the growing popularity of central heating, kitchens are often very much warmer than they used to be.

Warm foods should always be cooled to about room temperature before being put into the refrigerator—otherwise other foods may be spoiled and running costs go up. For the same reasons, the door should never be open for long, and should be fitted with a rubber or plastic gasket to ensure a tight fit, which will not allow warm air or water vapour to enter. Any free moisture in the refrigerator tends to be condensed as ice on the evaporator (i.e. the part of the freezing unit which is inside the refrigerator chamber). Naturally the efficiency of the freezing unit will go down sharply as the ice on the evaporator becomes thicker. Consequently it is important to minimize free moisture in the cabinet by putting all foods containing water (which includes nearly all foods) in tightly covered jars or boxes or in polythene bags closed with a rubber-band or wire. Another reason for this precaution is that the foods will tend to dehydrate: lettuce, for example, would lose its crispness and should therefore be covered. Some foods can normally be kept frozen in the ice-box at the top of the refrigerator, whilst meat, fish and poultry should be kept just below the ice-box, as this is the coolest part of the cabinet proper. The enzymes of raw fish, in particular, are still fairly active at refrigerator temperatures, and fish should therefore not be kept for more than 24 hours. Fruits and vegetables should preferably be enclosed in boxes or polythene bags and placed near the bottom of the cabinet. Potatoes should not be refrigerated (as discussed later). Cheese should also be wrapped in a moisture-proof container, but should be allowed to warm up to room temperature before being eaten in order to improve the flavour. Eggs should be placed in well-fitting plastic containers to prevent dehydration and deterioration in quality. Pastry is improved by chilling the ingredients first, and by holding the made-up pastry in the refrigerator before baking. It is not advisable to use the refrigerator for storing bread, which stales more quickly than normal. This is discussed later.

In spite of all precautions, it will be found that ice always accumulates on the cooling unit and the refrigerator should therefore be regularly defrosted, and thoroughly cleaned and dried before re-use. It is unwise to over-fill your refrigerator, as this interferes with the natural convection currents which ensure a reasonably uniform temperature in the cabinet,

It must also be remembered that fat-containing foods such as cheese, butter, milk and eggs tend to absorb odours very readily. It is probably best not to use the refrigerator for storing onions and other strong-smelling foods, but if stored, they should be very well wrapped.

Home-freezers. The rapid growth and popularity of quick-frozen foods have resulted in the manufacture of deep-freeze refrigerators for the home. These home-freezers may be combined with refrigerators or they may be separate units. The latter may be of the upright type, resembling the domestic refrigerator; or the chest type, with a hinged lid that opens upwards. When the lid is open the cold air in the chest stays in position because it is heavier than the warm air above, which is not the case with upright or cabinet-types. The latter, however, are more convenient to use. For quick-freezing, food is placed in the coldest parts of the freezer—in the case of the chest type these are at the bottom and sides, while the cabinet type has some shelves for freezing, usually between $-5°F$ and $-10°F$ ($-20°C$ and $-30°C$), and others for storage, normally $0°F$ to $-5°F$ ($-17°C$ to $-20°C$). Frozen foods are stored in the centre of the chest type.

The deep-freezer can be used in two ways: it can be used to produce one's own frozen food from fresh produce which can be grown in one's own garden or bought when in season and cheap, especially if bought in bulk; and the freezer can also be used to store manufactured frozen food, which again can be bought in bulk at a competitive price.

A very wide variety of foods can be deep-frozen at home, but certain precautions have to be observed, which are standard practice in the commercial process. In particular, the food should be packed in moisture-proof containers such as waxed cartons, polythene bags, aluminium foil, or specially made wrapping paper (for joints, etc.), which must in all cases be properly sealed, and should be as small or as thin as possible, to allow for the most rapid possible rate of freezing. Vegetables and some fruit should be blanched, while meat is best chilled and hung for several days after slaughter and before freezing. It must be remembered, however, that the efficiency of commercial quick-freezing techniques referred to in Chapter 6 cannot be achieved in the home. Consequently, there is likely to be more damage to the cell structure of the food, which results in loss in firmness of texture after thawing (see p. 98).

Food Spoilage

Fruits and Vegetables. Fruits and vegetables do not keep particularly well on the whole because they contain a considerable amount of water—about 80%. Since fruits and vegetables are living, enzyme activities continue at ordinary temperatures to produce maturation and ripening changes, as well as respiration which involves breaking down sugars and starch with the production of carbon dioxide.

The *texture* of fruits and vegetables tends to deteriorate if the latter are stored too long or in too warm conditions. One of the principal reasons for this is that the pectin which stiffens the honeycomb system of cells to a large extent in fruits, and to some extent in vegetables, is broken down by enzymes in the cells to much softer chemical compounds, giving the characteristic texture of over-ripe fruit, or wilted vegetables. If the fruit is bruised, the intact cells are broken open and the enzymes released to attack and break down the pectin. Incidentally, the same type of enzyme which makes fruit mushy—*pectinase*—is used by home wine makers to soften fruit pulp in order to ease the extraction of juice, and also to help produce a clear sparkling wine.

Bruising of fruit, referred to above, not only spoils the texture, but produces undesirable changes in *colour*. Apples and pears in particular turn brown when damaged, and they share with potatoes the tendency to brown rapidly when cut surfaces are exposed to air. Once again this is due to the release of enzymes known as *oxidases* which then proceed to oxidize—with the aid of oxygen in the air—certain constituents (phenols) to produce brown pigments. This may be represented as follows

$$\text{phenols (in cells)} + \text{oxygen (in air)} \xrightarrow[\text{oxidase enzyme (in cells)}]{\text{aided by}} \text{brown colours}$$

This can be a great nuisance to housewives as well as to food manufacturers who wish to hold peeled and chipped potatoes before frying, or peeled and minced apples prior to mixing with other ingredients for mincemeat. Methods for discouraging this enzymic browning are shown in Table 7.1.

Ready peeled or chipped potatoes can be purchased which have been

CHANGES IN FOOD

TABLE 7.1. CONTROL OF ENZYMIC BROWNING

Factors which discourage enzymic browning	Treatment of fruit or vegetable
Destruction of enzyme	Dip in hot water (blanch)
Exclusion of air	Submerge in cold water—salt water is better
Acid conditions	Hold in water containing citric acid or lemon juice
Chemical reducing agent	Hold in sodium metabisulphite solution or in vitamin C solution

protected from enzymic browning by being dipped into a solution of one or more of the above substances and dried.

Nutritive quality. The most valuable nutrient in fruits and vegetables is vitamin C. Unless refrigerated, this vitamin is steadily lost during storage. The acid in fruit helps in the retention of vitamin C, but in some fresh vegetables the loss is quite rapid. These include spinach, lettuce, peas, broccoli, cauliflower, and green beans. Spinach, for example, loses half its vitamin C in 3 days. Cabbage, however, loses about one-third of its vitamin C when stored at room temperature in 6 weeks.

Potatoes are of particular interest because they contribute approximately half of our total vitamin C intake. Figure 7.2 shows that the longer the potatoes are stored the lower is their vitamin C content. It will be seen that in end-of-season potatoes the vitamin content has fallen to about one-eighth of the original amount.

Finally, it should be observed that vegetables and fruits that have been roughly handled are likely not only to deteriorate in texture, colour and flavour, but also in nutritive value.

Fish spoilage. In a previous chapter (p. 21) it was shown that meat is of inferior quality if the animals have not been rested before slaughter, because there is less lactic acid produced. Fish spoil much more readily than meat because inevitably they struggle while being caught so that there is less lactic acid. The typical smell of bad fish is due to an unpleasant ammonia-like substance called *trimethylamine* which is produced by the action of bacteria on nitrogenous compounds in the fish muscle. Raw fish does not keep very well in the ordinary refrigerator because those enzymes which are responsible for spoilage are still fairly active at refrigerator temperatures.

Staling of bread. Staling represents a serious economic loss to the baker and a nuisance as well as an expense to the housewife. Losses due to staling a few years ago in America were between 5 and 6% of production. When bread goes stale, the centre or crumb of the loaf becomes harder, and the crust becomes leathery at first and then hard later, while the

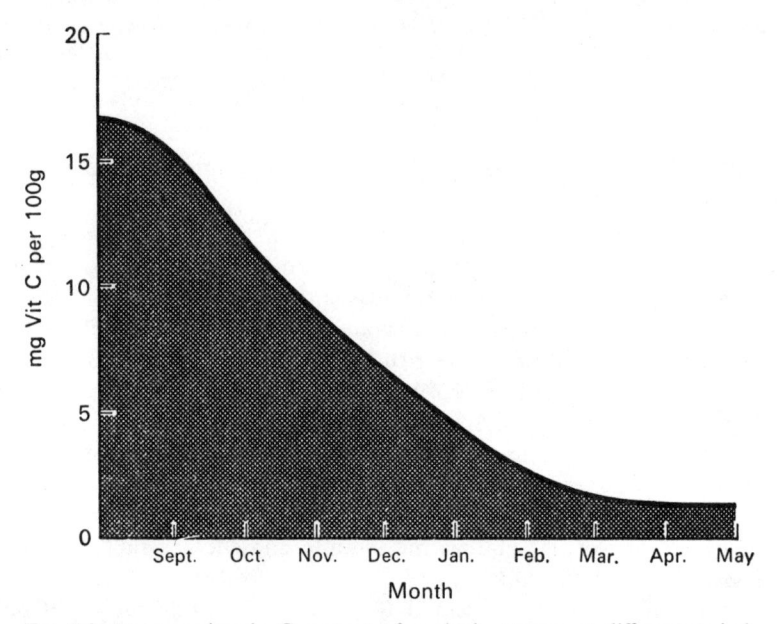

FIG. 7.2. Average vitamin C content of cooked potatoes at different periods of the year.

typical aroma of fresh bread disappears and an unpleasant flavour takes its place.

Although drying out takes place, this is a result rather than a cause of staling. The cause is thought to be a physico-chemical change in the structure of the starch. When the dough is baked in the oven, the starch grains absorb water, swell and soften (i.e. gelatinize). When the bread stales, the starch slowly changes from this softened state, because the individual starch molecules slowly join together to form giant molecules which no longer possess the ability to hold a good deal of water, and in losing it, become hard and crystalline. This change can be reversed by damping the stale bread and re-baking it.

The change from fresh to stale starch depends very much on temperature as can be seen from the shape of the graph in Fig. 7.3.

It will be seen that at the temperature of a domestic refrigerator—say 45°F (7°C)—the rate of staling is much higher than at room temperature, say 65°F (18°C). On the other hand, at very low temperatures the rate

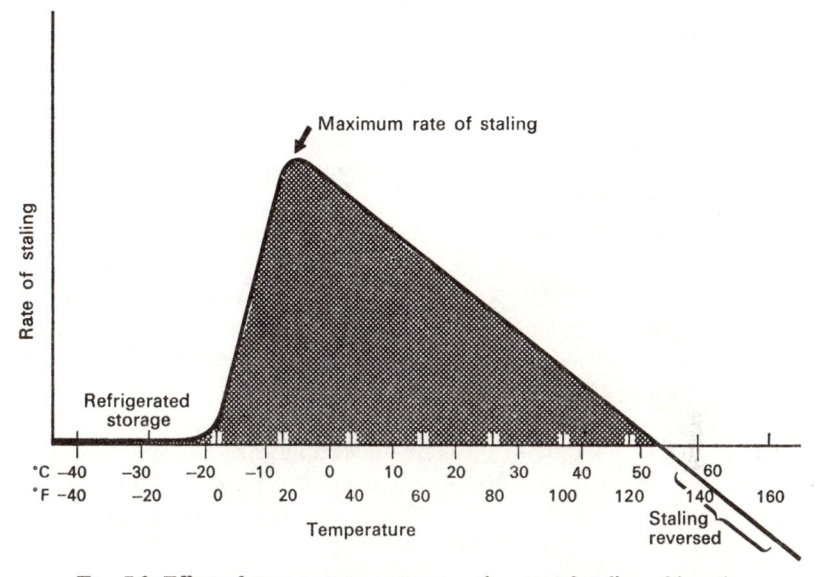

Fig. 7.3. Effect of storage temperature on the rate of staling of bread.

of staling is almost zero, so that whilst a refrigerator is ruled out for storing bread and rolls, a deep freeze would be quite suitable for rolls, though not so suitable for large loaves which take a long time to freeze. Many bakers use this technique for rolls and buns. The principal commercial method for increasing the shelf life of bread is to incorporate some fat, or some GMS (glyceryl monostearate). Both of these additions soften the bread and delay the starch changes described above.

Fat deterioration. Fats and oils and fatty foods are subject to various types of spoilage. Reference has been made in this chapter to the tendency of such foods to pick up other odours. This applies to the larder as well as the refrigerator, and strong odours may penetrate such wrappings as paper, cardboard or polythene. The major form of spoilage of fats is rancidity, of which there are two types—hydrolytic and oxidative.

In *hydrolytic* rancidity, water is essential and plays a part in the breakdown of the fat molecules into fatty acids and glycerol:

$$\text{FAT} + \text{WATER} \xrightarrow{\text{influenced by enzymes, moulds or bacteria}} \text{FATTY ACID} + \text{GLYCEROL}$$

This chemical reaction is catalysed by the enzyme *lipase*, which may be present in the food itself—e.g. oats, nuts, meat; or produced by moulds or bacteria which have infected the food. The glycerol is tasteless, but the fatty acids produced by most types of fats in food have a sour or soapy taste, but no appreciable odour, except in the case of butter and milk products. In these cases there is a strong and typical smell—reminiscent of bad cheese (actually, in the case of cheese, unlike other foods, the presence of a *small* amount of fatty acids contributes towards the characteristic flavour desired in the matured product). Since enzymes are destroyed by heat, this type of rancidity can be prevented by heating the food. For this reason, steam treatment is incorporated in the process of manufacture of oat flour. Keeping food dry is also an insurance against this form of spoilage.

In most cases rancidity that has been produced in foods which have been kept for a long time—especially under non-refrigerated conditions—is of the *oxidative* type. This produces nauseating odours and tallowy flavours and is not usually enzymic in nature. It is the result of the action of oxygen upon the double bond of unsaturated fats (see p. 17). Peroxides of the fatty acids are produced which are themselves tasteless, but which break down chemically to produce a whole range of compounds with small molecules which are evil-smelling and tasting.

The process of oxidative rancidity is accelerated by warmth, light and certain metals, especially copper. Hence cheese, butter and cooking fats are protected to some extent by being wrapped and kept in the refrigerator. Fats that have been hydrogenated (see Chapter 4) are saturated and are immune. Since oxygen is essential to this type of rancidity, its exclusion by vacuum packing or tight sealing is also a form of protection.

Nature has her own way of protecting some foods. These contain natural anti-oxidants, of which vitamin E is a notable example, found in nuts, wheat germ, and oily seeds. Man, not slow to copy nature, has also produced some synthetic anti-oxidants, which the manufacturer of fats is permitted to add within certain limits. These are very few in number and are carefully vetted to ensure that they have a completely clean record.

Finally, it should be emphasized that *all* foods containing fats are subject to rancidity, including eggs, dried milk, ham, bacon, cheese, biscuits, and nuts. The housewife is reminded that the best precaution against rancidity is to keep the food in stock for as little time as possible, and preferably to use the refrigerator.

Methods of Cooking

The objects of cooking food can be briefly described as the use of heat in order to produce improvements in appearance, texture and flavour which will make the food more palatable and more easily digested. It is possible, of course, to live on raw food and, before he discovered fire, early man probably used to live on wild fruits, berries and nuts, together with eggs and raw meat from the animals he killed, supplemented by fish and shellfish if he lived near water.

No one knows how cooking first started. It might have been due to the discovery of the intriguing flavour of animals that had been killed in a forest fire, or in a tree that had been struck by lightning. According to Charles Lamb, the origin of roast pork is contained in an ancient Chinese manuscript which relates that mankind lived in a golden age called Chofang (meaning cook's holiday) so called because meat was eaten raw. This lasted for 70,000 years until one day the hut of a young swineherd, who lived with his pigs, happened to catch fire. A delicious aroma came from the embers and after poking the pigs' bodies to see if they still lived, he sucked his fingers and discovered the delights of roast pork.

The source of heat may be the result of combustion of coal, gas or oil; by electric heating elements contained in a hotplate or electric oven, or by a microwave cooker.

Methods of heat transfer. The heat may be transferred to the food by *conduction, convection, radiation,* or by the energy of a microwave oven. Conduction is the method of transfer of heat by contact; convection is the transfer of heat as a result of the flow of a liquid or gas travelling from the hotter to the less hot parts of a room, oven or saucepan; and radiation is the emission of heat in the form of waves from hot objects. They travel at the same speed as light waves, which they often accompany, and with which they have much in common. The heat from the sun reaches us by radiation which, like light, is absorbed by dull black surfaces and reflected from white or bright metallic surfaces. Radiated heat will travel through gases, clear liquids or glass without heating them, or through a vacuum. For efficiency as a conductor the best utensil is copper. Aluminium pans conduct heat more slowly, and steel containers more slowly still; whilst glass is a very much less efficient conductor than any of the metals, but compensates for this by transmitting heat from the source by radiation, which of course is not transmitted through metals. For efficient conduction to take place from a hot surface to another surface such as the bottom of a frying pan, it is important that there shall be as large an area of contact as possible—hence it is an advantage for the bottoms of pans to be thick and flat, without curves or buckling.

Cooking in air. Cooking can be carried out in various media or no media at all. Grilling, roasting and baking take place in air. Grilling consists of placing the food below or above a red-hot surface. When under the heater, the food is heated by radiation only, which tends to produce a rapid browning action on many foods—the heat being more slowly conducted through the surface of the food downwards. This is essentially the same as toasting, and as the heating effect is largely superficial, such grilled foods are usually reversed, or rotated slowly on a spit. When the chef uses his grill, or "salamander", the food being above the grill, heat is transmitted to the food by convection currents as well as by radiation, with consequent increased efficiency.

Roasting and baking are essentially the same, i.e. cooking in a closed oven at temperatures ranging from 250°–500°F (120–260°C). The difference is primarily that the term "roasting" tends to be used more for meat, while "baking" tends to be used for bread, cakes and biscuits. Roasting usually implies a more humid atmosphere, though it would be wrong to describe baking as cooking by dry heat, because here, too, the oven atmosphere needs to be moist. This is particularly important at the beginning of the bake, so that moisture condenses on the cold dough. This helps in heat transfer and plays a part in the formation of the crust. These cooking methods involve transfer of heat from the heat source in the oven by radiation, conduction and convection. Heat is transmitted directly on to the container through which it is conducted and thence passes through the food itself. Convection currents of burnt gases, or air, help to make the temperature in the oven fairly uniform. It has been shown that in a gas oven about 23% of the heating was due to radiation, and in an electric oven about 42%; both operating at about 420–450°F (216–232°C). Both ovens, however, produced scones which were equally good. In the baking of bread and cakes, the radiant heat from the top or crown of the oven is especially important in producing the golden-brown crust. Too moist an atmosphere produced by roasting meat in the same oven is thought to reduce the browning of the baked goods. Although copper is a better conductor of heat than iron, an experiment showed that a cake in a dull black steel tin was baked in 26·8 minutes, compared with 34·1 minutes for a copper baking tin; whilst a stainless-steel tin needed 34·0 minutes. This would appear to show that the speediest baking was due to the rough, black surfaces which absorbed more radiated heat than the bright, shiny ones. The effect of covering the tin in order to avoid fat splashing when roasting meat cuts down the efficiency of the roasting process by minimizing the effect of radiation. In an experiment it was revealed that a 12-lb turkey cooked at 450°F (232°C) took half an hour longer to cook when covered with a shiny aluminium foil (which reflected back the heat) than when it was uncovered.

Cooking in water. This involves boiling, simmering, or stewing. In each case the medium transferring the heat is water. The water receives its heat mainly by conduction through the sides and bottom of the pan. Water is a poor conductor of heat, and it passes on the heat by convection currents, which equalize the temperature, and become very vigorous when boiling commences. Water has a high heat capacity, that is, it requires more heat than any other liquid to raise the temperature (for the same weight of material).

Cooking in steam. Steam is the cooking medium for the processes of steaming, "waterless" cooking and pressure cooking. In steaming, the food is cooked in the steam from added water, whilst in "waterless" cooking the steam originates from the food itself. Cooking food in plastic bags is really a form of waterless cooking—it has the advantage of preventing the transmission of flavours from or to the sealed food. One can see the advantage of cooking kippers by this method. The pressure cooker is a device for reducing cooking times by increasing the pressure, so that the boiling point of the water is automatically raised, as is shown in the accompanying table.

TABLE 7.2. BOILING POINTS OF WATER AT DIFFERENT PRESSURES

Pressure (lbs/in^2) above normal atmospheric pressure	Temperature, °F	°C
0	212	100
5	228	109
10	240	116
15	250	121

This procedure is also used in home bottling and commercial canning to destroy micro-organisms at higher temperatures (see Chapter 6). In cooking by steaming the food is heated up as a result of the steam condensing on the food, and releasing the large quantity of heat (latent heat) contained in the steam.

Cooking in fat. The use of fat as the cooking medium involves frying, which may be either shallow or deep fat frying. The former is really a type of baking in which the liquid fat prevents local burning by convecting away the intense heat of the frying pan, and also prevents the food sticking to the metal. Because of the shallowness of the fat, and the poor conductivity of most food, the latter must normally be turned over to ensure some degree of uniform cooking; whereas in deep fat frying the vigorous convection currents make for a more even distribution. The temperature is not limited to the boiling point of water and can be so high that cooking can be rapidly completed. In most foods this high temperature results in rapid drying-out of the surface, and the production of a hard, crisp surface, usually brown, and the absorption of a fair amount of fat, which raises the calorific value of the food quite substantially (fat having two and a quarter times the calorific value of protein, starch and sugar).

The temperature must not be allowed to rise so high that the fat begins to smoke. At this temperature it splits firstly into fatty acid and glycerol (as explained earlier), which is followed by the glycerol decomposing into a substance called *acrolein* which causes intense irritation to the eyes and nose.

Microwave cooking. The use of microwaves for cooking involves no medium for the transfer of heat. Although first recognized as valuable for cooking food in 1947, it is only in the last few years that there has been any serious attempt to use them in Britain. Microwaves belong to the electromagnetic wave series, of which radio, light, and infra-red heat waves all form a part. Whereas short wireless waves have a wavelength of about 10 metres, and visible light about one-millionth of a metre, microwaves have a wavelength of about one-tenth of a metre. The system of heating is also sometimes called High-Frequency Heating, because these very small or microwaves have a very high frequency—about 2450 megacycles (or 2450 million times) per second.

In such an oven the microwaves are generated by a complicated electric instrument called a Magnetron which beams on to the food and penetrates this to a depth of 1–3 inches. The molecules in the food are forced to oscillate at very high frequencies, which raises its temperature. Metal containers cannot be used as they reflect the rays, whereas glass, china, paper and plastic transmit them, without being affected. Because this process does not rely on conduction, or convection of the material being heated, it is normally possible to heat the whole of a food simultaneously. A leg of lamb, for example, may be cooked in about 20 minutes, but the outside will not have been browned. Instead of being heated to a very high temperature—as in roasting—the surface will probably be cooler than the interior because of loss of heat at the surface.

Microwave or dielectric heating as it is also sometimes called can be used in three ways for preparing food:

(a) cooking from the raw state;
(b) reheating of prepared refrigerated food;
(c) reheating of prepared food from the deep freeze.

The limitation in preparing food from the raw state is that surface browning is not possible except by conventional means. But it can cut down the time of preparation considerably. Prepared refrigerated food can be cooked ready to eat in a few minutes, especially if the food is in a plastic disposable dish, which does not get heated and from which it can be eaten. Snacks and meals can be prepared and deep-frozen for months. When required they can be de-frosted by the microwave oven, held for a while to equilibrate, and then heated for a few minutes, or seconds, by microwaves ready to eat. It is not practicable to heat deep-frozen food in one step to the hot state, as it is liable to contain isolated cold spots. Nevertheless, microwave ovens, which look rather like small electric ovens, have enormous advantages, particularly in industrial catering, where they can result in considerable saving of time. They can be used for automatic vending of meals, which can be heated up by the purchaser himself. They are also being used in baking biscuits, combined with infra-red heating, and in the manufacture of crisps to prevent overbrowning. When they become cheaper they will be a great boon for the busy housewife, especially if she is a breadwinner as well.

Changes in Cooking

It has been suggested that the modern kitchen is beginning to look more like a laboratory. Perhaps this is not such a strange phenomenon when we consider that after all, the cook or housewife is dealing with mixtures of chemicals called food, and subjecting them to processes which lead to all sorts of physical and chemical changes. Unrecognized though she may be, the housewife is a chemist of sorts. Let us take a look at some of the changes which take place as the result of the cooking processes we have been considering. A convenient way to do this is to consider a meal of roast beef, cabbage, roast and boiled potatoes, followed by a dessert called Pineapple Cream.

Cooking of meat. Meat consists essentially of a large number of long muscle fibres lying parallel to one another in bundles, the fibres being sheathed in connective tissue; and the bundles of fibres are also bound together by connective tissue called *collagen* (see Fig. 7.4 (a) and (b)). When meat is cooked, the collagen, being a protein, coagulates and on further heating is hydrolysed by water to soft, soluble gelatin. Some of the gelatin melts, and some dissolves in any water present. When meat is roasted, the watery solution drips out, taking with it other soluble substances such as vitamins and minerals, and dries on the outside. In boiling of meat, the solution goes into the water in the saucepan. In both cases, the production and flow of the gelatin causes the rest of the muscle fibres to shrink. Further shrinkage is caused by the muscle protein being denatured and coagulated—when it reaches a temperature of about 140°F (60°C). The overall effect is that on chewing the meat the muscle fibres separate easily and have now developed a short, brittle texture, which is easily masticated. Older meat contains tougher muscle fibres, and a higher proportion of a different type of connective tissue which is not hydrolysed in the cooking process. In roast meat, unlike boiled or stewed meat, the outer surface shrinks considerably to a tougher,

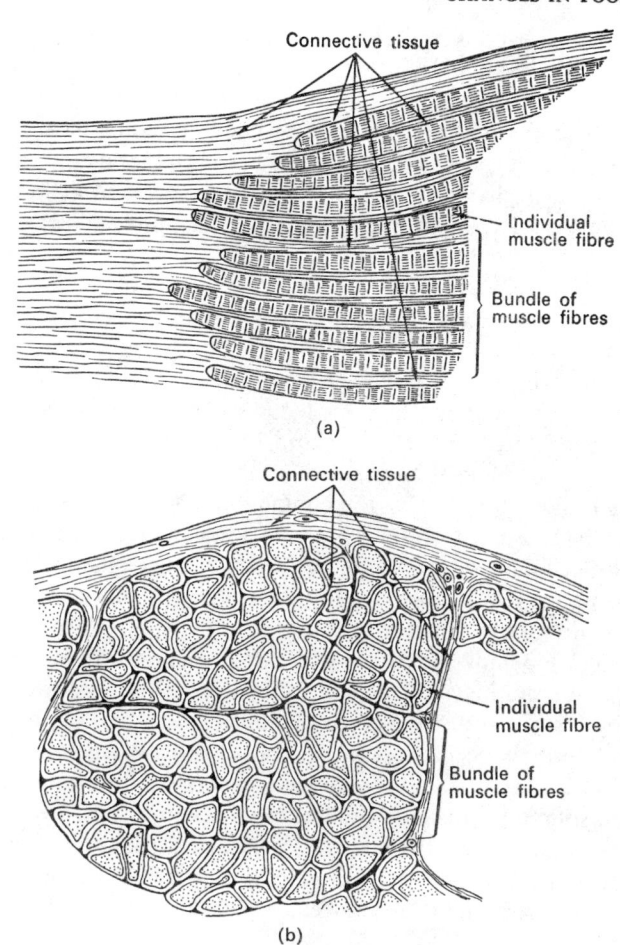

FIG. 7.4. Diagrams of muscle showing fibres and connective tissue. (a) Longitudinal section. (b) Transverse section.

crisper texture. Various methods are available for tenderizing tough meat —beating the meat to break the connective fibres is one way; but increased hydrolysis of the protein may be achieved by "marinading" it with lemon juice or vinegar, or by means of various tenderizing enzymes now on the market which break down and soften proteins. Meat can also be

122   FOOD SCIENCE

toughened by over-cooking. The coagulation of the protein continues, excessive shrinkage takes place, and the meat fibres can become so tough as to be virtually indigestible.

The *colour of the meat* also changes on cooking. When meat is cut, the fresh surface is a purplish-red, which becomes brighter as the main meat pigment *myoglobin*, discussed on p. 143, picks up oxygen from the air in just the same way as haemoglobin in the blood of the lungs takes up oxygen. This, of course, is easily reversed.

On heating myoglobin, the iron atom in the centre of the molecule becomes oxidized irreversibly by a more permanent mechanism than the picking-up of oxygen mentioned above. This profound chemical change is accompanied by a sharp change from red to brown. Providentially, this change occurs at about the same temperature as that of the denaturation of the muscle protein during cooking, i.e. about 140–145°F (60–62°C), so that the brown colour is an indication that the meat is cooked.

Cooking of potatoes. During the cooking of vegetables some softening takes place as the result of absorption of water by cellulose, starch and pectin. The cellulose does not undergo any further change, unlike the starch and pectin. On further heating the starch granules swell and gelatinize. In so doing their texture changes from hard lumps to a soft jelly. While this is happening the pectin which is present as a reinforcement of the cellulose in and between the cell walls in a rather tough form, is hydrolysed by the hot water and converted into a softer, more soluble form. This results in the cells separating more easily—hence, it becomes easier to bite and masticate. When boiling potatoes the water dissolves more of this soluble pectin and produces more gelatinization of starch, thus producing a softer texture than in roast potatoes. Stickiness or gumminess which occurs with certain varieties of potatoes is due to the gelatinized starch escaping from the ruptured cells.

Non-enzymic Browning

Roast potatoes are usually well rolled in hot fat to provide a skin which cuts down the escape of moisture. Roasting of potatoes, like toasting of biscuits and baking of bread and cakes, produces a golden-brown colour by a rather similar process, which also gives the food a pleasant flavour. Potatoes, like flour, contain a small amount of the simple sugar, referred to in Chapter 2, called glucose. When this is heated with a protein or an amino acid, the two substances combine together, form a complex which

TABLE 7.3.

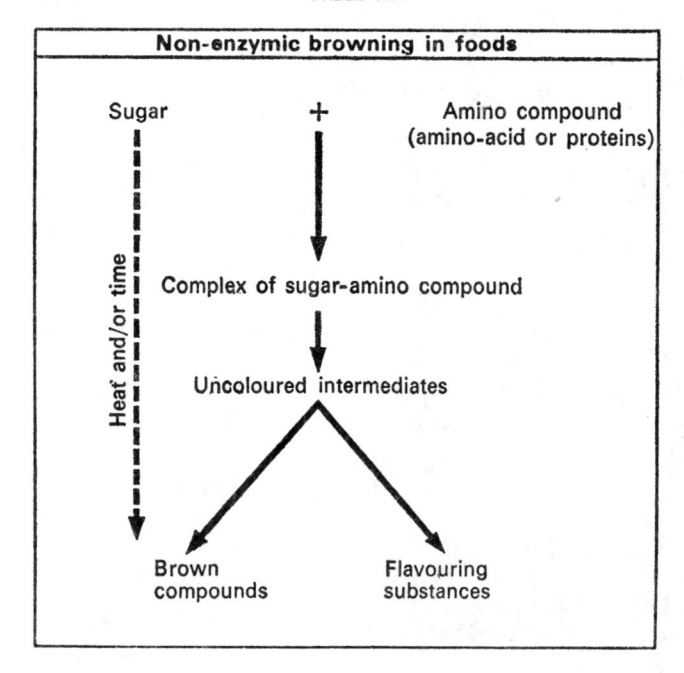

```
┌─────────────────────────────────────────────┐
│         Non-enzymic browning in foods       │
│                                             │
│   Sugar            +      Amino compound    │
│                           (amino-acid or proteins) │
│                                             │
│              ↓                              │
│   Heat and/or time                          │
│      Complex of sugar-amino compound        │
│                                             │
│              ↓                              │
│      Uncoloured intermediates               │
│                                             │
│             ↙   ↘                           │
│       Brown       Flavouring                │
│     compounds     substances                │
└─────────────────────────────────────────────┘
```

TABLE 7.4. EXAMPLES OF NON-ENZYMIC BROWNING IN FOODS

Desirable	Undesirable
Toast	Condensed milk (storage)
Bread crust	Dried milk (storage)
Corn flakes	Dried egg-white
Frying of chips	Over-browning of chips
Crisp manufacture	Over-browning of crisps
Coffee roasting	Dehydration of vegetables
Malt kilning	

breaks down to produce brown colours and in addition a whole series of flavouring substances which give the roasted or fried food its distinctive flavour, as shown in Table 7.3. Because this does not involve enzymes, it is distinguished from the enzymic browning, discussed earlier, by being termed "Non-Enzymic Browning". Although the colour is also brown, its chemical nature is quite different, and is accompanied by flavour changes, sometimes pleasant and desirable, sometimes not, as is shown in Table 7.4.

When potatoes containing an unusually high content of sugar are fried the production of the brown colour on the outside takes place so rapidly that the starch is not gelatinized or the pectins hydrolysed inside the chips, so that they still taste raw. If frying is continued in order to cook the interior, the outside looks burnt, and has an unpleasant flavour. Although this tendency is more marked with certain varieties, the high content of sugar is more commonly brought about by the conditions of storage. Two main enzymic processes take place during the storage of many living plants such as potatoes, starchy vegetables and wheat. They are shown in Table 7.5.

TABLE 7.5. EFFECT OF TEMPERATURE ON ENZYMIC PROCESSES IN STORED POTATOES

No.	Substance acted upon	Enzymes	Products	Effect of low temperature on rate
1	Starch	Starch hydrolysing enzymes	Sugar	Slight slowing down
2	Sugar + oxygen (from 1)	Respiration enzymes	CO_2 and water	Almost complete cessation

In the case of potatoes, the reaction 1 carries on quite smoothly: but as fast as the sugar is produced, it is broken down by respiration (reaction 2) provided the temperature is 50°F (10°C) or above. There is then no build-up of sugar. If the temperature is down to about 40°F (4°C), reaction 2 almost stops. Since reaction 1 is still going on, it will be seen that sugar tends to accumulate, with the result that excessive browning may take place during frying. It follows from this that the refrigerator is not the best place to store raw potatoes for long periods if they are intended for frying. If the potatoes were stored for a long period at 50–55°F (10–13°C) there would be no undesirable accumulation of sugar, but there would be other disadvantages. The respiration rate would be high, leading to a loss in the dry weight and therefore shrinkage of the potatoes, and it is probable that there would be considerable sprouting. The latter can be suppressed by special anti-sprouting substances; and the manufacturer of chips or crisps overcomes the weight loss problem by storing the potatoes under normal cool conditions, but for the last 2 to 4 weeks they are stored at 50–55°F (10–13°C). Another way to overcome the problem has been found by part-frying the crisps in a conventional oil frier, stopping before browning commences. The frying is finished off by use of a continuous microwave oven. As this heats up the whole crisp simultaneously there is not the same danger of over-browning on the surface. Other advantages of this method are that sweet varieties of potatoes can now be used, there is little loss of weight during storage, and the product lasts longer before developing rancidity compared with conventionally fried crisps.

Apart from the effect on colour and flavour, non-enzymic browning can also affect the *nutritional value of foods*. This is because firstly, the amino acid *lysine*, which is an essential amino acid discussed on page 41 is often involved in this reaction. Since this is already in short supply in cereal foods (see Chapter 3) the effect of this type of browning in a cereal food can lead to loss of nutritionally useful protein. This destruction is not very great when bread or cakes are baked, but is particularly high in the browning of corn flakes as a result of the intense heating necessary to toast them. This is mitigated by the fact that we normally eat corn flakes with milk, which is rich in lysine, and can therefore make up for this deficiency. Another nutrient which is affected is vitamin B_1 (thiamine). Because this has an amino group, it acts in the same way as an amino acid in combining readily with sugars in the browning reaction. Small losses occur in baking, but the very high loss which occurs in corn flakes manufacture may be made up by the addition of this and other vitamins as a bonus to some brands of corn flakes before packaging.

Returning to our boiled potatoes. These have been standing about in the meantime, and a certain amount of discoloration or blackening may have taken place. This "after-cooking blackening" is a feature of some varieties of potatoes and has nothing in common with the non-enzymic browning due to the sugar–amino-acid reaction. As they have been well cooked it is not enzymic in nature. Nevertheless, it is related to enzymic browning. It has now been demonstrated that this type of discoloration is also the result of the oxidation of certain phenolic substances in the potato by air. But instead of enzymes this oxidation appears to be catalysed by iron salts. Further, if the potatoes have a high citric acid content, which often happens, this colour change is less likely to take place. In fact it can be controlled by immersing the potatoes briefly in a weak solution of citric acid.

Cooking Changes in Cabbage

When cabbage is boiled in water, the texture is softened in much the same way as the potatoes—by swelling of the more plentiful cellulose, gelatinization of the starch, and hydrolysis and conversion of the tough pectic substances into soft pectin. The outer leaves of cabbage are tougher and more difficult to soften because they contain more cellulose. If the cabbage or other vegetable is old, the texture may be even tougher and more resistant as a result of being partly impregnated with woody tissue.

Colour changes. When the cabbage is first placed in salted hot water, there is an initial brightening due probably to the wetting of the fine hairs on the surface and the release of the *chlorophyll* (described in Chapter 8) from its protein partner which has been coagulated as a result of the heat treatment. If the cabbage is cooked for too long a time, the bright green colour slowly changes to an olive-green or olive-brown colour. The extent of the change depends on the time and temperature of the cooking and the acidity or alkalinity of the water used. Acids are present in the vegetable itself and these combine under the influence of heat with the magnesium atom in the centre of the chlorophyll molecule, replacing it with two atoms of hydrogen and converting it into the green-brown *phaeophytin* as shown in Fig. 7.5.

Volatile acids are partly responsible for this change, so that removal

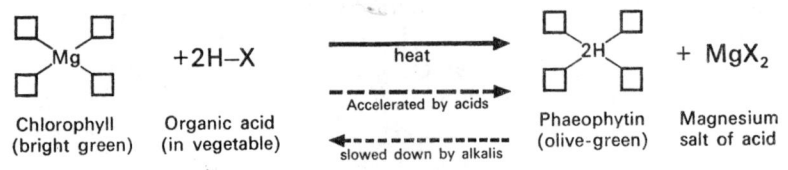

Chlorophyll (bright green)	Organic acid (in vegetable)		Phaeophytin (olive-green)	Magnesium salt of acid
Mg	+2H−X	heat → (Accelerated by acids) ← slowed down by alkalis	2H	+ MgX$_2$

FIG. 7.5. The change in colour on heating chlorophyll in green vegetables.

of the lid and the escape of these volatile acids results in less colour change. Baking soda (bicarbonate) added to the water partly neutralizes these organic acids and results in a brighter green vegetable. Bicarbonate may be responsible for greater losses of vitamins, so that only a little should be used: the best method of retention of the green colour is to keep the cooking-time short. In a pressure cooker the colour change is much more marked because of the higher temperature. Commercial pressure-cooking of peas and other green vegetables for canning inevitably leads to the production of the brown phaeophytin, which explains why artificial green colour is normally added to canned peas.

Prolonged cooking of cabbage also affects *flavour*. Volatile flavouring substances are partly lost or dissolved in the cooking water, and there are some mild-tasting sulphur compounds which decompose, on continued heating, to produce hydrogen sulphide and other unpleasant substances.

The *nutritional value* of the vegetables is also affected by continued cooking. The main value of fruits and vegetables in the diet is their content of vitamin A (in the form of beta-carotene) and vitamin C. The beta-carotene does not dissolve in the water and is practically unaffected by the cooking process. Vitamin C, however, is very soluble in water and is rapidly oxidized by air especially in the presence of an enzyme which is also contained in the cabbage. Iron utensils also increase the destruction rate of the vitamin. It is clear that in order to retain the highest amount of vitamin in the vegetable the following precautions should be taken:

1. Use as little water as possible (cooking water losses) in a saucepan with a tightly fitting lid.
2. Boil vigorously (high temperatures destroy the enzyme).
3. Cut the cabbage into as *large* pieces as convenient with a sharp stainless-steel knife (large pieces cut down cooking water losses and enzyme action).
4. As soon as possible place cut cabbage in the boiling water and bring the whole to the boil as rapidly as possible (rapid enzyme destruction and exclusion of air).
5. Boil for the shortest possible time.
6. Serve as soon as possible (keeping cooked greens hot produces oxidation of the vitamin (see Fig. 7.6)).
7. Use the cooking water in gravy or soup (this may contain a good deal of the total vitamin C).

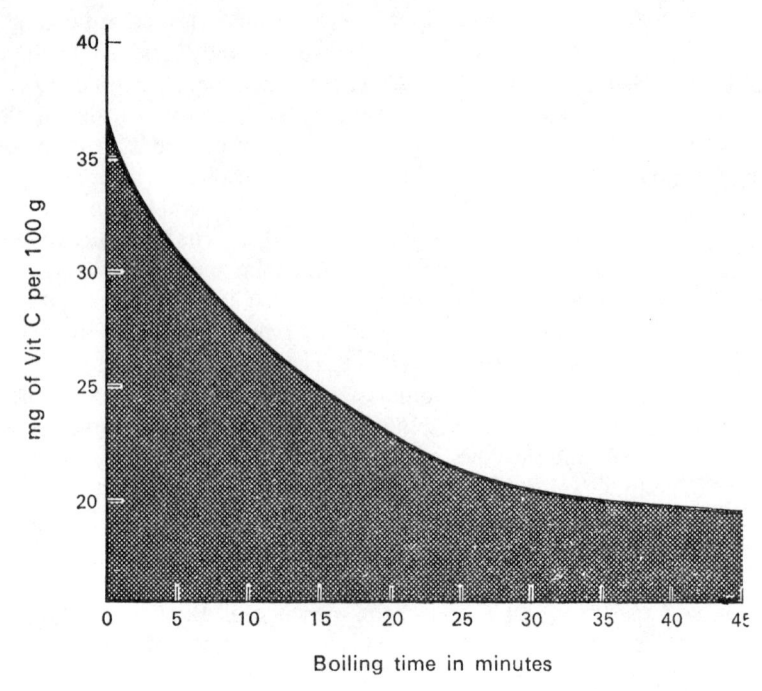

FIG. 7.6. Loss of vitamin C in brussels sprouts during cooking.

TABLE 7.6. EFFECTS OF COOKING VEGETABLES UNDER VARYING CONDITIONS ON VITAMIN C AND BETA-CAROTENE CONTENT

Vegetable	% of vitamin retained							
	Pressure cooked		Water to cover		$\frac{1}{2}$ cup water		Waterless cooking	
	Vitamin C	Carotene	Vitamin C	Carotene	Vitamin C	Carotene	Vitamin C	Carotene
Cabbage	75·5	96·8	44·3	73·3	57·4	89·7	68·4	95·6
Carrots	79·1	88·4	63·1	84·5	75·1	86·3	72·5	98·9
Cauliflower	75·5	89·8	47·3	80·7	54·0	83·7	70·7	97·4
Peas	73·7	89·7	51·3	83·2	70·0	89·4	78·8	91·2
Potatoes	57·3	86·3	41·0	78·9	48·4	80·5	79·4	85·8
Spinach	61·7	74·8	49·1	80·7	51·7	87·2	70·0	91·3

The significance of different methods of cooking and their effects on the retention of vitamin C and beta-carotene are shown in Table 7.6. As far as vitamin C retention is concerned, pressure and waterless cooking are equally efficient; whilst using the larger amount of water produces the greatest loss of the vitamin.

The Dessert

Following this we deserve a mouth-watering dessert. None could be better than this delectable Pineapple Cream (or if you prefer it *Crème d'ananas*). The recipe is as follows:

> 1 fresh pineapple or 1 tin of pineapple.
> 1 gill cream.
> 2 teaspoonsful of gelatine.
> Whites of 2 eggs.
> Chop the pineapple into very small pieces and put them into a large mixing bowl. Add 2 tablespoons pineapple juice; then the cream. Mix well. Dissolve the gelatine in 2 tablespoons of hot water and when melted, add to the contents of the bowl. Now stir until the mixture is almost set. Whisk the whites of the eggs until they become very stiff. Then fold into the mixture.
> Fill the pineapple creams into glasses and ice before serving.

This recipe serves to illustrate a number of interesting points. There could be quite a marked difference between the use of fresh pineapple and canned pineapple. Fresh pineapple contains an enzyme called *bromelin* which attacks protein and breaks it down to smaller molecules. The effect of this on the gelatine solution, which is a protein, is that it is unlikely ever to set, as the enzyme would have weakened the gel-forming properties of the gelatine. If tinned pineapple is used, the heat used in canning it would have destroyed the enzyme, so that the gelatine gel would set in the normal way. If fresh pineapple is used, it is advisable to cook it first before adding to the gelatine mixture.

It will be recalled that when the meat was cooked in the first course the effect of heat on the connective tissue, collagen, was to break it down to gelatine. Commercially, gelatine is made from bones which contain large quantities of collagen, by treatment with acid and lime to hydrolyze it to gelatin.

The white of egg can be obtained direct from fresh eggs or dried egg whites could be used. In the manufacture of this product there is a danger that the small amount of glucose in it will react with the protein albumen, which represents the bulk of the dry egg-white. This would lead to the sugar-protein browning reaction discussed earlier, which would continue steadily during storage. To avoid this discoloration, the glucose is removed immediately after separation of the egg-whites, either by fermentation with yeast, or by treatment with a specific enzyme called *glucose oxidase*, which breaks down the glucose.

The meal, with a reasonable balance of calories, proteins, vitamins and inorganic elements is now ready for digestion.

Suggestions for Further Reading

BROWN, M. A. and CAMERON, A. G. *Experimental Cooking*, Arnold, 1976. A book of experiments.
CALLOW, A. B. *Cooking and Nutritive Value*, Oxford University Press, 1945
CAMERON, A. G. *The Science of Food and Cooking*, Edward Arnold, 1973.
COBB, V. *Science Experiments you can Eat*, Penguin, 1974.
GRISWOLD, R. M. *The Experimental Study of Food*, Constable, 1970.
HMSO, *ABC of Cookery*, HMSO, 6th edn., 1962.
JOHNSON, K. *Deep-freezing for the Housewife*, Pitman, 1968.
MAPLETON, L. *A Guide to Microwave Catering*, Northwood Industrial Publications, 1967.
MINISTRY OF AGRICULTURE, *Domestic Preservation of Fruits & Vegetables*, HMSO, 3rd edn., 1958.
MINISTRY OF AGRICULTURE, *Home Freezing of Fruits & Vegetables*, Advisory Leaflet No. 434, HMSO, 1962.
PAUL, P. C. and PALMER, H. H. *Food Theory and Applications*, Wiley, U.S.A. 1972.
SPENCER M. *Chemical changes during cooking, processing and storage of food*, Nutrition and Food Science, 1973, (April), II.
SWEETMAN, M. D. and MCKELLAR, I. *Food Selection and Preparation*, Wiley, 4th edn., 1954.

CHAPTER 8

Flavour, Colour and Texture

However nutritious a meal is, it needs to be attractive in flavour and appearance if it is to be eaten and the nutrients made use of. In other words, it must stimulate the appetite. The cook, baker, confectioner, and food manufacturer realize the importance of presentation of food as well as of correct flavouring.

For most people wining and dining are among the major enjoyments of life. To be enjoyed, food must be of good eating quality or palatability. That the surroundings play a part is evidenced by experiments recently carried out in an American university involving medical students, in which it was shown that the flow of digestive juices from the stomach is improved when the surroundings and service are pleasing.

Our appreciation of any experience depends upon its impact on our senses; for example, our enjoyment of a play is dependent on the senses of sight and hearing; but we also ought to be in a comfortable seat, hence the senses of touch and of temperature are also involved. In the same way the palatability of food may be judged on the basis of the kinds, quality and intensity of sensory impressions made.

Among the sensory properties of food the following may be listed:

1. Flavour, which may be broken down into
   (a) taste,
   (b) odour or aroma.
2. Temperature—sensations of heat and cold.
3. Appearance.
4. Texture—or "mouth-feel"—affecting the sense of touch.

The art of food preparation, small or large scale, is the art of skilful combination of these properties to please the eye, the nose and the palate.

Flavour

Flavour is a complex of sensations that we derive from food, including particularly the sensations of taste and smell. If you have a cold your flavour sensations are often blunted, because the "smell" or olfactory apparatus is temporarily out of action; you are unable to get the tang of a cigarette, and the fragrance of a lemon is completely lost. Similarly, when you burn your tongue with hot soup, or too much curry, the "taste" part of the flavour sensory apparatus may be temporarily obscured, and you may miss the sweetness or sharpness of the dessert which follows. It is possible by suitable tests, to isolate these two sensations and learn something about them individually.

The Taste Sensation

The organs of taste are concerned with the non-volatile components of food—sweetness, saltiness, sourness, and bitterness. These taste sensations are therefore responsive to chemical stimulation. For a substance to affect the taste sense it must be already in solution or dissolve in the saliva, since a completely dry substance in a dry mouth will not produce much response.

The cells associated with taste are in the taste buds, and lie mostly in grooves around little projections on the upper surface of the tongue (Fig. 8.1 (a) and (b)). These sensitive cells are in bundles from which slender hairs emerge through the pore of the taste-bud, and make contact with the stimulating substance. The message is then sent back through one of the nerves of taste to the brain.

Several thousands of taste-buds are distributed over the tongue and soft palate, and are mainly associated with distinguishing the four basic tastes: sweet, bitter, salt, and sour. The sensitivity to the different tastes is not uniform all over the tongue. The areas most sensitive to sweetness and saltiness are on the tip of the tongue; those most sensitive to sourness along the edges; while bitterness is tasted most strongly at the back of the tongue. It is interesting to note that a baby has a large number of taste-buds at the tip of the tongue, which enable it to appreciate the sweetness of its mother's milk. As it grows older, the number of these taste-buds decreases, while those at the base of the tongue increase, which appears to be related to the preference for less sweet foods with increasing age. The overall number of active taste-buds decreases slowly at the age

FLAVOUR, COLOUR AND TEXTURE

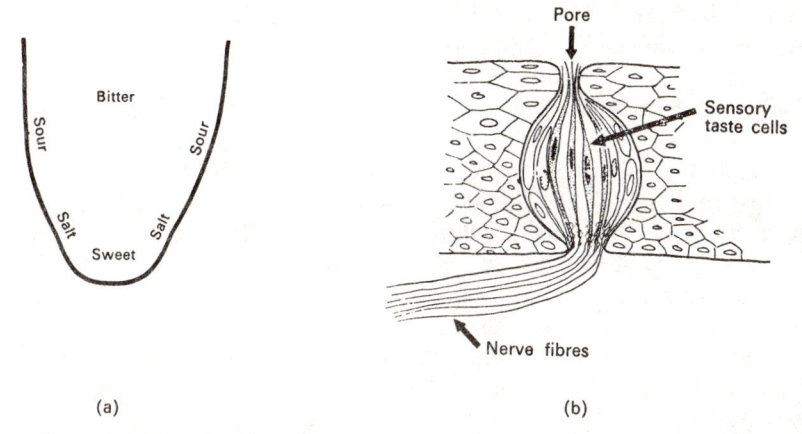

FIG. 8.1. (a) Distribution of taste-buds over the tongue. (b) Diagram of a taste-bud.

of 45, and more rapidly at about 70 years of age. This may well be related to the reduction in the activity of our sense of taste as we get older.

Sensitivity to different "tastes" varies considerably; for example, sweetness can be detected in a solution of sugar of 1 part in 200; saltiness in a solution of 1 part in 400 of common salt; sourness in a solution of hydrochloric acid of 1 part in 130,000; and bitterness can be detected in a solution containing only 1 part of quinine in 2,000,000 parts of water.

The Smell Sensation

Whilst humans possess several thousand taste receptor cells, they have many millions of the cells sensitive to smell or odour. These olfactory receptor cells, as they are called, are mostly in a cleft on each side of the septum, in the upper part of the nasal cavity. They lie in a yellow-coloured area of about one square inch and are slender, spindle-shaped cells ending in a bunch of fine hairs which project into the surface layer of the mucous membrane, which is maintained in a moist condition.

Our sense of smell is well-developed, but in many animals it is much more acute; a large part of the brain being concerned with smell. For such animals this is a question of survival, as the nose warns them of enemies, and directs them to food. This is hardly the case with civilized man; but nevertheless, there are certain substances containing sulphur which can be detected at a level of one part in 30 billion; or vanillin (found in vanilla) at a level of one part in 10 million.

Substances which vaporize when exposed to the air are termed "volatile". Liquids such as alcohol, ether and turpentine are in this category, and so are some solids like camphor and naphthalene, though to a lesser extent. Many volatile substances excite the sense of smell; whilst non-volatile substances such as metals, salts and carbon do not vaporize and have no smell. When we want to smell something we sniff, and in so doing draw in a little air, which is wafted over the olfactory clefts in the nose. The molecules of the volatile substances are drawn in with the air and enter the layer of fluid covering the mucous membrane—not unlike the mechanism of taste. They then stimulate the fine sensitive hairs of the olfactory cell which send their message through the olfactory nerve to the brain.

When food is in the mouth molecules of the volatile flavour compounds present are carried by diffusion and convection into the still air of the upper nasal cavity over the olfactory clefts, and so stimulate the olfactory hairs. The sensation is combined with those of the taste buds and the result is a composite impression of the flavour of the food one is eating.

Physiologists like Professor Adrian have studied taste and odour response using animals such as the rabbit, the frog and the opossum. Their work suggests that the olfactory system may work in a way similar to that of our sense of hearing. The inner ear receives a complex sound wave, which is broken up into simple components, each of which excites a small group of receptors. In the nose, similarly, each simple chemical component of a complex flavour may excite a small portion of the olfactory receptors. The pattern is then gathered and built up again in the brain in the same way as a complex sound. But whereas the ear has about 30,000 nerve fibres, the nose has about 80–100 million olfactory fibres. Odours would therefore appear to be more complex, and more difficult to analyse, than sounds.

Other Senses

In addition to the organs of smell and taste, there are other sensitive organs all over the mouth. These respond to the astringency of wines; the pungency of mustard, pepper and curry and the "coolness" of peppermint. We are also conscious of the texture of foods—the crispness of biscuits and corn flakes, the stickiness of toffee, the smoothness of good-quality chocolate or ice-cream. Part of the system in the mouth is a built-in thermometer. Hot chocolate and cold beer are delicious; tepid chocolate and warm beer would produce revulsion in many of us. Certainly the temperature of food plays a highly significant part in our appreciation and enjoyment of it.

Substances which Taste

If we exclude the senses of smell and touch, temperature and pain, and confine ourselves solely to the sense of "tongue taste", we find that we are left with the four basic tastes mentioned—salt, sour, bitter, and sweet. The investigation of the primary tastes was made possible by the recent development of the electro-physiological method on animal preparations. This consists of a determination of the minute changes in electrical potential produced in dissected taste nerves when various solutions were placed in contact with the taste-buds. This has confirmed the existence of the four basic or "nodal" taste sensations.

Research workers recently extracted proteins from the taste receptors of cows' and pigs' tongues. They found that one protein from the sweet-sensitive receptors formed complexes with sugar and saccharin. The strength of the bond that was formed with various sugars was proportional to the sweetness of the sugars. Another protein from the back of the tongue, which is more sensitive to bitterness, was found to form complexes with various bitter substances. Again, the strength of the bond was in the same order as the intensity of bitterness. Their electrical characteristics were quite different, which may be the key to the impression recorded in the brain as a result of the stimulus produced by these complexes being transmitted along the nerve fibres.

Saltiness

Common salt is an important component in the flavour of cooked and baked foods. It is not only common salt that stimulates the "salt" taste-buds; all salts stimulate them to some extent, especially chlorides, bromides and iodides, which are all members of the same chemical family. Sulphates and nitrates also taste salty, e.g. saltpetre, which is potassium nitrate.

It is well known that a preference for salt may be due to a physiological need for it. This applies particularly to people working in very hot conditions, which causes them to sweat profusely. The sweat contains a high proportion of salt, which must be replaced, and which leads to a salt hunger. This is why stokers, boiler-makers, and miners often drink large amounts of salty water. If they did not do so they would be liable to suffer from a rather unpleasant disease called miner's cramp, which is caused by a deficiency of salt dissolved in the fluid bathing the muscle fibres.

Sweetness

Our sense of sweetness may be stimulated by a number of different types of chemical compounds. Sugars themselves are a part of a larger group of organic chemicals containing several hydroxyl (OH) groups. These are often sweet. For example, glycerine, which has three hydroxyl groups, is fairly sweet; whilst ethylene glycol—the substance used as antifreeze—which contains two hydroxyl groups—is also sweet; but, it should be added, it is also poisonous!

Not all sugars are equally sweet. The sweetest of the common sugars is fructose, or fruit-sugar, found in many fruits, which is about 30% sweeter than cane sugar, whilst lactose, the sugar in milk, is the least sweet, and has only about one-sixth the sweetness of cane sugar.

But substances with completely different chemical patterns may also be sweet. Two well-known sweeteners are saccharin, which is about 300 times as sweet as cane sugar, and cyclamate, which is about 30 times as sweet. These are discussed in Chapter 9.

Bitterness is a characteristic shared by many quite different chemical compounds. One group of bitter substances includes quinine, strychnine and nicotine. Caffeine, which is quite different chemically, is also bitter.

Sourness in foods is more obviously related to the chemical structure than are the other sensations, for this is only found in acid foods. The sharpness or tartness of vinegar and lemons is due to the presence of organic acids. The effect on the palate is possibly due to the hydrogen ions which are produced when acids dissolve in water.

Temperature affects our sense of taste. Thus, a sugared drink appears to be sweeter when hot than when cold. Similarly, a lemon drink seems to taste more sour when it is hot than when it is cold. As opposed to this, cold tea and coffee appear to be more bitter than when hot. Ice-cream in the melted state appears to be sickly sweet because of the extra sugar needed to make it appear sweet enough when frozen.

The different taste sensations are not completely separate, but react on one another. For instance, bitterness and sweetness tend to counteract each other: we put sugar into coffee and tea to lessen the sensation of bitterness. Conversely, marmalade would seem horribly sweet if the bitter principles of the Seville type of orange were not included. This is why the housewife is advised to boil the pips with water to extract these bitter compounds and add them to the marmalade boil. For the same reason, sugar lessens the impact of sourness in lemons. In general the blending of one type of flavour with another decreases the harshness of individual flavours and helps to round off and balance the flavour of the food as a whole.

Aroma in Foods

Whereas there are four basic "taste" sensations, there are many thousands of separate odour sensations, and there has been no successful attempt to classify them. They must, as explained earlier, be reasonably volatile, and therefore the major food constituents such as sugars, starch, fats and proteins produce no aroma response; nor, for that matter, do vitamins and minerals affect our sense of smell. The aroma substances in food are only present in small amounts but, unlike vitamins, have no direct nutritional effect. They consist of organic chemicals belonging to groups well known to the organic chemist such as fatty acids and alcohols.

Natural Flavours

The actual amounts of these flavorous substances in our food are very tiny. It would take about a ton (1000 kg) of many foods to produce 1 g (1/28 oz) of these compounds, and in some cases only 1/10 g could be extracted. Some of these compounds are known to us in other forms. Amyl acetate, or "pear drops", used as a solvent for cellulose paints is commonly found in fruits. So also is acetone, also used widely as a solvent. The smell of rancid butter is due to fatty acids; but these unpleasant-smelling substances help to make the delicious aroma of a fine Camembert cheese. The "bad egg" smell which haunted us in our chemistry laboratory days—due to hydrogen sulphide—is quite common in cabbages, cauliflower and even in beer. There are, in fact, many thousands of such compounds, and in any one food there may be hundreds of different flavour compounds. Some which have been found as normal constituents in one food would be repugnant in another; for example, hydrogen sulphide, normal in beer, would be a sign of spoilage when found in meat or pickles.

But the unpleasant nature of many of these substances on their own is masked by their small concentration and by the balance which is exerted on them by the complex of other flavour substances.

"Not so natural" Flavours

In addition to the natural blend of aroma substances in food, many new ones are produced as a result of storage, cooking and processing. Many of them are lost to the air on heating, because they are so volatile, and many of them will not stand up to heat, which destroys their chemical nature. This is why strawberry flavour, consisting of more than 150 identified substances, loses its unique character when heated.

Cooking and storage may produce entirely new flavours. Good examples of this are the effect of toasting bread, or roasting coffee; both treatments produce essentially the same type of flavour change. New flavours are produced as a side-effect of browning, discussed on p. 122. Our palate is very sensitive also to flavour changes which take place as a result of spoilage. Meat which has gone bad through bacterial action, for example, may produce certain nitrogenous and sulphur compounds which smell revolting. In this case, we have a built-in safeguard against being poisoned, but unfortunately, we cannot always rely on this. Because the odorous food components are so easily lost on heating, especially when steam is also produced, the housewife is often advised to cook at a low temperature, or for a short time in order to minimize these losses. Strawberry jam, for example, should be boiled as quickly as possible, and when spices or essences are used in cooking they should be added as late as possible with minimum heating to conserve the essential oils. Roast meat that has been wrapped in aluminium foil retains more of the inherent flavour than when it is unwrapped.

Flavour investigation. The increase in our knowledge about aromatic flavours in foods is in no small measure due to a new technique of analysis called Gas Chromatography. This was discovered in 1952, and consists in principle of placing a tiny drop of the volatile liquid, or some of the vapour above the food under examination at the top of a long column packed with fine granular material, and passing a current of gas, such as nitrogen, or argon through the column. This slowly drives the vapour under test down the column, which is so constructed as to separate the individual components present. As they emerge at the bottom of the column, each separate chemical is detected by a sensitive device which produces a tiny electrical impulse, which is amplified and is recorded by a pen on a moving drum. In this way a series of peaks are obtained, each representing a separate component of the flavour in the liquid examined. As little as a hundred-millionth of a pint of liquid can be analysed in this way.

Copying nature's art. It is largely as a result of the impetus given to research into the composition of the very complex mixtures of chemical compounds which are responsible for flavours in food, that corresponding advances have been made in the tricky job of making up mixtures of chemicals which will resemble the natural flavours. The task of manufacturing the individual chemicals that have been separated from natural flavours and identified by the gas chromatograph and other instruments, and blending them in the right proportions is a highly exacting one. The harmonizing of these separate substances has been likened to the work of the conductor of an orchestra, and indeed this is the mental attitude of those concerned, the individual components being called "notes".

Some commercial food flavours are simply extracted from the foods, but they are expensive to produce; others are made entirely from synthetic chemicals, but they often tend to possess a rough or raw flavour. Probably the most successful flavours from a commercial point of view are those that are blends of the synthetic and the natural, which have a fairly harmonious balance, and at the same time are reasonably low in price.

Flavour intensifiers. Among substances used for flavouring purposes are meat and yeast extracts, and soya sauce. These all contain protein material which has been hydrolysed, or broken down to their constituent amino acids. These mixtures of amino acids have been known for many years to be excellent in their flavouring properties. Some 60 years ago, a Japanese named Ikeda discovered that one of the commonest constituents of these flavourings, called *glutamic acid*, was particularly effective in flavouring food. The salt of this amino acid, called *mono-sodium glutamate* (MSG) had an even more attractive meat-like flavour. MSG is now manufactured on a large scale all over the world, but especially in Japan, where they call it AJI-NO-MOTO, or the "Essence of Taste". On investigation, it has been found not to possess a great deal of flavour of its own, but has the curious property of enhancing certain food flavours, especially meat and chicken. It is used extensively in soups and other foods, and is present in flavouring mixtures sold to the housewife, such as Aromat. Being an amino acid, it has hitherto been regarded as harmless; but recent evidence suggests that there may be unpleasant effects when large amounts are ingested.

Ribonucleic acid, or RNA, has been shown to be intimately connected with the synthesis of protein in the living cell. It has been shown that a group of substances derived from RNA, called *Ribonucleotides*, which are present in yeast extract have the same flavour-enhancing property as MSG, but are ten times as powerful: they are more effective still when they are mixed with MSG. Both of these types of substances appear to affect all the four kinds of taste-buds in the mouth, but it has been suggested that, in some way, they stimulate them to increased sensitivity to certain flavours.

An even more unusual effect is provided by the berries of the "miracle" fruit from West Africa which are used by West Africans to sweeten sour maize bread, palm wine and beer. It appears that this is not due to any intrinsic sweetness on its part but to a protein called *miraculin* which is present. It has been shown that when it is eaten along with lemon, lime or rhubarb, the sour taste is converted to a sweet taste after 1 minute. This obviously has interesting possibilities. As miraculin contains only 7% sugar, one could sweeten the sourest of fruit without adding extra sugar!

Colour of Food

> *What* is the matter with Mary Jane?
> She's crying with all her might and main.
> And she won't eat her dinner—rice pudding again—
> What *is* the matter with Mary Jane?
>
> From the poem "Rice Pudding" by A. A. Milne

Mary Jane's mother undoubtedly explained patiently to her wayward daughter that the rice pudding tasted delicious—she sampled some to show her—also that it was very good for her and would help her to grow into a big girl. "Just taste it, and you'll like it", she certainly begged. But Mary Jane wasn't convinced. It just didn't look very appetizing, and she wasn't even going to taste that nasty, messy-looking stuff.

Everyone concerned with food preparation or manufacture realizes how important it is to make good food look attractive as well as ensuring that it must have good eating quality. Sales go down drastically when discoloured foods are offered for sale. This is, of course, related to the fact that many foods, such as meat, fruit, and vegetables, often change colour as a result of being stored for too long or under unsuitable conditions. The colour of foods certainly prejudices our preferences, and may even distort our sense of flavour. For example, a number of people who were asked to identify the fruit flavour used in a bright red jelly were certain it was raspberry. In fact, it was a banana-flavoured jelly. For this reason, when food firms are launching a new food and carry out tasting tests, it is quite common to eliminate colour differences between the samples being tasted by illuminating them with coloured lights. Another example to illustrate the need for this was shown when a bakery firm wanted to evaluate the preference for a new type of egg-containing roll. To test out the tasting panel's prejudices on colour, they submitted to them four samples of rolls, all containing the same amount of egg. The same recipe was used in each case, except that synthetic egg colour was used in varying amounts. The taste panel showed a clear preference for the two yellowest rolls.

Colours Natural to Foods

Fruits and vegetables. As a rule these have particularly attractive colours, and it is not surprising that so many artists like to use them when painting "still life". The commonest colouring compounds in this group are chlorophyll, carotenoids and flavonoids. Many of the pigments in vegetables are found in small packets around the margin of the cells. One of these is *chlorophyll* which is responsible for the bright green of lettuce, cabbage and green peppers. Chlorophyll plays the part of a catalyst in the process of building up, in green plants, organic compounds such as sugar and starch from carbon dioxide in the air and water from the soil, under the influence of sunlight. This is the process called *photosynthesis*, and is the basis of the production of all food from simple components.

There are actually two forms of chlorophyll: one is blue–black and the other is blue–green. The combined pigments appear slightly yellower because of the presence of some yellow pigments called *carotenoids*, which always accompany chlorophyll, but which are masked by the vivid green of the latter. The molecule of chlorophyll is ring-shaped, and contains a single magnesium atom in the centre. (see Fig. 7·5, p. 126) This is why soil which is poor in magnesium, produces plants with sickly looking leaves.

In the autumn, the bright green colour of the leaves disappears, leaving the yellow to brown carotenoids. This change is produced as a result of enzymes which attack the chlorophyll and is also partly responsible for the jaded appearance of lettuces, peas or cabbages that have overspent their time languishing in the greengrocer's shop on a hot summer's day. The colour changes which take place during cooking green vegetables are discussed in Chapter 7.

Carotenoids are a large family of yellow, orange and red pigments, all soluble in fat. They are found along with chlorophyll, in green leaves, and are also present in carrots (hence the name), swedes, peaches, apricots, peppers, tomatoes and bananas.

An important member of the family is beta-carotene. This is a brilliant orange–yellow pigment, which is closely related to vitamin A, because it is easily changed into that vitamin on being eaten (see p. 44). Other carotenoids possess either no vitamin A activity or only a trace. *Lycopene* is a close relative of beta-carotene, and it is the bright red pigment of tomatoes and red peppers. The yellow colour of maize and freshly milled wheat flour is also due to carotenoids.

One of the important features of carotenoids is that they are organic compounds with long unsaturated chains, which are responsible for their bright colours. This unsaturated property is easily destroyed by oxidation in air, or by hydrogenation. Oxidation is responsible for the loss of the bright colour of dehydrated carrots.

During the ageing of flour, or bleaching by oxidizing agents, the carotenoid colour is bleached, producing a white flour which in turn will make a whiter loaf. Palm oil, extracted from the palm fruit of Western Africa, is a bright orange colour due to the presence of carotenoids, including a good deal of beta-carotene. As the law stipulates that margarine must contain vitamin A, palm oil is very often used in its manufacture, thus giving to the margarine a rich golden colour, and a proportion of the total vitamin A (from the beta-carotene). Butter is yellow due largely to the presence of beta-carotene, though there is also some vitamin A present as well —but not contributing to the colour. It should be emphasized that the yellow colour of egg yolk, although due to carotenoids, does not include beta-carotene to any extent, so that it is quite wrong to suppose that the depth of colour of the yolk is in any way related to the vitamin A content. The vitamin A content is due to vitamin A itself. It need hardly be added that the pigmentation of the shell of brown eggs is also not related to beta-carotene, or vitamin content. In order to produce richly coloured yolks, certain carotenoids can be fed to chickens to produce just this effect.

The third group of colours found in fruits and vegetables, the *flavonoid* pigments, are water-soluble, and unlike the other two are found dissolved in the water cell-sap. A sub-group called *anthocyanins* is responsible for reds, blues, and violets found in a wide variety of fruits—plums, grapes, damsons, blackcurrants, raspberries, strawberries and other berry fruits. The same sub-group also includes the pigment found in many flowers and buds. The red–blue balance of these colours can be affected by acids and alkalis as well as by the presence of metals; hence red cabbage which is boiled in tap-water turns blue, whilst the addition of vinegar turns it red. Red fruits which are cooked in an aluminium saucepan frequently become bluish in colour.

A second sub-group called *flavones* is responsible for pale yellows in some onions, asparagus and apples. Alkaline tap-water is liable to cause them to turn a deep yellow–brown colour on cooking, which can be prevented by adding an acid such as cream of tartar or a little lemon juice to cooking water to whiten them. (Mary Jane's mother please note: yellowing of rice is also prevented in this way.)

Tannins are related to flavonoids, and are not necessarily coloured, but are often responsible for colour changes. They give unripe fruits their astringent flavour, which is slowly lost during ripening owing to the effect of enzymes on the tannin. As sugars are released in the process, the loss of astringency is accompanied by an increase in sweetness. Tannins are responsible for the colour and some of the flavour of tea. In a cup of tea the protein in the milk and the tannins in the tea precipitate each other producing the typical cloudy appearance, whilst the use of lemon in place of milk clarifies the tannin and lightens its colour.

The colour of meat is partly due to a red pigment in muscle called *myoglobin* and partly to any residual blood, which is coloured by a closely related pigment called *haemoglobin*. Both of these pigments have the property of combining with oxygen which has been drawn into the lungs and of releasing it in the body for the purpose of providing energy from our food. These pigments are somewhat similar to the leaf pigment chlorophyll, but have an atom of iron in the centre of the molecule instead of magnesium. Just as leaf colour is affected by the availability of magnesium, a shortage of iron in the diet leads to a shortage of these red pigments, and hence to anaemia.

Colours Added to Food

So far we have been considering colours which are found naturally in foods, but it must be borne in mind that colours are often added to food to give it a more attractive appearance. Until the middle of the nineteenth century vegetable, mineral, and even animal colours were used quite widely: these included such colours as saffron, iron oxide, and cochineal respectively.

The narrow range of colours available was increased when Perkin in 1850 discovered how to make colours artificially—the so-called aniline or coal-tar dyes. Colour after colour was synthesized in the second half of the nineteenth century in a brilliant cavalcade of rainbow hues. They were brighter, more concentrated, offered more variety, and were more stable than most of those used previously.

Unfortunately, it soon became clear that though wonderful for the textile industry, not all of these colours were harmless when eaten in food. The whole position of food colours is now therefore rigidly controlled by food regulations (1966), which only permit certain colours to be used that have passed searching toxicological tests. These include some of natural origin, such as carotene and chlorophyll, which have already been discussed. Annatto, made from the seeds of a South American plant, is used for colouring butter and cheese. Saffron is obtained from the dried stigmas of the Saffron Crocus, and has both flavouring and colouring properties, though medicinal properties have also been claimed. In the British Museum a seventeenth-century tract extolling the "Vertues and Uses of the Cordial Spirit of Saffron" says that it will "preserve against the injury of corrupted Air, or against the Violence of any Distemper. ... For such as have taken too Cheerful or too Liberal a Cup over Night, and thence become indisposed the next Morning: let such at their rising take three Spoonfuls thereof, or more, as they think fit, and walk after it."

Cochineal (or carmine) is a permitted colour. Vegetarians may be interested to know that this is made from female cactus-feeding insects which are killed by being dropped in hot water, or by the fumes of burning sulphur. They are then dried in the sun and made into an infusion called carmine. Caramel or "black jack" is the brown colouring and flavouring produced by heating glucose with ammonia or caustic soda until the required depth of colour is obtained.

The colours used more frequently by the food industry and also sold

FLAVOUR, COLOUR AND TEXTURE   145

to the housewife are the synthetic, or coal-tar colours. These are under constant review from the point of view of safety. They are extremely concentrated: a pinpoint is enough to give a deep colour to a half pint of water. All but two of the twenty-five permitted colours are water soluble.

Some people have queried the ethics of adding colour to foods. But it has been shown that in many cases making food more attractive in appearance improves the enjoyment of a meal. Peas, for example, that change from a bright green to a drab olive-green colour on canning do not sell well, and the consumers in Britain have shown that they prefer such peas coloured to resemble the fresh vegetable. Custard, jellies and ice-cream are more likely to tempt us if they are appropriately coloured. Margarine would look most unsightly if colour was omitted, and we were offered something that looked like cooking fat to spread on our bread. As mentioned in Chapter 4, this helped to keep down the sale of margarine in the United States.

Food Texture

Perception

We are very sensitive to the physical state of the food we eat as well as to its flavour. How irritating it is, for example, to come across grains of sand when eating insufficiently washed spinach or sultanas. We may receive an unpleasant shock when we eat a toffee which has been too long in store. Instead of the firm chewy texture we expect, our teeth sink into a mass of crystallized sugar, which may well have a rancid taste into the bargain. Similarly, we like our bread to be reasonably firm without having the brick-hardness of stale bread, or the sogginess of wet cottonwool.

The sense organs associated with the above sensations are contained in (1) the palate, tongue, and gums; (2) around the roots of the teeth; and (3) in the muscles and tendons used in mastication. The sense organs resemble those found in other mucous membranes and in some part of the skin, such as that of the nipple and the penis. They respond to touch and may also be concerned with pain. During biting and chewing the teeth are very slightly displaced in their sockets and the areas and extent of compression of the membranes under the teeth are detected by the sense organs. If you carefully observe your own movements during biting and chewing you will notice that the tongue plays an important part in the operations—rolling the food across the gums and the hard and soft palates. As the texture of the food changes during mastication, this is recorded by all three groups of sense organs. The increased surface area of the food exposed by this process releases taste and smell substances, which are detected and transmitted to the brain along with the texture sensations, until the instruction is given to the muscles by the brain to swallow the now fully masticated food.

Factors Affecting Food Texture

From the point of view of texture, foods can be roughly divided into two kinds: (a) those that still contain the basic structure of the plant or animal from which the food comes, e.g. meat, potatoes, cabbage, nuts; and (b) those foods that have completely lost the native plant or animal structure, such as bread, jam, butter, ice-cream. Very few foods in both groups are free of water—even if there is only a very small percentage present.

In the first group, the texture is very much determined by the fact that living tissue is composed of cells. The main cell structure is held together by the cell walls—protein in the case of most animal tissue—carbohydrates for most plant tissue. The tougher these cell walls are, the tougher is the consistency of the foods, because biting and chewing such a food involve biting your way through cell walls. Nevertheless, the contents of the cells also affect the texture and include protoplasm, a watery "solution" containing protein. This is really a special sort of solution, in which the dissolved particles are so large that it makes the solution thick, slow-moving, or "viscous", and even if diluted it could not be filtered through parchment membranes as a true solution could. Such "solutions" are distinguished from true solutions, such as sugar solutions, by being called "colloidal" solutions.

Colloidal solutions. A large proportion of foods of the second group (non-cellular) are also colloidal in nature, especially in the ready-to-eat form. Colloidal systems consist of two parts: fine particles of one substance (the dispersed phase) distributed in a second substance (the dispersion medium or "solvent"). The particles of dispersed phase are always fairly large, that is, larger than the particles of a true solution, but smaller than those of a suspension. In a suspension, say of sand and water, the sand would very quickly drop to the bottom, but a colloidal solution of starch in water is reasonably stable. Examples of colloidal systems found in food are shown in Table 8.1.

FLAVOUR, COLOUR AND TEXTURE 147

TABLE 8.1. COLLOIDAL SYSTEMS FOUND IN FOOD

Dispersed phase		Dispersion medium (solvent)	Name of system	Example
Solid	in	Liquid	Sol	Starch "solution" Gelatine "solution"
Liquid	in	Solid	Gel	Blancmange Gelatine jelly
Liquid	in	Liquid	Emulsion	Milk Mayonnaise
Gas	in	Liquid	Foam	Beaten egg-white Whipped cream
Gas	in	Solid		Meringue Cake

"Sols" which resemble true solutions may be made by simply dissolving the solid material—e.g. starch, gelatine, or pectin—in water. It often helps to heat the mixture, and it is usually necessary to stir well to ensure that all the solid dissolves. A "gel"—or jelly—behaves like an elastic solid. It can often be made by cooling the "sol" produced above, as in making custard, blancmange, gelatin jellies, or jam (a pectin "gel"). Usually the reverse change is produced by heating. In the "gel" the particles of colloidal material—starch, gelatine, pectin—join together to form a three-dimensional network of interlacing fibrils which hold the liquid immobilized inside it. Hence the elastic and sometimes plastic property of the gel. Very often, in course of time, the gel exudes liquid—weeping or *syneresis*. Examples are strongly acid jams and jellies, junket, and meat.

Emulsions. Emulsions consist of one liquid dispersed in another liquid with which it is normally immiscible. The dispersed liquid can be seen under a microscope to consist of tiny droplets. For example, alcohol dissolves completely in water and cannot form an emulsion with it. But oil or fat does not mix freely with water, and it is possible to produce an emulsion of oil in a watery liquid or vice versa. If oil is vigorously shaken with water the emulsion so formed rapidly separates leaving us with a two-layer system. To make a more permanent emulsion, a third substance must be included to act as a sort of matchmaker to these two unwilling partners. This matchmaker is termed an emulsifying agent, or emulsifier. Emulsifiers belong to a group of substances called surface-active agents, which also includes detergents. Their special ability to reconcile two opposing systems is due to the fact that their molecules have two portions: (1) a "water loving" *hydrophilic* (H) portion; and (2) a "fat-loving" *lipophilic* (L) portion (see Fig. 8.2). As a result of the attraction which each phase—i.e. water and oil phases—of an emulsion has on one portion of the emulsifier, the latter acts as a bridge between the two phases, which

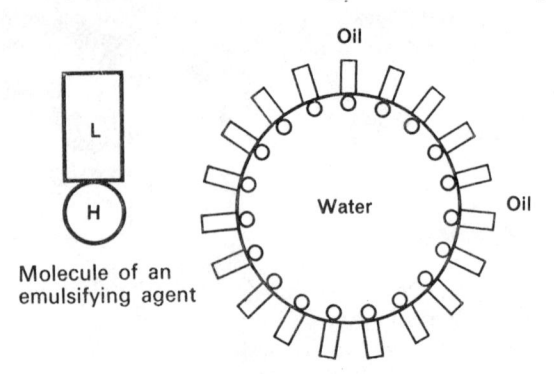

FIG. 8.2. Structure of a water-in-oil emulsion—showing the stabilization of a water droplet in oil by an emulsifying agent.
H = hydrophilic portion. L = lipophilic portion.

in its absence shun each other like the plague. In this way, the tiny droplets of water which are produced by violent agitation of the oil and water mixture are held in position as shown in Fig. 8.2.

Milk is an example of an emulsion. The fat is dispersed in the form of globules in the water phase of the milk and is termed an "oil-in-water" emulsion. The emulsifying agent here is protein. When cream, which is also an "oil-in-water" emulsion, is agitated or "churned" the emulsion is turned inside out and a "water-in-oil" emulsion is produced. This new emulsion is butter, and the watery liquid which is also produced is buttermilk. Mayonnaise represents an oil-in-water emulsion in which the emulsifier is egg yolk. In this case, a special machine is often used to break up the oil into very fine particles.

Foams. Foams are yet another example of a colloidal system—this time, air-in-liquid. Like emulsions, the tiny air bubbles are stabilized by a "foaming agent", which has essentially the same structure as an emulsifying agent, and acts in much the same way. Beaten egg-white is a foam in which the protein *albumen* is the foaming agent. Whipped cream and ice-cream are further examples of foams. A meringue represents an example of a gas-in-solid system and is virtually a solidified form of the beaten egg-white with the addition of sugar. Mild heat in the oven coagulates or sets the protein of the egg-white, which thus loses its liquid nature, but retains its shape.

Fresh fruits and vegetables. These are composed of cells separated by thin walls of *cellulose* and another rather tough carbohydrate, *protopectin.* Inside the cells is the watery colloidal solution already referred to, protoplasm. As the fruit ripens, enzymes convert the tough protopectin into the softer, more soluble pectin, until it reaches the stage of good eating quality, when the fruit is fairly firm, but not too soft. The pectin is now in the form of a gel. If, however, the fruit is not eaten, enzymes continue to soften and break down (hydrolyse) the pectin to simpler substances which are no longer in colloidal form but are in true solution. The structure of the fruit breaks down, the crispness is lost and it is rather unpleasant to eat. This unpleasantness is increased because sugars and acids, so characteristic of ripe fruit, also break down and may give rise to quite nasty-tasting substances. The effects of cooking on the texture of vegetables is discussed in Chapter 7.

Texture of Cakes

A good confectioner prides himself above all on the lightness of his cakes. The tenderness of cake texture as opposed to the relative firmness of bread is brought about by the craftsman's skill, to which is allied the use of certain materials, including low-protein flour, and specially treated fats. It is clear from microscopic studies that cake batters belong to the foam type of colloidal system (discussed earlier) and contain minute air bubbles enclosed in fat. A good foam structure is necessary and fat is therefore probably the most important ingredient responsible for texture in good quality cakes. It is therefore important to use the right type of fat. Fat increases the leavening power of the baking powder in the batter and improves the final tenderness. The firmness of the baking fat gives strength to the batter, and reduces its tendency to collapse under its own weight before the gluten and egg-white—which are both proteins—coagulate or set.

Whereas bread has a continuous gluten structure, and is therefore rather firm (see p. 60) in cakes and biscuits, the formation of a continnuous gluten system is prevented by fat. This gives cake—and to some extent biscuits—weaker structures which are easier to bite. This property of fats to produce low breaking strength is called *shortening power*. Hence baking fats are sometimes called shortenings.

The shortening power of a fat depends on a number of things, but especially its *plasticity*. Good cakes cannot be made out of liquid oil or hard hydrogenated fats: the ideal is somewhere between; that is a relatively soft or plastic fat. These are manufactured by mixing together a number of oils and fats with some hardened—i.e. hydrogenated fats. These are thoroughly blended in the molten state with an emulsifying agent such as GMS which is really a kind of fat. When the fat mixture is cooled while being vigorously stirred, the GMS gives it a light, creamy texture containing air bubbles in a fine state of dispersion. The GMS, together with the soft plastic fat, help to produce a smooth batter when the flour, egg and other ingredients are whisked together and also help to incorporate air from the whisking process—or carbon dioxide gas from the baking powder—to give the finished cake a light, spongy texture.

It will be seen, in conclusion, that flavour, colour, and texture all play an extremely important part in food palatability, and the methods and ingredients used to achieve high standards in each of these food qualities help to make eating one of the major enjoyments of life.

Suggestions for Further Reading

MACKINEY, G. and LITTLE, A. C. *Colour of Foods*, Avi, U.S.A., 1962. Fairly advanced.
MATZ, S. A. *Food Texture*, Avi, U.S.A., 1962. Of fairly advanced standard.
MERORY, J. *Food Flavourings: Composition, Manufacture and Use*, 2nd. ed., Avi, U.S.A., 1968. A comprehensive account.
MILNE, L. and M. *The Senses of Animals and Men*, Penguin, 1965.
SWEETMAN and MCKELLAR, *Food Selection and Preparation*, Wiley, 4th edn. 1965.

CHAPTER 9

Eating Chemicals

To MANY people the idea of eating chemicals is so obnoxious that it evokes an immediate emotional response which is without any rational basis. This is unfortunate, for it obscures the fact, which is fundamental to the whole of this book, that food itself is composed of nothing but chemicals. However, what is usually meant by chemicals in food is not the materials which form the bulky part of our diet—carbohydrates, fats and proteins—but those substances which do not normally form a part of food in its natural state. Such substances are usually present in only small quantities and they may either result from accidental contamination or from deliberate addition to "improve" the food in some way.

To say that chemicals in food are all bad is just as misleading as it is to say that money is the root of all evil. Like money, chemicals are neither good nor bad in themselves, but may be either good or bad according to how they are used. Without the use of chemicals most of the 6000 or so products that appear on the shelves of a large supermarket would not exist—and, much more important, many millions of tons of agricultural produce would be lost instead of being converted into useful food products. In this chapter we shall be concerned, not to condemn or approve chemicals as a whole, but to judge each use of chemicals in food on its merits. What is needed is a calm, rational and critical appraisal of the subject.

Changing Food Standards

In the past adulteration of food was widespread and had many disastrous consequences. For example, the industrial revolution in Britain led to an unprecedented move of population from country to town, and this was accompanied by changes in methods of food production. For the first time large-scale food production became necessary and this created conditions that were conducive to large scale adulteration of food.

Frederick Accum (see Suggestions for Further Reading) writing from London in 1820 gives a vivid picture of the adulteration of bread, alcoholic drinks, tea and coffee and many other foods that was widely practised at that time.

At that period bread was not only the basic item of diet but it was the one most subjected to adulteration. Bread was adulterated, for example, by the incorporation of sieved boiled potatoes in the flour, though the most serious example concerned the addition of alum to flour. The town-dweller, no longer content with the rather heavy brownish-coloured loaf made at home, was starting to show a preference for a loaf which was porous and light, and white in colour. In order to produce such bread, bakers were not slow to discover that instead of using expensive fine flour they could substitute cheaper, inferior flour provided that alum was added in order to whiten it.

Alcoholic beverages were also widely adulterated, especially porter, which was the townsman's favourite drink at that time. By law only malt and hops could be used in its manufacture but in order to increase its intoxicating effect unscrupulous brewers often added various drugs. Among the many toxic substances employed was a black, sticky material known as "black extract" containing the stimulant *cocculus indicus*, obtained from poisonous berries.

The recipe books of this time contain some extraordinary and alarming recipes of which that for preserving the green colour of green vegetables preserved in vinegar is typical. "To render pickles green, boil them with halfpence, or allow them to stand for 24 hours in copper or brass pans." It is not entirely surprising that records of that period record a number of deaths from copper poisoning!

In addition to the examples of adulteration given above many others could be cited, such as the addition of sulphuric acid to vinegar to increase its acidity, the dilution of milk with water and the addition of rice powder or arrowroot to diluted cream to thicken it. The growth of these and many other abuses caused Parliament in 1860 to pass an Act controlling the adulteration of food and drink. Since that date many further Acts have been passed to safeguard the quality and safety of our food. Today deliberate adulteration of food in industrialized countries is rare. Indeed, food manufacturers are only too aware that successful marketing of a food product can only be achieved if it is of high quality. The gradual rise in food standards over the last century can thus be attributed, not only to increasingly strict legal standards, but also to the growth of an increasingly critical and discriminating public.

Unintentional Contaminants

While it is true to say that deliberate adulteration of food is uncommon today in industrialized countries, it is unfortunately also true that unintentional contamination is widespread and often outside the control of food manufacturers. Some sources of contamination, such as radioactivity, packaging materials and the vast array of chemicals now used in growing crops and raising animals, are relatively new and present some serious threats to food safety. Others, such as contaminants from food-processing machinery and from the chemicals that are used as aids in food manufacture, are older and more obvious sources of contamination, but they, too, may present a serious health hazard.

Contamination of food by radioactive fallout from nuclear explosions is a serious modern problem. This type of contamination differs from all others in that it is quite outside the control of both those who grow food and those who manufacture food products. Indeed it is also outside the control of the scientists who make such explosions possible. It is in fact the result of political decisions made for political reasons.

When a nuclear device explodes, atoms of heavy metals such as uranium are split into smaller particles called fission products. These fission products contain unstable atoms, called radioisotopes, which spontaneously break down emitting radiation and particles that are highly injurious to living tissues. When a nuclear bomb is exploded in the atmosphere fission products are carried to high altitudes and settle down slowly, so that the fall-out from such an explosion may continue for as much as several years after the explosion has taken place. When fall-out products reach the ground they contaminate both soil and vegetation and thus become part of our food supplies.

Some radioisotopes break down so rapidly that they lose almost all their radioactivity before they reach the earth. Others, however, such as the radioisotopes of strontium (strontium-90) and caesium (caesium-137), remain radioactive for many years and thus contaminate vegetation and grazing animals and eventually find their way via food into our bodies. If they are absorbed by the body their radioactivity can cause severe harm.

Strontium-90 constitutes one of the most serious health hazards. Chemically it behaves just like normal strontium and the body treats them both in exactly the same way. Strontium is very similar to calcium and these two elements tend to be found together in the same foods. Foods, such as milk, which are good sources of calcium are therefore also liable to contain some strontium-90 following radioactive fall-out. After absorption in the body strontium-90 is deposited in bones where it can cause bone tumours or, by irradiating adjacent bone marrow, the disease leukaemia.

It is sometimes claimed that doses of strontium-90 and other radioisotopes below a certain critical value are not harmful, but this comforting idea is not supported by any convincing evidence and it seems prudent to assume that even the smallest doses of radioisotopes are harmful. Although it is encouraging that the major powers have agreed to discontinue exploding nuclear devices in the atmosphere it is unfortunate and regrettable that some nations are continuing such tests.

Another major source of food contamination concerns the increasing use of a wide range of chemicals to control and improve crops and animal husbandry. Such chemicals include insecticides, fungicides, herbicides, rodenticides, growth promotors and seed protectants for the treatment of crops and hormones, and antibiotics for the treatment of animals. Although the use of this rather bewildering array of chemicals is deplored by some, it is undeniably true that without them much food would be lost. Indeed some experts claim that commercial production of some crops would be impossible if chemicals were not used and that over 20% of cabbage production and over 30% of the potato crop would be lost.

On the other hand, the danger of treating crops and animals with chemicals should not be minimized. Modern agricultural chemicals are for the most part complex organic compounds that are often toxic to both animals and humans. In theory crops and animals are treated with chemicals in such a way that food when eaten is free from contamination. In practice chemical residues often remain in such food and two widely used insecticides—the well known and controversial chlorinated hydrocarbons DDT and dieldrin—have been detected in small amounts in soil, water, vegetables and animal tissues in all parts of the world. The extremely widespread nature of this contamination is emphasized by the fact that even the air we breathe contains traces of them. The main ways in which pesticides get into food are shown in Fig. 9.1.

DDT and dieldrin are soluble in fat and thus in the body they become concentrated in fatty tissues. Tests carried out in many parts of the world

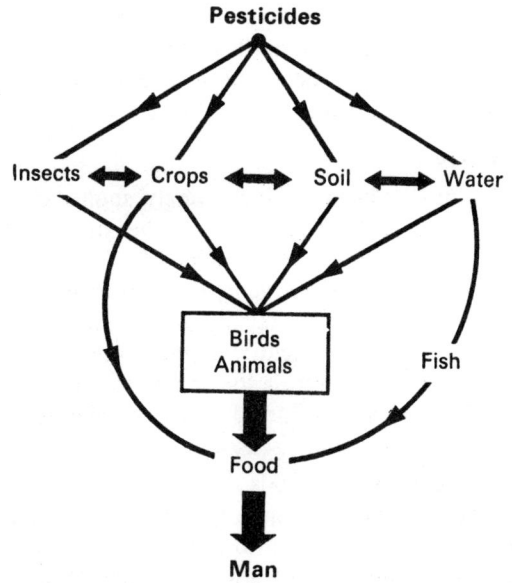

```
                    Pesticides
                        •
                   ╱ ╱ ╲ ╲
                  ╱ ╱   ╲ ╲
    Insects ⟷ Crops ⟷ Soil ⟷ Water
         ╲      ╲    ╱      ╱
          ╲      ┌─────┐   ╱
           ╲────▶│Birds│◀─╱
                 │Animals│   Fish
                 └─────┘
                    ▼
                  Food
                    │
                    ▼
                   Man
```

FIG. 9.1. Pathways by which pesticide residues reach man.

confirm that all human fat contains small quantities of DDT. It is believed that the small amounts present are not harmful but although harmful effects have not been demonstrated it seems wisest to err on the side of discretion and assume that even small amounts may cause harm. The presence of pesticide and other residues in food is a serious international problem. Although there seems to be no way of preventing contamination of food in this way, international bodies such as the World Health Organization have attempted to control the extent of contamination by prescribing limits for the amounts of many pesticide residues that may be present in foods.

Agricultural and radioactive contaminants are but two of the very considerable number of unintentional contaminants that find their way into food. Although contamination of food in any way is bad, the question of contamination must be considered in the light of any benefits that ensue. We have already mentioned the fact that without pesticides much food would be lost. Again, the use of modern packaging methods has led to some contamination of food by chemicals present in the materials used for packaging. For example, formaldehyde resins, which are added to paper to increase its strength when wet, may migrate from the treated paper to the foodstuff. Yet in the absence of such packaging materials the shelves of the modern supermarket would look decidedly empty.

Intentional Additives

As the food industry becomes increasingly sophisticated, producing an ever-growing range of food products, it relies more and more on the use of additives. Additives are used to modify flavour and texture, to sweeten food, to colour and preserve it; they are used as processing aids and as nutrient supplements and they are used to change storage properties and to control moisture and acidity. Some of these additives—notably preservatives, emulsifying agents, colouring matter and flavour and texture modifiers—have been considered in earlier chapters and we shall exclude these from the present discussion.

Nutrient supplements. When foods are processed there may be a loss of some nutrients, and additives may be used to restore such nutrients to their original level. For example, to produce the white flour that most people prefer, flour is milled in such a way as to reject the brown-coloured part of the wheat grain which, unfortunately, is rich in minerals and vitamins. To compensate for such losses, and to safeguard the nutritional well-being of the nation, the B vitamins thiamine and nicotinic acid and the minerals iron and calcium are all added to flour. The iron is often added as finely divided metallic iron and the calcium is added as purified chalk. Though this may seem rather surprising, it has to be remembered that sugar and salt are just as much "pure" chemicals as iron and chalk.

Where manufactured foods are used as substitutes for natural ones, nutrients may be added to the former to ensure that their nutritional value is at least equal to that of the natural product. The addition of vitamins A and D to margarine to ensure that its vitamin content is at least equal to that of summer butter exemplifies this use of nutrient addition. Although margarine manufacturers do not regard margarine as a substitute for butter, nevertheless it is often used in place of butter on account of its cheapness and it seems proper therefore to ensure that the less affluent members of the community who economize in this way should not suffer thereby. It is interesting to note that in an effort to improve the "image" of margarine an additional additive—namely butter—is sometimes used!

The all-round excellence of milk as a food is marred by its low content of certain nutrients including vitamin D; hence in some countries, including the United States but excluding Britain, extra vitamin D is added. Absence of this vitamin in diet causes rickets and its addition to milk has reduced the incidence of rickets in America. Many foods, such as breakfast cereals, baby foods and fruit juices, are fortified by the addition of vitamins. Indeed, although fortification of food with vitamins may be of nutritional benefit in some circumstances—as, for example, is the case with baby foods fortified with vitamins A, C and D—the practice has become so widespread and indiscriminate that it is often little more than a fashionable gimmick and an aid to selling.

Diets in some parts of the world are deficient in certain mineral elements, and in such areas mineral supplements can with advantage be added to suitable foods. For example, iodine deficiency, which causes goitre, is encountered in many inland areas. Sea-foods are the most useful source of this element and where these do not form part of the diet goitre may be endemic. To overcome this, iodine, often in the form of potassium iodide, may be added to salt in controlled amounts. Such salt is known as iodized salt. Table salt may also contain a further additive in the form of magnesium carbonate. This substance is not added because it confers any nutritional benefit but because it improves the free-running properties of the salt.

It is interesting that whereas many supposedly rational human beings appreciate and approve the addition of iodide to salt, they are not prepared to tolerate the addition of fluoride to water. Yet the arguments for the addition of both these substances to our diet are very similar. Both iodine and fluorine occur in food and water and they are both therefore a natural part of our diet. They are both of benefit to the body when present in small amounts, iodine being essential and fluoride providing effective protection against dental decay in children.

It is true that too much fluoride is harmful to teeth and that more than a certain amount is highly toxic, but this is surely only an argument against the indiscriminate addition of fluoride to water; not against its controlled addition where fluoride is known to be lacking. The addition of fluoride to water—known as fluoridation—is carried out so as to increase the fluoride concentration to 1 p.p.m.; an amount which extensive trials have shown to be the optimum. The scientific arguments in favour of fluoridation are overwhelming, but in spite of this the considerable public outcry against it has prevented it from being carried out in most parts of Britain. In the United States, on the other hand, the drinking water of over 30 million people is treated by fluoridation with beneficial results, especially to children.

Sweetening agents. Most people have a "sweet tooth" and find sweet foods attractive. Food manufacturers are only too ready to pander to this desire for sweetness by creating an ever-growing range of palatable sweet foods. The principal sweetening agent used is sugar, the average consumption of which now exceeds 2 lb per person per week in Britain, if both sugar and manufactured foods containing sugar are taken into account. In many ways sugar is an ideal sweetener; it is produced as a pure solid that has no colour, it is soluble in water and it has a "pure" taste not mixed with overtones of bitterness or saltiness. Moreover, it is a useful source of Calories and is easily digested by the body. In fact it has only one drawback—it is not sweet enough!

A chance discovery, made as long ago as 1879, produced the first synthetic sweetening agent. It proved to be very much sweeter than sugar; more than 300 times as sweet in fact. One evening a young German research chemist noticed that his supper tasted inexplicably sweet. He traced the source of sweetness to a substance on his hands that he had just synthesized in the laboratory. This substance later became known as *saccharin;* it proved to be a harmless white solid that is sparingly soluble in hot water. Saccharin did not prove to be a perfect sweetening agent, however, because although it is very sweet indeed, it is also bitter and leaves an unpleasant after-taste.

Almost 60 years after the chance discovery of saccharin another synthetic sweetener was discovered—again entirely by accident. At first, the new sweetener, known as *cyclamate*, seemed to have little chance of competing with saccharin as it is only about thirty times as sweet as sugar; that is it is only about one-tenth as sweet as saccharin. However, it soon became evident that cyclamates have a less unpleasant after-taste than saccharin and would therefore be useful in food both alone and mixed with saccharin.

The use of cyclamate in food has been the subject of fierce controversy, although it was used in certain dietary goods in the United States for about 20 years without any harmful effects being reported. There is evidence, however, that cyclamate does not always pass through the body unchanged although it is thought that the breakdown products formed are harmless in the small amounts likely to be produced. Although the evidence against cyclamate is slender and unconvincing, its use in food was banned in the United Kingdom, the United States and some other countries in 1969.

Saccharin is the only synthetic sweetening agent used extensively in food, and it is the only one permitted in Great Britain. It is used mainly because it can produce the requisite sweetness in food more cheaply than sugar and also because, having no Calorific value, it is suitable for use in diabetic and other special dietary products. Research into other possible sweetening agents is continuing and substances which are more than 3000 times as sweet as sugar have been reported. However, there is no sign that such new sweeteners are likely to be used in food in the near future.

Flour improvers. There is a remarkable difference between present-day bread and the unleavened bread of earlier days. One has a light open texture and an even white colour while the other is brownish, heavy and rather hard. These very different products are both made from flour and water, unleavened bread being made from these ingredients alone whilst with the other a number of additives are employed. The most obvious additives used in bread are salt to improve taste and yeast to aerate the dough. The use of these two additives is hallowed by long tradition and they are generally considered therefore to be above suspicion. The modern loaf, however, could not be made unless certain other additives were used and it is against these that objection is sometimes made.

Freshly milled flour has a slight yellow tinge and yields a weak dough that produces poor bread. This has been known for many years and in the past it was overcome by storing the flour for several months before using it to make bread. During storage atmospheric oxygen acts on some of the proteins which form the dough to give the latter increased strength and elasticity; it also produces a whiter loaf. As we mentioned earlier certain unscrupulous bakers used to add alum to flour to give it a white colour.

It was discovered that the long storage period required to produce flour suitable for making bread could be dispensed with if the flour was treated with small quantities of substances known as "flour improvers". Before 1946 the most widely used flour improver in Britain was Agene (nitrogen trichloride), but at that time it was discovered that dogs fed on flour which had been treated with Agene developed fits. It was shown that the fits were induced by a substance formed by action of Agene on one of the amino acids in flour. Although extensive feeding trials failed to produce any evidence that Agene-treated flour produced any harmful effects on men, Agene was withdrawn and its use is no longer permitted.

Most bread made today uses flour that has been treated with flour improvers such as potassium bromate and ammonium persulphate. The exact way in which flour improvers work is not known, but it seems likely that they join some protein molecules together so increasing their molecular weight. Such an increase in molecular complexity would be expected to produce an increase in the strength of the dough. Certain flour improvers, such as chlorine dioxide (Dyox), not only improve the flour but also bleach it, giving it the desired white colour. Where flour improvers which are not bleaching agents are used, a bleaching agent such as benzoyl peroxide may be added.

Although some people prefer to think of bread as a natural food—whatever that may be—the fact remains that if fresh bread is to be made generally available in the form of the white loaf that most people prefer, some additives must be used in its manufacture. In addition to flour improvers and bleaching agents, anti-staling agents are often used in bread-making. In fresh bread the starch molecules are arranged in a completely haphazard and random manner, whereas in stale bread they are arranged in a more orderly way. Anti-staling agents may act by combining with components of starch in such a way as to prevent the starch molecules from taking up an orderly arrangement. As mentioned earlier, calcium, iron and vitamins are also added to white flour to increase its nutritional value.

In recent years many new uses have been found for additives reflecting continuing technological innovation within the Food Industry. Thus *propellant* and *packaging gases, humectants, anti-caking agents, anti-foaming agents, firming agents, liquid freezants* and *release agents* are but some of the new types now recognised. Although some of these names may sound a little mysterious, their uses are easy to appreciate. Humectants, for example, are substances that absorb moisture and so can reduce the effect of humidity on a food such as baking powder. Anti-caking agents help prevent particles of food from adhering to each other to improve their flow properties during processing while firming agents keep the tissues of fruit and vegetables crisp and firm. Inert gases are added to packets of instant food, such as dried potato, to prevent oxidative changes that would occur if air was present.

The Ethics of Using Food Additives

As we said at the beginning of our discussion, the subject of food additives is one which provokes many people to strong emotional responses. Indeed people who eagerly swallow comparatively large amounts of chemicals in the form of patent medicines allow their imaginations to run riot when they contemplate eating comparatively small amounts of chemical additives in their food. However, the examples of food additives given earlier should serve as a basis for a rational discussion of the ethics of using food additives.

The examples already given should be sufficient to demonstrate that food additives often fulfil a useful function. Indeed, if we accept that our present way of living—in which most people are part of large urban communities—is to continue, and that living standards will rise, then food additives are more than useful: they are essential. Moreover, as consumer demand becomes more sophisticated, the amounts of food additives used must increase. This pattern is already apparent from the growing number of food products available and the increasing demand for additives by manufacturers. The total number of additives now available and permitted in food approaches the very large number of three thousand. The largest group of additives is that comprising natural and synthetic flavours of which over 1,300 are permitted in food. This reflects the prime importance given to flavours by the Food Industry and the great advances made in identifying the tiny amounts of numerous chemicals present in natural flavours. The results of such analyses have allowed much improved synthetic flavours to be formulated.

Although the number of additives used in food is large and increasing, the actual amounts consumed are extremely small. In a year a person in Great Britain eats only about 3 lb. of additives and in the U.S.A. only slightly more. Although added colour is one of the prominent additives in present day convenience foods annual consumption per person is only about 1/7 oz. so that in an average life time our total consumption only amounts to 10 oz.

People who condemn the whole idea of using food additives often do so on the grounds that it involves "tampering" with food, so making it unwholesome in some way. Such "natural food" addicts are not just idealists, they are very confused, for they fail to realize that many traditional foods which they would regard as "natural foods" are often very far from being in their natural state. It is just that the chemicals used in their treatment have been used for so long and become so familiar that they are no longer thought of as additives.

Such processes as salting, smoking and pickling carried out to preserve food, and the addition of natural flavouring and colouring agents to make it more attractive have been carried out for so long that they are regarded as natural and harmless. Yet in reality they are in exactly the same category as additives of more recent origin and the same rigorous standards of testing should be applied. Such testing was recently applied to *safrole*, a flavouring agent extracted from sassafras bark and used for many years in America to flavour root beer. The tests revealed that this traditional additive could produce liver cancer in rats and its use was therefore prohibited.

From a rational point of view the use of additives in food is acceptable provided that they serve some useful purpose and are not harmful. A joint committee of the Food and Agriculture Organization (FAO) and the World Health Organization (WHO) which considered this problem came to the conclusion that the use of additives was justified where they fulfilled one or more of the following functions:

1. maintaining nutritional quality of food;
2. enhancing keeping quality or stability with a reduction of food wastage;
3. making food more attractive to the consumer in a manner which does not lead to deception; and
4. providing essential aids to processing.

These different functions can be illustrated in terms of the different additives used in flour. The addition of mineral elements and vitamins to flour serves to compensate for losses incurred during milling; anti-staling agents improve keeping quality; bleaching agents produce a white flour that is attractive to the consumer and, finally, the use of flour improvers aids processing by reducing the time taken for the flour to mature. Without the use of these additives large-scale manufacture of the type of loaf that the public finds attractive would be impossible.

To accept the use of food additives where they clearly confer one of the benefits mentioned above is not to approve their wholesale use or any use at all unless it is carefully controlled. In the past such control has been inadequate and has been the cause of some health hazards. The possible hazards of using Agene as a flour improver and safrole as a flavouring agent have already been mentioned. Many other examples of food products being banned after they have been used for a considerable time could be mentioned. For example, a considerable number of food colours have been withdrawn because it was found that, when taken in large amounts, they produced harmful effects on test animals. A substance called *coumarin* was used in America for nearly 75 years in synthetic vanilla flavours before it was banned when it was found to cause liver damage in rats and dogs.

The control of additives in food is being gradually improved and tightened and testing procedures are becoming more rigorous. In Britain, all matters relating to the composition, description, labelling and advertising of food are considered by the Food Standards Committee. This committee has published a large number of reports on a wide range of foods and additives, and it is clear from these reports that the safety of all additives is very carefully considered. Although these reports have no legal authority they often form the basis of legislation which imposes legal obligations on food manufacturers and others. Such legislation lays down what additives may be used in food, and often defines the maximum amounts that may be present in individual foods.

Britain is now a member of the European Economic Community which intends to harmonise the food laws of member countries. Such laws are prescribed in the form of legally binding Regulations and less obligatory Directives. The process of harmonising the food laws of the U.K. with those of the EEC is a complex and lengthy one, but the first of such new legislation relating to additives, namely colouring matters, preservatives and antioxidants, have already been issued. In due time Britain's membership of the EEC will bring many changes to existing food legislation.

In order to try to formulate food standards on an international basis the FAO and WHO have set up a permanent commission known as the *Codex Alimentarius*. The subject of food additives and contaminants is to be given particular attention and it is to be hoped that such an international body will contribute to improving food standards all over the world.

Finally it must be made clear that in certain circumstances additives should be banned. It is often very difficult to know where to draw the line because the benefits of using a particular additive may be very evenly matched with the disadvantages. In general, it seems to be wisest to err on the side of caution and to ban an additive which is a borderline case. The WHO/FAO committee which considered the question came to the conclusion that situations in which the use of additives would not be in the interest of the consumer, and should not be permitted, include the following:

1. when faulty processing and handling techniques are disguised;
2. when the consumer is deceived; or
3. when the result is a substantial reduction in the nutritive value of a food.

The use of additives for the purposes outlined above deserves nothing but condemnation. Although such additives may be completely harmless, their use cannot be condoned because instead of conferring some benefit they deceive the consumer. Such blatant deceptions as the addition of alum and sieved potatoes to flour, drugs to alcoholic beverages and sulphuric acid to vinegar, are happily things of the past. Nevertheless, some present practices are not above suspicion, though they may take a sophisticated form. For example, it is possible to create a food product that gives an impression of richness while having little nutritional value. Synthetic cream and meringues made largely from cellulose derivatives come into this category. Again, additives may be used to give a food some property that the consumer associates with the presence of traditional ingredients. The addition of yellow colouring matter to cakes, for instance, gives an impression of richness that is traditionally associated with the presence of eggs. Colour may also be added to processed foods to give an impression of high quality and freshness. Green colouring matter may be added to canned dried peas so that they simulate the colour of fresh ones. Indeed, the colour of some canned peas is a good deal brighter and greener than that of the freshest of garden peas!

In conclusion we may say that additives may be harmful or beneficial, they may promote or hinder good nutrition. As we cannot live in modern society without them, we must ensure that their use is controlled so as to gain the benefits while eliminating the abuses.

Suggestions for Further Reading

ACCUM, F. *Treatise on Adulterations of Food, 1820.* Re-issued by Mallinckodt, USA, 1966.

BIRCH, G. G. et al. (Ed.) *Sweetness and Sweeteners*, Applied Science Publishers, 1971. A Symposium Report.
FAO/WHO *Report on Pesticide Residues*, HMSO, 1973
FURIA, T. E. (Ed.) *Handbook of Food Additives*, Chemical Rubber Co., U.S.A., 2nd edn., 1972. A comprehensive account.
GOODWIN, R. W. L. (Ed.) *Chemical Additives in Food*, Churchill, 1967.
LUCAS, J. *Our Polluted Food*, Charles Knight, 1975.
PYKE, M. *Technological Eating*, Murray, 1972.
Royal College of Physicians, *Fluoride, Teeth and Health*, Pitman Medical, 1976.
SPENCER, M. *Food Additives*, Postgraduate Medical Journal, 1974. 50, 620.
SPENCER, M. Chemical changes during cooking, processing and storage of food, *Nutrition and Food Science*, 1973 (April), II.

CHAPTER 10

Fads, Fallacies and the Future

FOOD is not just a basic necessity of life; it is something that is woven into the fabric of life in many different ways and it has great significance apart from its food value. Eating is not just a nutritional exercise; it is a social occupation and it forms an indispensable part of hospitality in all parts of the world. We may or may not subscribe to the Indian belief that food cooked with love tastes better than food cooked with indifference, but we recognize that emotional forces do play a part in our attitude to food. It seems probable that fads and fallacies play a greater role in determining our views about food and eating than in any other sphere of our lives.

In primitive societies, taboos, religion, prejudice and magic all have an important influence on what is or is not eaten. Magnus Pyke in *Food and Society* records that "The Abipones of Paraguay eat jaguars, bulls and stags to make them strong, brave and swift—and avoid eating hens and tortoises for fear of becoming cowardly and slow; the Miris of Assam prize tigers' flesh to make themselves fierce—but forbid it to their women; the Kansas Indians relish dogs' flesh on the grounds that by eating it they become brave and faithful. Caribs abstain from pigs' flesh lest their eyes become small, and the Aino people of Japan, who believe the otter to be a forgetful animal, refuse to eat it lest by doing so they lose their memory!"

Tradition and prejudice, rather than reason, are important factors in determining what people in under-developed countries will or will not eat and this often has unfortunate results. For example, recent years have witnessed some tragic famines in India the basic cause of which has been the failure of the rice crop that provides the basis of the local diet. Even in these extreme circumstances attempts by famine-relief workers to substitute wheat for rice have failed due, in part at least, to the people's dislike and suspicion of an unfamiliar food. In Malay villages young children suffer from lack of protein and one might assume that this is because high protein foods, such as meat, fish and eggs, are scarce because of their high cost. Such a rational explanation is quite untrue, however, the real reasons being prejudice and lack of understanding. Mothers are prejudiced against fish because they believe it gives the children worms and, through lack of understanding, they spice their meat to such an extent that their children cannot eat much of it.

In developing countries where the educational standard is low, it is to be expected that nutritional knowledge will also be low and it is inevitable that custom and prejudice will prevail. It may be hopefully assumed, however, that in advanced countries—where information about nutrition has been more widely disseminated—decisions about diet will be governed by sound nutritional knowledge. Such hopes are unfortunately often proved to be groundless. Indeed, in nutrition, as in other spheres, people's actions are often in direct conflict with their knowledge. For example, the connection between smoking and lung cancer is widely appreciated and yet this knowledge has done nothing, or almost nothing, to reduce the amount of tobacco and cigarettes smoked. People who believe that certain foods are nutritionally good often reject such foods in favour of others that they believe to be inferior. For example, four out of five people believe that brown bread is better than white and yet nine out of ten people actually eat white bread in preference to brown!

It might be supposed that America, with its high standard of living and intensive educational system, would be the home of wise dietary decisions based on sound nutritional views. Yet in practice this does not seem to be altogether true, and a recent report suggests that modern media are widely used to spread misleading nutritional information. It is suggested that of all forms of quackery prevalent in America today that relating to nutrition is the most thriving. For example, fashion and nutritional misinformation, rather than informed opinion, have been the cause of the slimming craze. Sensational gimmickry was the cause of the rise and fall of chlorophyll as a desirable ingredient of toothpaste and certain foods. It is evident from these examples that education and knowledge are not in themselves effective in motivating our actions.

How many people, when questioned about what motivates them in the selection of the food they eat, could honestly say "Nutritional knowledge"? The answer is, very few indeed. Most people would agree that factors such as price, appearance, taste, smell and palatability affect their choice of food, but there are other less obvious factors which also play a part although they may go unrecognized. The subconscious effects of advertising condition us to select a particular food, or a particular brand in preference to another; psychologists have studied our reactions to different sizes, shapes and colours and food manufacturers design their packaging accordingly. Our own personal likes and dislikes will also affect our choice. The conclusion is that though some of us may like to think that we are governed by reason and nutritional knowledge, the facts suggest that this is true to only a small extent.

In Britain, attempts at improving nutritional education are hindered by an anti-scientific, back-to-nature pressure group which is still active and whose views are still given credence. Parts of the national press still favour emotional and sensational discussion of food topics. The following headings are typical of the emotional approach favoured by one popular author:

Murdered Food
Modern bread—Public Enemy No. 1
The poisons on your plate
Health-destroying white bread

The same author quotes as the unalterable law of sound nutrition that "only those substances which are of plant or animal origin should be used as food". In other words such people believe that the only acceptable sort of food is "natural" food. To them vitamin C in an orange is in a different, and altogether more desirable, category from vitamin C made in the laboratory, even though both substances are identical in all respects.

As we saw in the last chapter there is a good deal of confusion about the concept of a "natural" food. It seems that to most people a food which is traditional and to which they are accustomed is "natural" while anything new is "unnatural". On this basis bread baked at home using wholemeal flour without the aid of flour improvers or other additives is a good example of a natural food. If in addition the flour was grown without the use of any chemical fertilizers or other artificial aid then it becomes a perfect example. Our rather odd views about what is natural and what is unnatural are well illustrated by the old lady who was asked what she thought about people travelling to the moon. She replied, quite seriously, "I don't thinks its natural. People should stay at home and watch television as the Good Lord intended."

Those who favour "natural" foods argue that not only should they be of plant or animal origin, but that they should be grown in a "natural" way, that is, only organic manures and composts should be used. It is true that fertile soil contains humus composed of organic material derived from decaying plant and animal matter, but it also contains mineral salts. Moreover, it is this inorganic material that provides the nutrients needed to support plant life. Both organic and inorganic matter are present in fertile soil and where a soil is rich in humus but deficient in mineral elements it seems irrational to object to the addition of these inorganic elements to the soil in the form of artificial fertilizers. The argument against "unnatural" fertilizers is based on the fallacy that substances such as ammonium salts which are made naturally in the soil differ in some mysterious way from the same salt made in the laboratory.

The rational position about organic manures and composts is that, while they are invaluable for food production, they are available in such limited amounts that if we relied on them entirely we should be unable to maintain, still less expand, food production. In these circumstances, the use of synthetic fertilizers is not only desirable; it is essential.

The argument of "natural" versus "unnatural" is a false one and a product of muddled thinking. For example, the merits or otherwise of the rearing of chickens on mass-production lines instead of on free-range can be argued on various grounds. We can argue that one is more cruel than the other, that the birds, or their eggs, are more tasty or of higher nutritional value when the birds are reared in a particular way. But because the selective breeding of chickens for eating or for egg production is in itself an artificial process it is not meaningful to argue that one method is "natural" and that the other is "unnatural".

Vegetarianism

When the "natural" versus "unnatural" argument is applied to diet it takes the form that animal foods are "unnatural" while vegetable foods are "natural". There are, of course, many other arguments put forward in support of vegetarianism. Some people believe that a vegetarian diet is more healthy than a mixed one, others think that the slaughter of animals for eating is unethical, and some people are prohibited from eating certain animals because of their religious beliefs. Prejudice and taboos may also deter people from eating certain animal foods.

Strict vegetarians eat no food whatever that is of animal origin. This means that eggs, milk, cheese, butter, fish and meat are all avoided.

Planning a satisfactory diet for such people is rather like planning a journey for someone who will not travel by road, rail or air! The main difficulty of planning a strictly vegetarian diet is that, because animal protein cannot be used, very few sources of high-quality protein are available. It will be remembered from Chapter 3 that high-quality protein foods furnish all the essential amino acids in approximately the proportions needed by the body. On the whole, most vegetable proteins—with certain notable exceptions such as soya beans—are of low quality. This does not mean that protein needs cannot be met using vegetable protein alone, but it does mean that the vegetables used need to be chosen with care. A vegetable in which certain essential amino acids are missing needs to be supplemented by others rich in them.

The world shortage of animal protein has prompted much research into ways of making mixtures of vegetable protein having both high protein content and high protein quality. One of the earliest of such mixtures, known as "Incaparina", contains about 25% protein, whose quality compares well with proteins of animal origin. Incaparina mixtures are based on ground, cooked, maize to which cottonseed and soyabean flours are added together with certain minerals and vitamins. Although Incaparina, and other similar vegetable mixtures, have been developed as a means of overcoming the world shortage of animal protein, they show that it is possible for strict vegetarians to satisfy their protein needs.

Vegetarian diets suffer from being very bulky, because they rely heavily on carbohydrate-rich foods with a high water content. Such foods are not only deficient in protein but often in mineral elements and vitamins as well, so that constant care is needed to maintain a good balance in the diet. The majority of vegetarians, however, exclude only animal flesh from their diet and continue to eat such animal products as cheese, butter, milk and eggs. This makes it relatively easy to plan a balanced diet, and vegetarian diets of this sort do not differ greatly from ordinary ones except that cheese, being a concentrated high-quality protein source, is relied on to a greater extent than in normal diets and nuts and soya foods are used as additional sources of protein.

Slimming

Many people slim for the simple reason that it is fashionable to be slim, and, because slimming is "in", endless pages of print have been devoted to the subject. In the spate of information and opinions a good deal of misinformation has been included and some very odd notions are prevalent. It remains a fact that many people are too fat and this is objectionable because, apart from aesthetic reasons, it imposes a strain on the heart and other organs. Statistics show that for men who are 10% overweight the risk of death is increased by 13%, while for those who are 30% overweight the risk is increased by 42%.

The figures given above show that for many people slimming is not desirable only as a matter of fashion but also as a matter of health. Traditional slimming methods are mainly concerned with reducing Calorie intake by cutting down the amount of food eaten. The theory behind this is that people become fat when the energy intake derived from food is greater than the total energy output. The food which is surplus to the body's energy requirements is stored as fat in the fat depots of the body. In this connection it is important to reiterate the fact that it is not only fatty foods which contribute to fat reserves. Excess carbohydrate can be broken down into fatty acids which can then be built up into fat molecules. This is illustrated by the following verse;

> Jack Sprat could eat no fat,
> His wife could eat no lean,
> But both got fat from eating sugar,
> Strange as this may seem.

It is evident that fat reserves may be depleted by reducing the Calorie intake to below the output. Alternatively, the Calorie input can be maintained and the output increased by the performance of more physical work. Unfortunately the latter method may not produce the desired result because vigorous exercise tends to increase the desire for food and drink, the satisfaction of which may well involve an intake of Calories greater than those expended.

The results of recent research suggest that the simple traditional theory of obesity outlined above does not present the complete picture. It seems to be an over-simplification to suggest that one theory can be applied to everyone. It appears that on the one hand some people do not grow fat even when they eat large amounts of food while on the other hand some people grow fat easily. It is believed that people who do not grow fat easily are able to increase the rate at which their bodies use food when they eat more, while those who do grow fat easily have difficulty in using up carbohydrate for producing energy and convert carbohydrate into fat rather than into energy.

In planning any slimming diet the aim is to achieve an efficient and attractive diet that differs as little as possible from a "normal" diet. For those who convert carbohydrate into fat rather than energy this can be done by severe limitation or elimination of carbohydrate without limitation of either fat or protein. Although such a diet would not be desirable for normal people—who need carbohydrate to ensure that fat is completely broken down—it seems to be satisfactory for most fat people. Such a diet can be made both palatable and attractive and it has the additional merit that although carbohydrate consumption must be reduced, the overall intake of food is not limited.

Most people who slim by changing their eating habits adopt a low-carbohydrate diet. Table 10.1, which is based on a survey involving nearly 400 people, shows that 83% cut down on starchy foods and 20% cut out or reduced the amount of sugar that they added to their food. Sugar is the most obvious food to cut down because, being pure carbohydrate, it contributes nothing but Calories to the diet, whereas starchy foods such as bread and potatoes contribute other nutrients such as protein, vitamins and minerals as well as Calories.

TABLE 10.1. CHANGES MADE IN FOOD HABITS BY SLIMMERS

Change made	Men (%)	Women (%)	Total (%)
Eat less starchy foods	80	85	83
Eat less or cut out sugar	20	20	20
Eat less	17	14	15
Eat special slimming foods	13	14	14
Eat more fruit	9	12	11
Cut down fluids	10	5	6
Cut down meals	1	3	2

J. C. McKenzie

It is a simple and inescapable fact that people get too fat because their Calorie intake is too big. Any attempt at slimming must be based on a reduction in the intake of Calories. If this is achieved simply by reducing food consumption the slimmer will feel perpetually hungry and will not be inclined to continue the diet for long. The result is that the slimming diet, originally undertaken with enthusiasm, is soon given up in despair and little, if any, lasting benefit results. It is to be regretted that many of the gimmicky and fashionable diets proposed in popular papers are of this sort. The very term "slimming diet" is probably unfortunate because it suggests something artificial whereas, to be effective, slimming must involve a permanent change in everyday eating habits.

There are several other methods of slimming which may be used to supplement the basic one of changing eating habits. One rather drastic and artificial method is to adopt a *formula diet*; that is one which is calculated to contain sufficient of all nutrients to maintain health but which supplies less than the required number of Calories. Such diets have the merit that they can be exactly controlled, but they are very monotonous because they are based on a single food. Such formula diets are available as drinks, powders and biscuits and are usually made from high protein foods, such as soya flour and skim milk powder to which minerals, vitamins and some carbohydrates are added. Formula diets are so different from normal diets that they cannot be maintained for long and they are best regarded as "shock treatment" aimed at breaking bad eating habits so that new and better ones can be established.

Use of the synthetic sweetening agent saccharin, discussed in the last chapter, makes it possible to replace sugar in foods by substitutes having no Calorific value. Low-Calorie foods, such as fruit drinks, confectionery and canned fruit, are readily available and can be used to reduce Calorie intake without inconvenience. When fruit is canned or jam is made without sugar, some substance must be added to give the food "body". Substances such as glycerol or sorbitol are sometimes used for this purpose, in which case the Calorific value of the food may be just as high as if it had been made with sugar. Although such foods are useless for slimming purposes, they are useful for diabetics.

Some materials give bulk and body to food without adding to its Calorific value, and such substances are obviously important in devising products for slimming. Agar and alginates, both extracted from seaweed, cellulose, and pectins obtained from fruit, are used for this purpose. These are all polysaccharides which pass through the body without being digested and so have no food value. They are used to give body to "syrups" used with canned fruits, to thicken ice-cream and synthetic cream and whips, and to add bulk to low-Calorie foods.

The replacement of energy foods by bulk having no Calorific value reaches its logical conclusion in the production of "foods" which provide bulk but which have no nutritional value whatever. These are not foods at all in the true sense of the word but, because they fill the stomach, they reduce desire for food. A derivative of cellulose used for this purpose is able to absorb fifty times its weight of water and once it has been consumed it swells in the stomach and gives a feeling of fullness. The danger of such preparations is that they lead to a reduction not only of Calories, but of all other nutrients as well. Some of these preparations are fortified with vitamins, but even so they should only be taken under proper supervision.

Finally, drugs are available which aid slimming either by depressing appetite or by increasing the rate at which the body breaks down food. The use of such drugs is potentially hazardous and they should never be taken except on medical advice.

Whatever method of slimming is chosen—and four out of five slimmers change their diet—there is a good chance of failure. Nearly half of those who try to slim do not succeed and it is interesting that the reason they give for failing is rarely that the method adopted did not work. Most of the failures blame themselves; either they gave up too soon, or they did not follow the method laid down—or they simply did not have enough will power to keep going.

Fallacies abound in the realm of slimming, but one of the strangest fallacies is that there are some foods which, if eaten, actually make you slim. This is, of course, complete nonsense—eating food can make you fat but it cannot possibly make you slim—hence there are several restrictions on claims for slimming foods; it is a complete contradiction in terms. There are pills and potions that can be bought without prescription which some people believe can make you slim and slimming claims are made for some lotions and creams which you can rub into your skin; there are special garments on the market which claim that they can help to make you slim. All such claims are fallacious as is the idea that Turkish or other types of steam-bath can make you slim. Such baths can certainly make you lose weight through loss of sweat, but you will equally certainly put the weight back again by extra drinking afterwards.

Food and the Future

Can it be doubted that the greatest world problem—greater even than that of maintaining peace—is that of ensuring that every human being is adequately fed? In answering this question it needs to be remembered that although adequate food is the most basic of human requirements,

FADS, FALLACIES AND THE FUTURE   175

about one-half of the world population is hungry (while in contrast some well-developed countries have surpluses of basic foods such as wheat and butter). Figures relating to the rate at which the world population is expanding have been repeated so often that they tend to be taken for granted and treated with complacency. As a background to our discussion it is enough to be reminded that tomorrow there will be about 140,000 extra mouths to feed compared with today.

Even a superficial survey of the problem is enough to convince one of its immensity and complexity. Many ways of increasing food production are being tried; making better use of existing land, creating more arable land, introducing mechanization, applying mass-production methods to crops, fish and animals—these are but a few of them. In our present discussion we are concerned, however, not so much with ways of increasing output as with ways of making better use of the available food. The advance of science is making it possible to devise new methods of processing and preserving food and it is also leading to the evolution of new foods. Although these new methods and new foods are still in the process of being developed, it is to be hoped that some of them at least will soon be making a significant contribution to solving the "hunger problem".

New Ways of Preserving Foods

Freeze-drying, discussed in Chapter 6, is an example of a recently developed method of preservation that has gained general acceptance and which is being exploited commercially at the present time. Another method of preservation is currently being developed though, unlike freeze-drying, it has not as yet gained general acceptance; it is known as *irradiation*. The name itself is enough to give rise to suspicion as it has unpleasant associations for many people and, as pointed out in the last chapter, radiation from nuclear explosions can have harmful effects on the human body. On the other hand, we also need to realize that even without nuclear explosions we are subject to some radiation effects, as these are a natural part of our environment. Such effects give rise to naturally radioactive carbon and potassium in our bodies, though the amounts present are so minute as to cause us no detectable harm.

The amounts of natural radiation received by our bodies are minute compared with the amounts required to preserve food and it is because such large doses of radiation are needed that it is so important to investigate carefully this new method of food preservation before allowing it to be used on a large scale. Much research has already been done and in the United States irradiation of food is now permitted for selected purposes. In Great Britain, however, irradiation of food intended for human consumption is not yet allowed.

Irradiation of food is carried out by exposing the food to high-energy radiation which penetrates it and brings about certain changes within the food. The radiation may either be in the form of a beam of negatively charged particles—electrons—which are accelerated to very high speeds or it may be in the form of electromagnetic radiation known as gamma rays, which are similar to X-rays, except that they have a much greater penetrating power. When such radiation penetrates food it brings about various desirable effects. For example, it kills micro-organisms and insects that contaminate the food and it reduces sprouting in stored potatoes. In addition irradiation has the merit that it produces no heating effect and can be applied to food after it has been packed into containers made of a wide range of packaging materials.

It is important to know how irradiation affects the nutritional properties of food, and experiments show that losses of nutrients are small and roughly similar to those incurred during cooking or canning. It is also important that we should know if the consumption of irradiated food could prove harmful in any way. It might be suspected, for example, that if food is treated with large doses of radiation it might itself become radioactive. Experiments carried out to test this idea show that if moderate doses of radiation are used, no induced radioactivity can be detected. On the other hand, if very high doses of radiation are used, it is thought that induced radioactivity might constitute a health hazard. It is evident, therefore, that any use of radiation for preservation must be subject to careful control.

Finally, it must be admitted that the high hopes entertained for preserving food by irradiation have not been realized. This is largely due to the effect which the radiation has on the taste and smell of food. The radiation used is of such high energy that it brings about chemical changes in food which often result in a marked deterioration of taste and smell. These changes may not only be unpleasant but also harmful, though so far no evidence of such toxic effects has been observed. In the long term, when the snags of this new method of preservation have been ironed out, radiation should be able to make a useful contribution to increasing food supplies.

New Ways of Processing Food

Protein, particularly animal protein, is one of the most expensive nutrients and, on a world-wide basis, is in short-supply. As was mentioned in Chapter 3 one of the most serious deficiency diseases in poor and developing countries is *kwashiorkor*, and this unpleasant disease which afflicts so many African children results from not eating enough protein. As we mentioned earlier in the chapter, the current world shortage of animal protein has stimulated much research into ways of making vegetable protein mixtures of high nutritional value. Whereas animal protein is in short supply thousands of tons of vegetable protein, in the form of grasses and oilseed residues, for example, go to waste, and successful attempts at converting such waste materials into edible protein have been made.

The reason why vegetable materials such as grass are not eaten is that they consist largely of cellulose which man is unable to digest. Coconuts, copra and grasses are available in large amounts and although all these materials contain a large proportion of indigestible fibre or cellulose, the protein can be extracted from them. Methods for extraction are still being developed and have not yet been used on a large scale. One difficulty is that the protein concentrate produced is not very appetizing as it lacks both taste and smell. In addition it is usually lacking in one or more essential amino acids, though this drawback can be overcome by blending proteins from different sources, or by the addition of the missing amino acids in synthetic form.

Huge amounts of vegetable material are grown to provide edible vegetable oil for making margarine and other fats. After the oil has been extracted from the vegetable matter a residue rich in protein is left. At present residues of this sort are used as animal food or fertilizer or even thrown away as waste. It has been estimated that the amount of protein contained in such oilseed residues is sufficient to provide twice the world's deficit of protein. Soya beans, groundnuts and cottonseed are the chief materials available and, provided that the oil is expressed with care and any harmful materials removed, the residue that is left can be milled to form an edible flour containing as much as 50% protein. As with protein concentrates obtained from coconuts and similar sources, the quality of the protein needs to be improved by adding synthetic amino acids or by blending different protein flours to ensure that all the essential amino acids are present in suitable proportions. Various products of this type have been developed and Incaparina, mentioned earlier in the chapter, is commercially available.

Although the quality of protein in most vegetable material is low, that of soya beans is an exception. Soya beans, and soya bean flour, have been a valuable source of high quality protein in the diets of Japan and China for many centuries, and they are now being cultivated increasingly in other countries, particularly in the United States. Although soya beans are grown primarily as a source of vegetable oil, new methods of processing them have been developed. One of the greatest problems associated with new protein sources is the difficulty of getting them accepted by the people who would benefit from eating them. In order to try and circumvent such difficulties soya-bean flour is used to make products resembling meat. Two types of product are available; the cheaper is usually called textured vegetable protein (TVP) and is made by converting the flour into a dough and extruding it through a nozzle at a high temperature and pressure which produces the desired texture. Alternatively the protein from the soya beans is spun into fibres which have a slight resemblance to meat fibres, and these are moulded into suitable meat-like shapes and textures, such as cutlets. After adding various ingredients such as fats, flavourings and colours the mixture is cooked.

Vegetable proteins are regularly used in schools, hospitals and canteens usually as a meat extender to replace part of the meat in traditional dishes. It is recommended (Food Standards Committee, 1974) that in the U.K. not more than 10% of meat should be replaced by vegetable protein, though in the U.S.A. the limit is 30%. Vegetable proteins are also being used as components of simulated meat products such as stews, curries and burger and burger-style dried mixes. Although previously found mainly in Health Food Stores such products are now available in supermarkets.

New Types of Food

Writers, whose undoubted enthusiasm has not been matched by an equal sense of proportion, have raised many false hopes about the development and use of new foods. Much development and research have gone into ways of making new foods, and many of the biological and chemical problems associated with their manufacture have been overcome. While these scientific advances are undoubtedly important, other factors —particularly economic and sociological ones—are equally important.

In short, though many novel foods can be made, they often cannot be made cheaply enough or attractively enough for them to contribute much to the world's need for more food. Those who fear the day when our diet will be reduced to a little pile of tablets may be reassured to know that the dreaded day lies in the indefinitely remote future.

One method of making new food is based on the principle that unicellular organisms such as yeast, algae and fungi may be cultivated on liquids just as more conventional plants may be grown on land. Indeed there are certain places in the world where this is already done and in a remote part of the Sahara, for example, the inhabitants collect a green slime made up of millions of minute algae. The slime, which grows at the surface of ponds and lakes, is dried in the sun and the powder formed is used as the basis of soup. Although this food may not sound particularly appetizing, it is nevertheless a rich source of high-quality protein!

The advantage of using algae, or similar minute organisms, as a source of protein is, firstly, that they can be cultivated in media which are cheap, and secondly that they multiply very rapidly. At present various types of industrial waste are being used as media and these include molasses and waste hydrocarbons produced during oil refining. Several of the major oil companies have built large-scale protein-from-oil plants, and have successfully reared cattle and poultry using the products.

Chemical methods for making new foods have been developed to a greater extent than any other, and every type of nutrient can now be synthesized. For example, several vitamins can be made synthetically even though they are complex substances and some foods, such as margarine and bread, contain added vitamins of synthetic origin. Amino acids can also be synthesized and, as we mentioned earlier in this chapter, they are added to vegetable protein foods which are deficient in certain essential amino acids. Although many of the chemical problems of making vitamins and amino acids, and also of fats and carbohydrates, have been solved, the methods of making them have not been developed on a large scale, because they cannot compete economically with the corresponding natural product.

Synthetic food has been made in large quantities only when economic factors have been of secondary importance. This occurred in Germany during World War II when fatty acids were made from hydrocarbons derived from coal or petroleum. The fatty acids were combined with glycerol obtained synthetically from petroleum to form fat. The fat was of inferior quality and some people suffered ill effects from eating it; it was only used because the circumstances made it necessary.

Many times in the past the progress of science has caused men to think that science alone can solve all their problems. An example occurred in France in the last century. The following is a slightly paraphrased extract from a speech made by the Emperor Napoleon to the Paris Chamber of Commerce in 1811. "I am informed from recent experiments that France will be able to do without the sugar and indigo of the two Indies. Chemistry has made such progress in this country that it will be able to bring about as great a change in our commerce as the discovery of the compass. I do not say, gentlemen, that I do not wish for maritime commerce and colonies, but we can abandon these for the time being, until England returns to just and honourable principles, or until I can dictate to her terms of peace."

The fact is that in France and every other Western country we are not only unable to do without natural sugar, but comsumption of it continues to increase by leaps and bounds. It is true that we have the scientific ability to synthesize sugar and many other foods, but the evidence available suggests that the contribution which such foods will make to satisfy the world's urgent need for more food will only be on a small scale. Scientific marvels can nowadays be achieved—as witness the sending of men to the moon—and are only dependent on man's will. In terms of science the problems of overcoming world hunger can certainly be overcome. In terms of man's will it is not at all certain that they will be overcome. If men willed it, not only could science be harnessed to improving the world's food supply but available food could be used in a much more rational and equitable way. It is not science that will decide— it is us.

Suggestions for Further Reading

BIRCH, G. G., PARKER, K. J., WORGAN, J. T. (Eds.) *Food from Waste,* Applied Science Publishers, 1975. A Symposium Report.
CAMERON, A. G. *Food: Facts and Fallacies,* Faber and Faber, 1971. A detailed discussion of some of the topics dealt with in Chapters 9 and 10.
CRADDOCK, D. *Obesity and its Management,* Churchill Livingstone, 1973.
DAVIS, P. (Ed.) *Single Cell Protein,* Academic Press, 1974.
JONES, A. *World Protein Resources,* Medical and Technical Publishing Co., 1974.
MINISTRY OF AGRICULTURE, FISHERIES AND FOOD. *Food Standards Committee Report on Novel Protein Foods,* HMSO, 1974.

PIRIE, N. W. *Food Resources Conventional and Novel,* Penguin Books, 1969.
PYKE, M. *Food and Society,* Murray, 1968. A stimulating and provocative appraisal of modern attitudes to nutrition.
STAMP, E. *The Hungry World,* E. J. Arnold, 1967. A simply written, well-illustrated account of hunger—its causes and how to overcome it.
YUDKIN, J. *This Slimming Business,* Penguin Books, 4th edn., 1974.

Appendix

METRIC AND IMPERIAL UNITS

The following table shows how non-metric units may be converted into metric equivalents.

	Non-metric	Metric equivalent
Energy	1 kilocalorie (Cal.)	4200 joules (J) 4·2 kilojoules (kJ)
Temperature	32° Fahrenheit (F) 212° Fahrenheit To convert °F into °C: −32° and then × 5/9	0° Celsius (C) 100° Celsius
Volume	1·8 pints 1 pint 1 gallon	1 litre (l) 1000 millilitres (ml) 568 millilitres 4·5 litres
Weight	1 ounce (oz) 1 pound (lb) 2·2 pounds	28·4 grammes (g) 454 grammes 1 kilogramme (kg)
Length	1 inch (in.) 1 foot (ft) 39·4 inches	2·5 centimetres (cm) 30·5 centimetres 100 centimetres 1 metre (m)

Index

Acetic acid, as a preservative   101–103
Acrolein   118
Additives   6, 153–164
   intentional   156–164
   unintentional   153–156
Adulteration   6, 151–153
Aerobes   91
Aflatoxin   97
Agar, in slimming diets   173
Agene   2, 159, 163
Albumen   149
Alcohol   60, 79
Alcoholic beverages   79–86
Ale   81
Aleurone   56
Algae, as a source of protein   179
Alginates   173
Alimentary system   2, 8, 27, 28
Alum   151, 164
Amino acids   6, 41
   as nutrients   18–21, 31–32
   essential   31, 177
   in flavourings   139
   synthetic   179
   transport of   34–35
Ammonium persulphate   160
Amyl acetate   18
Amylase   33
   pancreatic   34
   salivary   34
Anaemia   48
Anaerobes   91
Animal fats   16
Annatto   144
Anthocyanins, in fruit   143
Anti-caking agents   160
Anti-foaming agents   160
Anti-oxidants   114–115
Anti-staling agents   160, 162
Appert, Nicholas   100
Apples   7, 13, 31

Aroma   137–138
Arsenic   25
Ascorbic acid see Vitamin C
Ash   7, 25
Aspergillus flavus   97
Atheroma   51
Aureomycin   51

Bacillus   97
   mesentericus   97
Bacteria   80, 90, 94–99
   aerobic   91
   anaerobic   91
   and food poisoning   90–94
   and food spoilage   94–97
   pathogens   90
   spirochaete   91
   spores   91
Baking   116–118
   biscuits   120
   bread   60–62
Barley
   diastase in   23
   in brewing   80
Basal metabolism   39
Beef   7, 31
Beer   80
Benedictine   85
Benzoic acid   103
Benzoyl peroxide, in flour   160
Beri-beri   44
Beryllium   87
Beta-carotene   142
   losses in cooking cabbage   127–129
Beverages   79
Bicarbonate   127
Bile, action of   33
Biological value of proteins   41
Biscuits   120
Bitterness   136

"Black spot" on frozen meat 98
Blanching 23
Blancmange 12
Bleaching of flour 160
Boiling 117
Bottling 99–100, 118
Bran 56
Brandy 84, 85
Bread 7, 59–64
  adulteration 152
  as a food 61
  breadmaking methods 60
  Chorleywood process 61
  consumption 63
  crumb softener 62, 64
  deep freezing of 109
  fermentation 60
  G.M.S. in 62, 64
  germ 63
  high protein 63
  home-baked 168
  "rope" in 62, 97
  staling of 112
  wholemeal 61, 62
Bromelin, in pineapple 129
Browning 17
  crust 60–64
  enzymic 110–111, 126
  non-enzymic 122–126, 130
  reaction 23, 28
Butter 17, 68, 156
  fat dispersion in 17
  in vegetarian diets 170

Cabbage 7, 31
  changes in cooking 126
  vitamin loss 128
Caesium 137, 153
  as a contaminant 153
Caffeine 77
Cakes, texture of 149–150
Calcium 4, 154
  added to flour 156
  the need for 48, 49
Calories 29, 30, 38, 39, 79
  intake 171
  requirements 38–40
Calorific value 14, 81
  of carbohydrates 30

  of fats 30
  of proteins 30
Canning 99–101, 118
Caramel 13, 14, 144
Carbohydrates 6, 7, 9, 13, 29, 104
  digestion of 36
  in the diet 37–40
Carbon atoms 6, 16, 18
Carbon dioxide, in champagne 84
Carotene 44, 69
  in margarine 67
Carotenoids 141–142
Catalysts 21
Cellulose 11–13, 174, 175, 177
  derivative, for slimming 174
  in potato 122
Chalk, added to flour 156
Champagne 84
Cheese 7, 17, 31
  in vegetarian diets 170
  manufacture 20
Chemical methods of new foods 179
Chemical preservation 101, 104
Chemicals in food 6, 131–165
Chickens, free range 169
Chicory in coffee 78
Children, protection of 42
Chips, frying 123–125
Chlorination of water 90
Chlorine dioxide, in flour 90, 160
Chlorophyll 126, 141–144
  effect of heat on 126, 127
  in toothpaste and foods 167
Chlortetracycline 103
Chocolate 7, 16
Chorleywood Bread Process 61
Cladosporium herbarum 96
Clostridium
  botulinum 91–94, 100
  welchii 92–93
Cobalamin 25
Cobalt 25, 50
Coca-cola 77
Cocculus indicus 152
Coccus 91
Cochineal 144
Cocoa 79
Coconut oil 66
Coconuts 177

INDEX

Codex alimentarius 164
Collagen 120, 129
Coffee 77, 78
Colloidal solution 146, 148
Colour
  added 144–145
  as an additive 162–163
  in food 164
  natural 141–143
  of food 140–145
Compost for growing food 169
Conduction 115–118
Contaminants 153–156
Convection 115–118
Cooking changes 120–130
  cabbage 126
  chlorophyll changes in 126
Cooking methods 115–120
Copper poisoning 152
Copra 66, 177
Cornstarch 12
Coronary thrombosis 50
Cottonseed 177
  oil 66
Coumarin 136, 163
Cream 17
  adulteration of 152
  in slimming diets 173
Crisps, frying of 123, 125
Cyclamates 2, 136, 158–159

DDT 154
Deep-freezing 109
  of bread 113
Deficiency diseases 50–51
Dehydration 9, 106, 107
  of bacteria 94
  of foods 99–101
  vitamins 25
Denaturation 50
  of proteins 23, 120
Diastase 23
  in flour 59
Dieldrin 154
Dielectric heating 119–120
Diets
  formula 173
  low carbohydrate 172

slimming 172–174
Digestion 23
  of a meal 32–37
Disaccharides 10
Distillation of spirits 84, 85
Double bonds 16, 17
Drambuie 86
Drugs for slimming 174
Dyox see Chlorine dioxide

EEC 163
Edible gums 13
Egg production 168
Eggs 7, 31
  colour of 142
  in vegetarian diets 170
  spoilage 96–97
Egg-white
  changes in cooking 129
  denaturation 20
Elements, trace 25, 26, 48–50
Embryo, of wheatgerm 56–57
Emulsification 13
Emulsifying agents 17, 147, 148
  as additives 161–162
  in margarine 67, 68
Emulsions 147–148
Endosperm 56
Energy 29–30
  reserve depots 30
Enzymes 21–22
  amylase 33
  bromelin 129
  effect of temperature on 107
  lipases 35
  pepsin 31, 33
  sucrase 22
  tenderising 121
  trypsin 31, 33
Essential oils 18
Ethics of using food additives 161

Fats 6, 7, 9, 15–18, 29, 33, 104
  animal 16
  chemistry of 15–18
  cooking in 118
  depot 30
  deterioration of 113–115
  digestion of 35

186 INDEX

flash point 17
frying in 16–17, 118
function in cakes 150
hardening 67, 114, 150
in the diet 39–40
saturated 16
synthetic 178–179
unsaturated 17, 37, 67, 114
vegetable 16
Fatty acids 15–16, 38–49, 114, 118
from hydrocarbons 179
unsaturated 51
Fermentation
in baking 59–62
in brewing 79–80
in manufacture of tea 23
in wine-making 82–83
Firming agents 160
Fish 7, 31
flour as animal protein 177
spoilage 111
Flash point of fat 17
Flavones 143
Flavonoids 141, 143
pigments 143
Flavour
effects of cooking on 138
intensifiers 139–140
Flavouring agents, as additives 161–162
Flavouring oils 17, 18
Flavours
natural 137–138
produced by cooking 138
synthetic 139
Flour
additives in 162
bleaching of 2, 148, 161, 163
fortification of 44
improvers in 159–160
presence of water in 8
production 55–59
Fluoridation of water 157–159
Fluorine 25, 157
the need for 49
Foams 148–149
Food
chemical 110–115
manufacture 55
micro-biological 94–97

new types of 178–179
poisoning 87–90
preservation 97–104
Regulations 1966 144
Standards Committee 164, 178
synthetic 179–180
texture 145
Formaldehyde resins 156
Formula diet 173
Freezants, liquid 160
Freeze-drying
of coffee 78
of foods 99, 175
Freezing denaturation 20
of foods 98–99
Fructose 11, 13, 19, 22, 23, 82
hydrolysis 23
Fruit
composition of 49, 60, 70
drinks 76, 77
juices 75–77
squashes 76
Frying 16–17, 118
Fungi 179

GMS 60, 62, 64, 67
in bread 113
Gas chromatography 138
Gelatin 129
biological value of 41
breakdown of 129
from cooking of meat 120
Gelatinization
in bread 112–113
of starch 12
Gels 147
Gelling 13
Germ of wheat 56–57
Gin 85
Glucose 6, 10, 34, 36, 59
as a source of alcohol 79–80, 82
blood 21
from glycogen 30
oxidase 130
sweetness 14
syrup from starch 12
Glutamic acid in flavouring 139
Gluten 57, 58, 60, 149
Glycerine 15, 16

INDEX 187

Glycerol 15, 16, 18, 114
  as replacement for sugar 173
Glyceryl monostearate *see* GMS
Glycogen
  liver 30
  muscle 21, 30
Grapes 82, 84
Grass as food 177
Gravy 35
Grilling 116
Groundnut 176
  oil 66

HTST process for milk 67
Haemoglobin 143
Hardening of fats 67, 114, 150
Heat transfer, methods of 115–120
Herrings 7
High frequency heating 119
High and low protein foods 31
Honey 6, 9, 31, 69
Hops 80, 81
Humectants 160
Hydrogen 6, 11, 18
  bonds 8, 12, 14, 20, 74
  sulphide 137
  swell, in canned foods 100
Hydrogenation of fats 67, 114, 150
Hydrolysis
  of fats 16, 67, 114, 150
  of polysaccharides 12
  of proteins 20

Ice-cream, thickening of 173
Improvers, of flour 160–162
Incaparina 170, 178
Infra-red heating 120
Insulin 11, 13
  amino acid sequence in 20
Intestine, production of B vitamins 45
Inulin, in chicory 11
Invertase
  action of 33
  in yeast 59
Iodine
  added to salt 157
  the need for 48
Irradiation of food 175–177

Jam 7, 9, 13, 31
  in the diet 73
  legal requirements 71, 72
  manufacture of 69–73

Ketosis 38, 39
Kilocalories *see* Calories
Kwashiorkor 41, 50, 177

Lactic acid 30
  in muscle 21
Lactose 10, 13
Lead sugar of 2, 87
Legislation 164
Leukaemia 154
Linoleic acid 38, 51
Lipase 114
Lipase, pancreatic 35
Lipophilic 148
Liqueurs 86
Liquid freezants 160
Low-calorie foods 173
Lycopene in tomatoes 142
Lysine 32, 41
  in browning reaction 125

MSG 139, 140
Magnesium 141
  in chlorophyll 126
Magnesium carbonate, added to salt 156
Magnetron, in micro-wave cooking 119
Malt 13, 23, 80, 82
Malting of barley 23, 80
Maltose 10, 13, 69
  digestion of 34
  from starch 23
  in fermentation 59
Margarine 17
  manufacture 64–68
  vitamin D content 47, 157
Marinading of meat 121
Marmalade 69, 72, 137
Mayonnaise 148
Meat 7, 31
  changes in 16, 21
  colour 122, 143
  cooking of 120–122
  spoilage 96
Mège-Mouriés 64, 65, 68

Meringues 165
  structure 149
Micro-wave cooking 118–120
Micro-organisms 87–97
Milk 7
  as an emulsion 148
  in vegetarian diets 170
  pasteurisation 96, 97
  sterilized 98
  vitamin D content 156
Minerals, the need for 6, 7, 48–50
Miracle fruit 7, 140
Miraculin 140
Molasses, in new foods 179
Monosaccharides 9, 10
Monosodium glutamate see MSG
Muscle protein 21
Myoglobin 122, 143

"Natural Foods" 168–169
New types of food 178
New ways of preserving food 175
Nicotinic acid 45, 57, 58
  in flour 156
Nisin 103
Nitrates, in meat curing 101, 102
Nitrogen 6, 18
  trichloride 2, 159–160, 163
Nutrient supplements 156–158
Nutritional value
  of cooked vegetables 127–129
  of processed foods 104
Nuts, as a protein source 170

Obesity 30, 50, 171–174
Oil refining 66–67
Oils 15–18
Oilseed residues, as a protein source 177
Olfactory clefts 137
  receptor cells 133–134
Oligosaccharides 9
Olive oil 16
Orangeade 76
Oranges, bitter 71
Oxygen 6
Oxy-tetracycline 103

Palm
  fruit 66
  kernel oil 66
  oil 66, 67, 142
Pasteur, Louis 88, 97
Pasteurization of milk 88, 96, 97
Pathogens 90
Peas, added colour to canned 165
Pectin 12–13, 110, 149
  in jam 69–70
  in potatoes 122
Pectinase 110
Pellagra 45
Penicillin 104
Pepsin 31
  action of 33
Peroxides in fat rancidity 114
Pesticides 154–155
Phaeophytin from chlorophyll 126
Phenols
  from smoking of food 102
  in enzymic browning 110–111
Phosphorus 6
  the need for 49
Photosynthesis 141
Pickles 102
Pineapple, changes in cooking 129
Plasticity of fat 150
Polypeptides 18–20, 23
Polysaccharides 9, 10–14, 20
Port 84
Porter, adulteration of 152
Potassium bromate 160
Potatoes
  added to flour 165
  after-cooking blackening of 125–126
  cooking of 122, 126
  enzymic changes in 124–125
  nutritional value of 125
  roasting of 122, 125
Pregnancy needs 42
Preservation of food 95–104
  chemical 101–104
  deep freezing 109
  dehydration 106
  new ways of 175
  refrigeration 108
Preservatives, action of 95–96
Pressure-cooking 117–118

INDEX 189

of vegetables   127
Processing of foods, new ways of   177
Propellant and packaging gases   160
Propionic acid, as a preservative   103
Proteins   6, 7, 18, 21, 33, 40–43
   deficiency   50, 177
   denaturation   20, 23, 120, 122
   digestion of   34
   high and low, in foods   31
   in soya   178
   in the diet   40–43
   nature of   18–21
   sparing action, of fat and carbohydrates   42
   vegetable and animal   16, 170
   world shortages of   166–167
Protopectin   149
Protoplasm   146
Psychrophilic organisms   96
Ptomaine poisoning   87, 88
Pyridoxine   45

RNA   140
Radiation
   a method of heat transfer   115–118
   high energy, for preserving food   176
Radio-isotopes, as contaminants   153
Rancidity
   hydrolytic   16–17
   oxidative   17, 114–115
Refrigeration   98–99
Refrigerators   98
   use of   107–109
Release agents   160
Riboflavine   45
   in tea   78–79
Ribonucleotides *see* RNA
Rice, polished   44
Rickets   47, 157
Rigor mortis   21
Roasting   116–117
"Rope" in bread   62, 97, 103
Rum   84

Saccharin   158–159
   in diets   173
Saffron   144
Safrole   162, 164

Salmonella   88, 93
   in eggs   96–97
Salt
   in breadmaking   59
   in margarine   67
   iodized   156
   loss of, in sweat   135–136
Salts   7
Saltiness   132–133, 135–136
Saturated fat   16, 67
Sauces   102
Scurvy   24
Scutellum of wheat   56, 57
Selenium   25
Semolina   57
Sherry   81
Simmering   117
Slimming   170–174
   baths   174
   diet   172
   drugs   174
Smell sensation   133–134
Smoking
   and lung cancer   16, 67
   of food   101, 102
Soft drinks   75–77
Sols   147
Sorbitol, as sugar replacement   173
Sourness   132–133
Soya
   as source of protein   170–178
   bean oil   66
Spirits   84
Spoilage of foods   94, 97
   bread staling   112
   fish   110
   fruits and vegetables   110
Spores, bacterial   91, 94
Staphylococcus   88, 93
Starch   11–13
   digestion of   34
   in potato   122
Steaming as a method of cooking   117–118
Sterilization
   of foods   88–91
   temperatures   92
Sterilized milk   98
Stewing   117

Straight dough system 60–61
Streptococcus lactis 103
Strontium-90 153, 154
Subtilin 103
Sucrase (invertase)
  action of 22–25
  in yeast 59
Sucrose 10, 13, 22, 23
  digestion of 34
  inversion of 22–23, 59
Sugar
  invert, in jam 71
  synthetic 180
Sugars 9–14, 158
  as preservative 95–96, 101, 102
  in flour 59
  in jam 71, 96
  rare 14
Sulphur dioxide
  as a food preservative 71
  effect on vitamins 103, 104
  in wine making 82
Sulphuric acid, added to vinegar 165
Sunflower seed oil 66
Sweat, loss of salt in 135–136
Sweeteners, artificial 158–159, 163
Sweetness sensation 14, 38, 134–136
Syneresis 147
Synthetic food 179

TVP 178
Tannins
  effect on flavour and colour 143
  in tea 77
Taste buds 132–133
  protein 14, 135
Taste sensation 132–133, 135
Tea 77–79
  instant 77, 78
Temperature
  effect on enzymes 107
  effect on micro-organisms 92–93
  effect on taste 136
  maintenance of body 29, 38
Tenderizing of meat 21, 121
Texture
  of food 143–150
  of fruits and vegetables 110
Textured Vegetable Protein *see* TVP

Theobromine 79
Thiamine *see* vitamin B_1
Tocopherols *see also* vitamin E 47
Toxins 91, 93
Trace elements 25
Trimethylamine 111
Trypsin 31, 33
Tryptophan 41
Turkish baths, and slimming 174
Tyrosine 41

Unicellular organisms 179
Unsaturated fats 17

Van Lowenhoek 88
Vegetable protein, addition of amino
  acids to 170, 179
Vegetables, structure of 149
Vegetarianism 169–170
Vinegar 102
  adulteration of 152, 165
Vitamins 24–25
  specific
  A 23, 24, 43, 44, 142, 157
    in margarine 67, 68, 142, 156
  B group 24, 43, 44
    from the intestine 90
  B_1 (thiamine) 25, 44, 57, 58, 156
    addition to flour 58
    cooking losses 125
    effect of sulphur dioxide 103, 104
    from intestine 90
  B_{12} 25, 50
  C (Ascorbic acid) 23, 24, 25, 43,
    45–47, 157
    cooking losses of 46
    effect of sulphur dioxide on 103,
      104
    in fruit juices 75, 76
    recommended intake of 46
    sources of 46
    storage losses 111
    uses, in bread 61
  D 24, 43, 47
    in margarine 67, 68, 156
    in milk 157
    sources of 46

E   24, 43, 47
   as anti-oxidant   114
   sources of   47
   synthetic   178
   the need for   43–48
Vodka   85
Votator   68

Water   6, 7
   as a beverage   75
   bacteria in   75, 90
   body's requirements   9, 37
   chemistry of   7–9
   properties of   7–9, 74–75
Waterless cooking   117
Wheat grain, composition of   56–57

Wines   82–84
   fortified   84
   sparkling   84
World Health Organisation   155, 163–164
World population expansion   175
Wholemeal bread   62
World War II   179

Xerophthalmia   44

Yeast
   and food spoilage   95–96, 101
   as food   179
   fermentation   23, 58, 59, 80, 82, 83

Zymase, in yeast   59, 79–80